IN THE INTERESTS OF SCIENCE

Adelaide Bartlett and
The Pimlico Poisoning

Kate Clarke

Foreword by Linda Stratmann

This edition 2019 (softcover)

Revised Third edition (2015, hardcover)
First edition published by Souvenir Press (1990)
Second edition published by Carrington Press (2011)

The right of Kate Clarke to be identified as the author
of this work has been asserted in accordance with
the Copyright, Designs & Patents Act 1988.

All rights reserved. No part of this book may be reprinted or reproduced
or utilised in any form or by any electronic, mechanical or other
means, now known or hereafter invented, including photocopying
and recording, or in any information storage or retrieval system,
without the prior permission in writing of the publishers.

ISBN: 978-0-9931806-7-5 (hardcover)
ISBN: 978-1-911273-67-7 (softcover)
ISBN: 978-0-9931806-8-2 (ebook)

Published by Mango Books
www.mangobooks.co.uk
18 Soho Square
London W1D 3QL

Non-Fiction
by the same Author

Murder At The Priory: The Mysterious Poisoning of Charles Bravo
(with Bernard Taylor) (Short-listed for the CWA's Gold Dagger Award)

Journal: Volume One (as Kate Paul)
(All subsequent volumes at the Mass Observation Archive/
Special Collections/Sussex University Library)

Who Killed Simon Dale? & Other Murder Mysteries

The Book of Hay (local history)

Deadly Service

Bad Companions

Lethal Alliance

Fatal Affairs

A Deadly Dilemma

Contents

Acknowledgements..i
Foreword by Linda Stratmann.......................................iii

Part One
1. Unusual Beginnings... 1
2. Feminist Flutterings 13
3. Love in the Afternoons... 20
4. A Change of Air 25
5. Edwin's Mysterious Illness..................................... 33
6. Signs of Hysteria.. 44
7. The Reluctant Worm.. 50

Part Two
8. On the Stroke of Twelve.. 63
9. A Strong Smell of Chloroform 70
10. Preacher in a Panic 82
11. Adelaide Stands Alone... 90
12. An Ingenious Tale 98
13. A Charge of Murder... 105

Part Three
14. Trial at the Old Bailey...................................... 115
15. Drawing Room Dramas 129
16. Leach in the Limelight 136
17. Doctors Take the Stand 148
18. A Powerful Plea 159
19. The Voice of Scepticism...................................... 170
20. Extraordinary Scenes... 179
21. Verdict of the Press... 194

Part Four
22. The Poisoner's Craft... 201
23. The Marriage Trap 212
24. Loose Ends.. 220

Bibliography.. 231
Index... 233

Yours Sincerely
Adelaide Bartlett

Acknowlegements

I would like to thank the following for their help and encouragement: David Barton, Noelle Beales, Professor David Bowen, Ivor Cantle, John Campling, Roger Capps, Evelyn Curtis, Anne Dewell, Andy Dixon, Milly Eagle, Dr Frank McGinty, Sasha Mahendra, Linda Stratmann, Tom Watt and Betty Young. I am grateful to Adam Wood, David Green and John A Vickers for their invaluable help with the update of this edition. My special thanks must also go to the crime writer, Mark Ripper (M W Oldridge) for his generosity in allowing me access to his researches at The National Archives.

I am indebted to the following for information freely given: The Wellcome Institute for the History of Medicine, the London Homeopathic Hospital, The Manor House Hospital, the Royal Archives, Windsor Castle, the Borough Librarian, Llanelli and the numerous other librarians who have kindly assisted me.

I would like to thank the following for permission to quote from published material: Michael Joseph Ltd for The Court of St James by E S Turner; Macmillan & Co for *The Prince Consort* by Roger Fulford; Cassell plc for *The Reminiscences of Lady Randolph Churchill*, edited by Ralph G Martin; Eyre & Spottiswoode for *The Life and Famous Cases of Sir Edward Clarke* by Derek Walker-Smith and Edward Clarke. Quotations from *The Pilgrim Daughters* by Hesketh Pearson, published by William Heinemann Ltd., are reproduced by permission of A P Watt Ltd on behalf of Michael Holroyd, CBE.

Quotations from evidence given in the trial at the Old Bailey are used throughout this book and unless otherwise credited are taken from Sir John Hall's *Trial of Adelaide Bartlett* in the Notable British Trials Series.

Foreword

The Pimlico Murder is one of the great classic cases in the history of crime, and for sheer drama, romance and mystery it stands unequalled amongst poison trials. The curious death of Victorian grocer Edwin Bartlett poses an extraordinary number of questions, only a few of which can be addressed with any certainty, many of which will probably remain forever unanswered. At the heart of the conundrum is his wife Adelaide, a young Frenchwoman who knew how to attract and fascinate men, excite their keenest sympathy, and induce them to believe the most unlikely and shocking tales, while carefully concealing a stony heart, calculating mind, lurid imagination and total disregard for the truth. Add to the mixture a besotted clergyman, a naive doctor, the power of mesmerism and a book with unusual advice on health, sex and marriage, and one begins to see the essential flavour of the case.

The mystery is also wreathed in the odour of chloroform, a chemical much beloved of writers of fiction, which enveloped Victorian society in hints of the erotic and mists of delusion. Adelaide's trial is the first known prosecution for murder by chloroform, and the properties of this unique substance and her understanding of them are central to the unfolding of events.

I first encountered Adelaide Bartlett in my avid reading of crime history many years ago, and when I decided to write about murder hers was the case I chose. I soon realised however that it abounded with numerous complexities and in order to understand what had actually happened as distinct from Adelaide's astonishing tales, and the elaborate theories that have arisen since, I needed to understand the Victorians. This meant acquiring an appreciation not only of how they lived their daily lives but how they thought, and most importantly what hidden meanings lay beneath their spoken words. If ever a case foundered on the prevailing habit of 'delicacy' - a veiled allusion to matters that could not be discussed openly which required the listener to assume the sense of what was being said - it was this one. To Adelaide Bartlett therefore I owe the start of my enduring fascination with the Victorian era, and subsequent writings set in that period.

No-one can seriously doubt that Edwin Bartlett was murdered, and the killer can have been none other than his wife, but the questions one must ask are: how did she do it, how did she get away with it, and what was her career thereafter? For after the trial, Adelaide disappeared, evaporated as completely as a drop of chloroform, and has never to date been traced. My early work on Adelaide remains unpublished, although it did lead to my first professional commission, and the results of my research were condensed into a chapter in my debut publication, *Chloroform: the Quest For Oblivion*. But a chapter cannot do justice to this remarkable case, and I am therefore delighted to welcome this re-issue of Kate Clarke's very thorough full-length account, which has been substantially revised with fresh material since it was first published.

Linda Stratmann, 2015

Linda is the author of twelve non-fiction books and six crime novels, with further publications planned for 2016.

www.lindastratmann.com

Part One

'Whether on the theory of guilt or innocence,
the whole story is marvellous.'
The Times, April 1886

'There is a peculiar fascination about a case of poisoning.
It is generally mysterious, the evidence is always circumstantial,
and, if a woman be concerned in it, there is almost
invariably a love story in the background.'
Sir John Hall: Introduction to
Trial of Adelaide Bartlett, Notable British Trials

CHAPTER 1
Unusual Beginnings

On 12th April, 1886, a young woman, dark-eyed and petite, stood in the dock at the Old Bailey charged with the murder of her husband.

She was the attractive, French-speaking wife of a South London grocer and of little importance socially, yet her maiden name was unusual, aristocratic even – Adelaide Blanche de la Tremoille.

Uncommon, too, was her alleged crime, for her husband, Edwin Bartlett, had died with his stomach full of liquid chloroform, a poison that was more generally associated with cases of suicide or accidental death, not murder.

But then, many things about Adelaide were extraordinary. Her name, the crime with which she was charged, the outrageous scenes at her trial – indeed, her whole life – might have sprung from the pages of a far-fetched novel. Even *The Times* felt moved to declare that 'whether on the theory of guilt or innocence, the whole story is marvellous.'

The crowds that flocked to her trial certainly thought so, and their voracious interest was finally rewarded by the sight of her defence counsel, the great Edward Clarke, sobbing with emotion as the verdict was delivered.

Much of Adelaide's background remains a mystery, but the following facts are beyond dispute. Her mother was an English woman called Clara Chamberlain, the daughter of William Robinson Chamberlain, a member of the Stock Exchange in the City of London. In 1853, Clara married Adolphe Collet de la Tremoille, Comte de Thouars d'Escury at St Leonard's Church, Shoreditch: the bride was nineteen years old and the groom a widower of thirty-five, described on the marriage certificate as a pensioned Naval Officer in the French Service. At the time of the marriage he was working as a teacher of mathematics. They had a son, Henry, the following year but by the time Adelaide was born on 19th December, 1855, the couple were living in France, at 9 rue Gourville in Orléans. Young Henry was baptised before they left London and they were back in Dalston by September the following year when Adelaide was baptised at St Mary's, in Hackney.

Although the illustrious name of her legal father[1] appears on Adelaide's French birth certificate, he was not, in fact, her biological father. In 1858, another son, Frederick, was born and two years later, another daughter, named Clara.

Sadly, Adelaide's mother, Clara, died on 14th November, 1866, in St Pancras, by now a widow aged thirty three. Five years earlier, she had been living in Hoxton with her four children – Henry, Adelaide, Frederick and Clara – and her seventeen year old sister, Ellen – whilst earning a living by teaching French.

When Clara died the family was split up and young Clara, aged six, went to live with her uncle, William Chamberlain, his wife Emily and their four daughters in Hornsey – she was to die in 1873, aged thirteen. It is not known what happened to eleven year old Adelaide or her two brothers after their mother died. It is possible that they were cared for in France by Adolphe de Thouars's family and perhaps it was at this stage in her life that Adelaide was sent to be educated at a French convent where she remained until she was brought to England in late adolescence.

Some thirty years after Adelaide's trial at the Old Bailey, Sir Edward Clarke revealed in his memoirs[2] that her true father was 'an Englishman of good social position.' Whoever he was, Sir Edward's previous silence on the subject, and the vast sum of money made

1 One of the Count's ancestors was Georges de la Tremoille, a favourite of Charles VII of France and arch enemy of Joan of Arc. The last of the line was accidentally burnt to death in 1932, which some might say, in the light of Joan of Arc's own fate, was a just historical revenge.
2 *The Story of My Life*, Sir Edward Clarke, QC, MP. John Murray, 1918.

available for her defence, albeit anonymously, inevitably served to perpetuate the mystery of the man's identity and speculation has flourished ever since.

Undoubtedly, the most popular guess has been that he was a wealthy and influential member of Queen Victoria's personal entourage. This was suggested by Yseult Bridges in her book *Poison and Adelaide Bartlett*, and endorsed by Mary S. Hartman in *Victorian Murderesses*, but no evidence was offered by either author to substantiate the theory, nor was any attempt made to suggest a possible identity. He was certainly rich enough to persuade Edward Clarke to defend his daughter, and his decision to remain anonymous may also suggest that he was not only a man of wealth and influence but one anxious to avoid public scandal.

When Adelaide was in her late teens, her natural father decided that it was time to arrange a marriage for her in England. Although her illegitimacy made this a rather delicate task, he was prepared to pay well for her respectability and in due course a suitable candidate was found.

On arriving in England, Adelaide stayed briefly in Richmond and from there she went to lodge in the home of one Charles Bartlett and his wife in Kingston-upon-Thames. His younger brother, Frederick, was also living in the house at the time and it was through Charles and Frederick that Adelaide was introduced to the middle brother, Edwin, the man her father had selected for her. At nineteen, no doubt Adelaide would have preferred to choose her own husband, but she was fortunate in that Edwin had a number of commendable characteristics – he was ambitious, extremely hardworking and, according to his father, possessed a 'merry disposition.'

Added to this, he was well-built, of attractive appearance, bearded, with fair hair and blue eyes, and was described as looking much younger than his years; he was also compassionate, collecting money in 'a jar in his office for distribution among the poor.'[3] He was, therefore, a perfectly acceptable choice of husband, yet one cannot help wondering whether he was perhaps a little too common-place

3   *The Lancet*, 22nd May, 1886. Article by Dr Alfred Leach.

to fulfil the romantic expectations of a young girl newly-released from life in a convent.

Whether there was any courtship between the couple is uncertain. Adelaide was to say later that she met Edwin only once before their marriage, although it must be remembered that she had a highly developed propensity for bending the truth when it suited her.

At the time of their meeting Edwin was in his thirtieth year and still living with his parents in Herne Hill, an area of South London made popular by the recent arrival of the railway which provided a popular link with the City. This innovation greatly increased the demand for housing, and by the end of the nineteenth century much of the open countryside south of the river had been built over, mainly with small terraced houses and shops. The spread of suburbia was welcomed, of course, by artisans and tradespeople alike – Edwin Bartlett, senior, was himself a builder, although not a very successful one.

As for Edwin, he had rejected his father's trade and chosen the grocery business instead, starting his career as an employee of one Edward Baxter, who owned a small shop in Herne Hill. The young man soon showed a flair for accountancy which proved very useful to Mr Baxter, and indeed, within three years he had become a partner in the business and the sign above the shop was changed to:

BAXTER & BARTLETT
Family Grocers
Wine and Provision Merchants

It was shortly after this that Edwin met Adelaide. There was, however, a major obstacle to their proposed marriage: when Edwin had accepted the partnership with Edward Baxter he had also entered into a verbal agreement whereby he would not marry for a period of three years, so that all his energies and material resources could be channelled into the costly and time-consuming task of developing the business.

Apparently Adelaide's father's agents, when arranging the marriage settlement, knew nothing of the 'tacit understanding'[4] between Baxter and Edwin. As for Adelaide, she objected most strongly to a long engagement and expressed a desire to marry as soon as possible. It was an awkward situation for Edwin, for if he insisted on a three-year engagement he ran the risk of losing his bride – and, it must be said, the considerable sum of money he would receive on their marriage. He had little alternative, therefore, but to renege on his gentleman's agreement with Baxter.

The marriage contract, drawn up between Edwin's solicitor, Edward Negus Wood, and Adelaide's father's agents, contained three stipulations – that Edwin should take sole responsibility for Adelaide after their marriage, that he should never refer to her origins, and that, in view of her youth, he should supervise the completion of her education. This last clause gave Edwin the perfect solution to his dilemma: he would send his bride away to school and keep the marriage a secret.

Instead of a local wedding, therefore, the ceremony was held at Croydon Parish Church on 6th April, 1875; Edwin's parents and brothers, his partner, Edward Baxter, and his friends, were not invited. The only two witnesses were Caroline James and William Chamberlain – the latter probably Adelaide's uncle, as her maternal grandfather of that name had died some years previously. Caroline James was Edwin's married sister who was living in Croydon at the time, and it was to her house that Edwin took his young bride for the wedding breakfast.

After refreshments had been taken, Edwin escorted Adelaide to a girls' boarding school run by a Miss Dodd, in Stoke Newington,[5] where she was enrolled as a pupil. Thus Edwin was not only honouring his promise to complete Adelaide's education, but was also able to keep her out of the way and continue to pursue, as far as Baxter was concerned, a bachelor existence.

Both men worked hard, and with the money Edwin received on his marriage to Adelaide he and Baxter were able to expand the

4   *The Westminster Times*, 20th February, 1886. Press Association.
5   By this time, Stoke Newington, with its spacious new houses and wide, tree-lined streets, had become a popular venue for educational establishments - from preparatory schools to colleges.

business by opening a new shop in Lordship Lane, East Dulwich. Following the success of this venture they opened yet another shop in the Brixton area, which was then one of London's most salubrious suburbs.

Adelaide remained at Miss Dodd's establishment for about a year. The three years of the agreement had still not expired, however, so Edwin was obliged to send her away again, this time to a Protestant convent in Belgium, where she remained for a further eighteen months. She said later that enrolment at the convent was at her request, so it may have been a joint decision by the couple that she should forsake her Catholic upbringing. As a committed member of the Wesleyan Church, Edwin may have felt that a period of study in a Protestant convent might bring Adelaide's religious beliefs more in line with his own.

During her absence Edwin did manage to visit her several times, but although his father assumed they stayed together in rented apartments during the holidays, this cannot be confirmed. Nor is it known whether the marriage was consummated during this period; Adelaide was to say that it was not until she had completed her studies and returned to England that they lived together as man and wife.

They wrote to each other regularly, although Adelaide's letters were concerned mainly with her religious studies and were not of an intimate or wifely nature. For the time being it seemed that Edwin was quite content for her to remain his wife in name only. The fact that she had by now developed into a beguiling and accomplished young woman makes his single-minded ambition and apparent lack of ardour somewhat remarkable.

So it was that while Adelaide kept faith with her textbooks in Belgium, Edwin continued to invest all his money and energy in the grocery business, forging ahead with some highly ambitious schemes. Within a few years he and Edward Baxter had opened a chain of six shops in the South London area and had also acquired a warehouse in the City for the importation of tea – no small achievement in such a short time.

Unusual Beginnings

It was not until the latter half of 1877, when Adelaide was in her twenty-second year, that she finally returned to England to live with Edwin as his wife. Their first home was a flat above the shop in Station Road, Herne Hill. The premises consisted of two shops joined together, in the shadow of the railway arch, with the names Baxter and Bartlett in bold lettering above the abundant window display, crammed with provisions of every description – choice teas which were individually blended for the more discerning customer, a wide selection of wines and cheeses, fresh butter from local farms, fancy cakes, and assorted sweetmeats. The rooms above the shop would have provided more than adequate accommodation for a young couple and two housemaids.

In many ways Adelaide was fortunate – she had a husband in a thriving business, a home of her own and many hours of leisure – yet one wonders whether she was really happy or at ease, surrounded by the bustling activity of Station Road, yet removed from it and alone for most of the day, without the companionship of fellow students or nuns to alleviate the boredom. It was said of her that her English was 'not very clear',[6] which probably excluded her from the spontaneous chatter that passes between neighbours and may have made it difficult for her to acquire friends.

But the marriage, at least, seemed happy enough. Adelaide performed her wifely duties without fault, rising early each morning to supervise Edwin's cold bath and cook his breakfast, and apparently organising her small household with thrift and efficiency. She began to show an interest too, in her husband's only hobby – the breeding of St Bernard dogs. Before long she had become proficient in animal care and even kept a fully equipped medicine chest for treating the dogs when they fell ill.

She must soon have realised, however, that whereas Edwin was totally absorbed in his work, her own existence, in many respects,

---

6   *The Westminster Times,* 6th February, 1886.

was often disagreeably dull. She spent most of her time alone, seeing little of Edwin who worked six days a week – ordering from wholesalers and importers, blending teas, attending to the accounts and travelling constantly between the warehouse and the various shops. He rested only on Sundays, and even then he was out attending church or caring for his dogs.

Being a fine needle-woman, Adelaide tried to fill the empty hours in sewing intricate pieces of embroidery; she also played the piano for hours on end and read a great many books. It was a lonely life and it's little wonder that she should eventually have gravitated towards the only young man who ever came to the flat, Edwin's brother Frederick.

It is not clear whether Frederick had a trade or whether he worked for his brother Charles, but his father later described him as 'not established in business' – a phrase that could mean he was a jack-of-all-trades or simply unemployed. In any case, Adelaide was attracted to him and their relationship blossomed.

One of Adelaide's duties was to exercise the dogs each day, a task she thoroughly enjoyed, only too glad to exchange the confined atmosphere of the parlour for the fresh air and open reaches of nearby Peckham Rye; had Edwin noticed that his wife seemed more lively and less withdrawn, he would have looked no further than the bracing exercise to account for the glow in her cheeks. In all probability, he noticed nothing.

Predictably, perhaps, the attachment between Adelaide and Frederick intensified during their daily rambles and in May 1878, having made no previous reference to any member of her family, Adelaide announced that she had an aunt who, moreover, had asked her to stay for a week. Edwin, preoccupied with work and his mother's recent illness, offered no objection to his wife spending a few days away from home.

The week's break seemed to agree with Adelaide for she returned home greatly refreshed – and Edwin suspected nothing. Or so it seemed, for when, a fortnight later, the aunt invited Adelaide to visit her again, he readily agreed and happily waved her goodbye.

Adelaide's return to her husband on 26th May passed without comment, for Edwin was anxious about his mother's health which was failing fast. Indeed, a few days later she died, leaving his father distraught and alone. Without consulting Adelaide, Edwin insisted that the old man should come to live with them in the flat above the shop, even going as far as to promise him a home for life.

The relationship between Adelaide and her father-in-law had never been warm and he, for his part, made little effort to conceal his resentment. Not only did he disapprove of her, but he was clearly suspicious of the clandestine marriage ceremony; the arrangement whereby the three of them lived together under the same roof was therefore doomed to end in disharmony. Indeed, no sooner had the old man moved into the flat then Adelaide walked out.

Puzzled by his wife's sudden departure, Edwin, together with his father, made enquiries as to her whereabouts. Old Mr Bartlett knew exactly where to start looking and it came as no surprise to him when he heard from his son Charles in Kingston that young Frederick was also missing. Not only that, he had recently been away from home twice before, and on each occasion Adelaide had also been away – supposedly visiting her aunt.

Even Edwin finally came to the obvious conclusion and the flight of the lovers was a brief one. Frederick, though full of romantic notions, was still young and had no money to support a mistress – nor was he the most lionhearted of suitors. Once he realised that his family had discovered the truth, he allowed himself to be shipped off to America in disgrace.

With Frederick steaming across the Atlantic, Adelaide had little choice but to return to Station Road, to face Edwin's irritating complacency and the open hostility of her father-in-law.

Her wings had been well and truly clipped.

It is possible that the lovers had made romantic plans with which to ease the pain of their abrupt separation, Frederick pledging to come back for Adelaide once he had established himself in America.

Such a notion is borne out by old Mr Bartlett's allegation that they wrote to each other secretly.

The affair with Frederick was soon forgotten by Edwin but his father had no intention of letting Adelaide's scandalous lapse pass unpunished. He was supported in his quest for vengeance by the neighbours, who were already discussing the affair with sanctimonious glee. Only too pleased to add his own venomous contribution, he told them that Adelaide had been receiving letters from his son in America.

Unfortunately for him, however, Adelaide came to hear of it and, knowing this information could only have come from the old man, was furious. She looked to her husband to defend her reputation, convincing him that if she acquired a bad name this would, in turn, reflect on him and might even affect his business. Edwin, being a shrewd businessman, albeit a gullible husband, was therefore moved to demand an apology from his father for maligning his wife's good name.

Though he loathed and mistrusted his daughter-in-law, old Mr Bartlett loved his son very much; he also relied upon him not only for his board and lodging, but also for financial support when he was out of work.[7] He agreed, therefore, against his better judgement, to sign a written apology which Edwin, a stickler for form, had drawn up by his solicitor, Mr Wood. It read as follows:

> 31st December 1878
>
> Having made statements reflecting on the character of Mrs Adelaide Bartlett, the wife of my son, Mr Edwin Bartlett, junior, which statements I have discovered to be unfounded and untrue, I hereby withdraw all such statements and express my regrets for having made them.
>
> I also apologise to the said Mrs Adelaide Bartlett and Mr Edwin Bartlett, junior, and acknowledge that all such statements are altogether unfounded and untrue. I authorise Mr Edwin Bartlett, junior, to make what use he pleases of this apology.

---

[7] According to Sir John Hall, in *Trial of Adelaide Bartlett*, 'he was largely dependent upon his son for his keep'.

With obvious reluctance, old Mr Bartlett signed the paper, although he later claimed that he signed it knowing it to be false.

The apology made, Edwin seemed satisfied that his wife's honour had been upheld, but Adelaide, though ostensibly appeased, harboured a grudge against her father-in-law from that day onwards.

After the old man's expedient retraction a surface calm was maintained at the flat in Station Road during the years 1879 to 1880. The only problem during this time seemed to be with Edwin's teeth. In 1878 he had allowed a dentist with butchering tendencies – a Mr Bellin of Brook Street – to remove some decaying molars; the dentist had then proceeded to saw off a number of perfectly sound teeth as far as the gum, so that Edwin's new dental plate would fit more comfortably! Dental treatment in the 1880's must have been excruciatingly painful and, rather than suffer any more of it, Edwin had allowed his teeth to decay.

Apart from this problem, however, Edwin was in excellent health. In November 1880, he was examined by Dr William Clapton on behalf of the British Equitable Insurance Company. The doctor found that he was 'suffering from no ailment whatever' and passed him, in terms of insurance, as a 'first class life.'

Physically, then, Edwin was in good shape but doubts were soon to be cast on his mental stability for in 1881 he suffered a form of nervous collapse. His partner, Edward Baxter, thought that too much physical work was to blame, since prior to his illness Edwin has been working excessively long hours laying a new timber floor in the warehouse. The doctor ordered Edwin to take a complete rest and recommended a sea voyage.

Taking his advice, Edwin made the trip alone, travelling from London to Edinburgh by steamer and then by train to Balmoral – whether this was the Victorian equivalent of a package tour or he had friends or relatives there is uncertain; he returned to London a fortnight later, as his father observed, 'wholly restored.'

Obviously, Edwin's doctor had thought it advisable for him to have a complete break from his work and, perhaps, from the prevailing tensions at home. Maybe Edwin had found that he was unable, after all, to forget Adelaide's flight with young Frederick. It must be remembered, too, that his father, though apologetic on paper, may well have raised the subject of the affair whenever he could, thus bringing still more disharmony into the home.

Life with Adelaide had not been easy, and Edwin was already under stress. Perhaps he had come to realise that he had taken on more than he had bargained for that day in April when he had married her for money.

CHAPTER 2

Feminist Flutterings

Adelaide's reading habits have a fundamental bearing on her story for her cloistered childhood and restricted adult relationships had made her especially susceptible to the ideas and philosophies presented to her in books. She read a great deal, but not for her the stylised moralistic tales to be found in *The Woman at Home Journal* and romantic novelettes of the day; she preferred more stimulating reading and became profoundly influenced by two progressive American writers, Dr Thomas Low Nichols and his wife, also a doctor, Mary Gove Nichols. They were two voices amongst the many forerunners of the early feminist movement, writing prolifically and in the frankest of terms on all matters relating to the physical and emotional health of women.[8]

The Nichols and their counterparts became almost cult figures for a small section of intelligent, middle class Victorian women who, more often than not, found themselves shackled to their homes and dominated, mentally and physically, by autocratic fathers or boorish husbands. The Nichols' doctrine, which offered them some comfort, was read avidly but not openly for it tackled subjects that were normally taboo. These writings drew attention to the misery of loveless marriages and men's selfish misuse of their conjugal rights. They even went so far as to suggest the use of contraceptive devices in certain circumstances, though only, of course, within marriage.

---

8 Mary Gove Nichols wrote an autobiographical novel, *Mary Lyndon*, about her first marriage which she described as 'loveless'.

More radical still was the assertion that even abortion, in some rare instances, might be considered morally justified.

In the 1870's such literature was certainly regarded as subversive for a young housewife like Adelaide, but with so many uninterrupted hours in which to read she soon graduated from the devotional texts of her convent days to the preachings of these enlightened, free-thinking sexologists from the New World. Feeling trapped and frustrated in the flat above the shop, alone for most of the day, and probably seeing herself as a prisoner of a loveless marriage, Adelaide read every word and experienced the first flutterings of liberation.

A book that had an especially strong influence on her was one written by Dr Nichols, which bore the remarkably long title, *Esoteric Anthropology: The Mysteries of Man – A Comprehensive and Confidential Treatise on the Structure, Functions, Passional Attractions and Perversions, True and False Physical and Social Conditions and the Most Intimate Relations of Men and Women.*

Contrary to the assumptions of the judge at Adelaide's subsequent trial, this book took a rather moralistic stand, advocating abstinence in marriage unless procreation was desired. Furthermore, it declared that the use of contraceptive devices was only justified if a women was 'compelled to submit to the embrace of her husband while her health or other conditions forbid her to have children.'

Far from being 'garbage' as Mr Justice Wills was to call it, the book was entirely sympathetic to both men *and* women and was not, as he declared, designed to incite the female population to 'abandon their natural instincts.'

When the book was published in America in 1853 it created quite a furore and enraged a great many readers. It is not known whether they were driven by pioneering zeal or by a desire to avoid their detractors, but the Nichols travelled to England shortly afterwards, settling in the prosperous spa town of Malvern, deep in the beautiful Worcestershire countryside. During the next twenty years they became part of the homeopathic and hydropathic movement in medicine that had become so popular with fashionable and wealthy Victorian ladies. Though the treatments prescribed were often rigorous, unpleasant and involved the use of douches, wet-packings, malodorous mud-baths and that most inelegant of contraptions, the sitz-bath, women still flocked to receive the punishment. Their obsession with finding unorthodox or even bizarre remedies for their indifferent health proved extremely lucrative for the doctors and proprietors of the alternative establishments which served them.

A prominent resident of Malvern at the time was James Manby Gully, the celebrated hydropathic doctor who featured so dramatically in the Charles Bravo poisoning case of 1876. He created a tremendous scandal by having an affair with one of his patients, a beautiful young woman who was the wife of Alexander Ricardo. Gully was sixty-two at the time and Florence only twenty-six. The relationship continued after Ricardo died and until Florence married again in 1875, this time to a young barrister, Charles Bravo. Four months later, Charles too was dead, poisoned by a massive dose of antimony. The sensational inquest that followed established that he had been murdered but failed to indicate who the killer might be, although suspicion was undoubtedly cast upon Florence Bravo and her companion, Jane Cox, and also, to some degree, upon Dr Gully.

Many years before this drama, however, in 1841, Dr Gully had been one of the pioneers of the hydropathic movement in England and co-founder of the Malvern clinic. He was renowned for his wisdom and healing powers, and at the height of his career his reputation was such that he could list among his patients eminent Victorians like Charles Dickens, Florence Nightingale, George Eliot, Alfred, Lord Tennyson and Charles Darwin. It would be difficult to imagine a more distinguished clientele.

Being part of such a flourishing industry, it is surprising that in 1873 the Nichols should have moved to Earls Court in London where, by 1879, Mrs Nichols had set herself up as a 'specialist advising ladies in all their problems, social and domestic, either by letter, in the strictest confidence, or by appointment at her private consulting rooms.'

Adelaide had now been married to Edwin for nearly five years and having digested the contents of *Esoteric Anthropology*, she consulted Mary Nichols at some time in 1879, probably by post. So much did she admire the Nichols' teachings that in her enthusiasm she made the mistake of lending her copy of *Esoteric Anthropology* to one of Edwin's friends, George Matthews. He was a silk merchant in the City and he and his wife, Alice, lived at 98 Friern Road, East Dulwich. Adelaide was obsessed with Dr Nichols's ideas, and it may have been to convert Matthews to the new learning that she lent him the book. This was a scandalous thing to do, for it dealt freely with sexual matters normally taboo in polite society, and when Mrs Matthews found the offending book in her drawing-room she was outraged and returned it immediately.

Adelaide, however, became so absorbed in the teachings that when she became pregnant soon after Edwin returned from his recuperative sea voyage, she consulted Mary Nichols once more, this time seeking advice on her confinement and help in choosing a suitable midwife to assist her. Annie Walker, a nurse who was sympathetic to the homeopathic cause, seems to have been Mary Nichols's choice for Adelaide subsequently engaged her to supervise the birth. No doctor was to be involved, but Nurse Walker was resident in the flat for four weeks before the birth.

It was a long and difficult labour and, fearing for the child, Nurse Walker begged Edwin Bartlett to send for a doctor. He refused, however, saying that he would rather not have any man 'interfering with his wife.' We cannot know whether it was also Adelaide's wish that the child be delivered without the intervention of a doctor or the administration of any allopathic drugs. A doctor *was* eventually called, but by the time he arrived the child had already come into the world – stillborn.

The pain of childbirth and the tragic death of the infant affected Adelaide badly and from that day she maintained she would never have another child. She said as much to Annie Walker, who stayed for three weeks after the delivery. The two women had become close friends during the confinement, and when Annie eventually left, she gave Adelaide a photograph of herself in her nurse's uniform.

Lacking any other intimate companions, Adelaide treasured this memento, displaying it in a silver frame on her mantelpiece. Friendships between women are often forged during periods of unhappiness and do not always survive once the crisis is past. The involvement with the nurse was very important to Adelaide at the time, but it did not remain so for long after they had gone their separate ways, although Annie Walker continued to visit her occasionally. It is a sad fact that Adelaide seemed unable to sustain close relationships and had failed to retain any friends from her school or convent years.

She was still at loggerheads with her father-in-law, and now, embittered by her loss, the old grievances came back into focus. His presence in the house irritated her, and at last she managed to persuade Edwin that they should move to a flat above one of his other shops; the one in Lordship Lane, East Dulwich, would, she said, be ideal. This marked something of a victory for Adelaide, for the new home was definitely not large enough to accommodate *three* people in comfort.

Clearly, then, old Mr Bartlett would have to go.

This incident illustrates Adelaide's ability to manipulate her husband when necessary. He had promised his father a home for life and reneging on that promise must have been a difficult decision for him. Father and son had always been very close, but Adelaide had somehow managed to loosen the old man's grip very efficiently indeed.

After leaving his son's flat, Mr Bartlett rented a small cottage – probably little more than a workman's hut – in St David's Mews, off Oxford Street, which was close to the building site in Berkeley Square where he was working. Convenient or not, his banishment left him saddened and more vindictive than ever. Nevertheless, despite Adelaide's hostility towards him, the old man was determined to keep in close touch with his favourite son and made a point of visiting Edwin at one or other of his shops every day.

Adelaide soon tired of living in the flat above the shop in East Dulwich, with its grey urban aspect and the relentless commercial hubbub in the street below. She longed for a more tranquil environment, and early in 1883 she and Edwin were on the move again. She had never really settled in East Dulwich and during the time she had lived there she had made only two friends – George and Alice Matthews, who were initially Edwin's friends, not hers, having known him for several years before his marriage.

Although they were obviously fond of Edwin and, on the whole, on friendly terms with Adelaide, their enthusiasm was somewhat cooled by the unfortunate episode with *Esoteric Anthropology*; it may have been with a certain sense of relief that Alice Matthews heard that the Bartletts were moving several miles away, to The Cottage, in the Merton Abbey area south of Wimbledon.

The Cottage was secluded, situated deep in the countryside, just two miles from the village of Merton. Its rustic charm contrasted favourably with the flat in Lordship Lane, and the outbuildings and surrounding fields provided excellent facilities for the St Bernard dogs. Though the village was small it had one great advantage – a railway station which enabled Edwin to travel north to his shop in Herne Hill each day with comparative ease.

Adelaide seems to have been no more gregarious in Merton than she had been elsewhere; having spent most of her life until her marriage in one institution after another, she may have found it difficult to relate to people from normal family backgrounds. Whatever the reason, she failed to cultivate the company of her new neighbours, and although Annie Walker called to see her now and then, she had few visitors. In the summer of 1884, George and Alice Matthews spend a week at The Cottage, but that was all.

The Bartletts employed a local couple, Mr and Mrs Furlong, as general servants, the man to take care of the garden and his wife, Mary Ann, to do the housework. This arrangement left Adelaide with little to do but amuse herself. The care of the dogs took up some of her time, but the remaining hours were spent, as before, in reading, playing the piano and sewing, and, for a while a least, she seemed relatively content. There even appeared to be a temporary truce between herself and her father-in-law during this period, and the journey from London to Merton Village did not deter him from visiting regularly. He was even invited to share Sunday lunch with them occasionally and much of the old resentment, it seemed, was gone.

By this time, however, tensions within the marriage were beginning to show. During one of Annie Walker's visits, for instance, Adelaide complained that although she played and sang in the evenings, Edwin didn't really appreciate her accomplishments and although her embroidery was beautifully worked he always thought she ought to do better.

Another source of irritation was Edwin's will, and Adelaide mentioned it several times to Annie Walker, even in her husband's presence.

'Don't you think it's a shame?' she once said. 'Edwin has made a will that his property will come to me provided I never marry again.'

Edwin Bartlett's will had been drawn up in 1875 as part of the marriage contract, so it may not have been on his insistence that this clause had been included. It may have come from her father's agents, thereby offering some protection against the type of unscrupulous suitor who might prey on rich widows. However, the Married Women's Property Act, amended in 1882, allowed women to retain their assets even if they remarried, so if this was the reason for the inclusion of the clause it was no longer necessary.

In view of the recent change in the law, therefore, Adelaide felt that her husband's stipulation was particularly harsh; the wording of the will rankled with her and she made no secret of her feelings about it. Her concern must have seemed premature, however, for Edwin was in robust health and unlikely, in the normal course of events, to die for many years.

CHAPTER 3

Love in the Afternoons

In 1885 the Reverend George Dyson was a young probationary minister attached to the Wesleyan Chapel in Merton High Street. He was twenty-seven years old, of average height and build, and had cultivated a large, drooping moustache. He was a man of academic ambitions and, whilst working as a minister, continued to study for a degree. It was said of Edwin that he had a great respect for learning, so that George Dyson's intellectual pursuits would have impressed him greatly. Adelaide, too, must have found his company stimulating.

Dyson first met the Bartletts when they attended his chapel. He saw them sitting amongst the congregation and afterwards he welcomed them to the area and later called on them at The Cottage in the course of his pastoral duties. They continued to attend chapel and he called on them again, in June, when he was invited to stay for tea and to come to supper the following Wednesday. Edwin Bartlett told him that he would like him to call more often. For about a week in June Dyson was in Dublin, taking his degree of Bachelor of Arts at Trinity College, and on his return Edwin told him that he wanted Adelaide to take up her studies again, asking Dyson to supervise them. In consequence, Dyson began to call on Adelaide from time to time and give her lessons in Latin, History, Geography and Mathematics.

The friendship developed rapidly. Adelaide not only received Dyson at The Cottage but accompanied him, with Edward's knowledge, to his lodgings in Wimbledon. The young preacher soon found himself on very intimate terms with both husband and wife.

Edwin may have hoped that the study of Virgil and the rainfall in New Guinea might disperse some of the feminist notions that were, by now, firmly lodged in Adelaide's mind. He must have seen the minister as a man to whom he could entrust his wife's education without fear of that trust being abused. Mr Dyson's clerical garb, however, did not guarantee immunity from temptation, for beneath the black serge was a man as susceptible as any other to the provocative guile of a pretty woman, especially one with lustrous dark eyes, a lively mind and an appealing French accent.

For her part, Adelaide was only too willing to study under the intense gaze of the young preacher, and persuading Edwin that it was an excellent way of keeping boredom at bay would have been no problem. Her influence over her husband was remarkable – she had engineered her reinstatement after the affair with Frederick, for instance, and evidently without recriminations (although possibly a lingering resentment on her side at his lack of jealousy). She had also persuaded Edwin to move house twice in as many years and had even managed to push her father-in-law out of the family nest once and for all.

So it was that Adelaide's tutorial sessions became an established routine, although Dyson did not call when there were visitors. In July of that year, for example, when George and Alice Matthews were staying at The Cottage, they saw nothing of George Dyson and claimed later that they 'never knew such a person existed.'

It was odd, too, that Edwin did not mention to his father that Adelaide was receiving tuition, despite the fact that they had always discussed their domestic arrangements quite openly within the family. Not that Edwin himself saw much of the preacher. The maidservant, Mary Ann, noticed that Mr Bartlett usually left the house at eight o'clock in the morning as she arrived for work, and did not return until six o'clock or even ten at night. She usually left at eleven in the morning, but sometimes she stayed to cook dinner. During July and August she observed the frequent lengthy visits of George Dyson, sometimes from as early as eleven in the morning, and noted how often he stayed to dine alone with Adelaide – as often as three times a week towards the end of August. Only once, on the last day of August, was Edwin there as well; on the other occasions Mary Ann would leave the house with the pair still sitting together in the dining-room.

To be left alone in this way was shockingly unconventional, even though the gentleman was a minister of religion and the lady a member of his congregation. It was the sort of indiscreet behaviour guaranteed to cause the maid to purse her lips, for surely such impropriety could only lead to temptation. 'You cannot doubt,' said Mr Justice Wills when Adelaide stood before him at the Old Bailey, 'that they got to that state of intimacy when in some fashion or other the possible death of the husband and the possibility of Dyson succeeding him were matters of familiar discussion.'

Indeed they were, and meanwhile the relationship between the three of them progressed swiftly – so much so that Edwin grew to love George Dyson 'like a brother' and seemed actively to encourage the unusual degree of intimacy between his wife and the young preacher.

Circumstances were soon to change this cosy threesome, however. Adelaide, now very attached to George Dyson, depended on him to alleviate the boredom of her marriage. Their friendship had changed her life, for she was no longer lonely, having found someone whose company was both pleasant and stimulating. She was very upset, therefore, when in July he warned her that he would be moving to Putney in September. He was being transferred to a larger chapel in the Upper Richmond Road, which, he felt, marked an important milestone in his career.

Hearing this, Adelaide realised that her halcyon days were soon to end. She was determined, though, to enjoy Dyson's company while she could, and entertained him throughout August. They spent most of the afternoons together while his pastoral flock was left to fend for itself. Edwin, too, was kept busy at Herne Hill, stocktaking and ordering specialities for the Christmas trade. So it was that while Edwin put in orders for the crystallised ginger, his wife and young Dyson enjoyed regular trysts, undisturbed, in the little cottage at Merton.

The conversations between the lovers were wide-ranging. They discussed, for instance, Adelaide's expert knowledge of drugs and her ability to interpret prescriptions. She also told Dyson about her nursing experience some years earlier, saying that she had nursed Edwin through a very serious illness and had suffered from exhaustion as a result. Dyson could not afterwards recall that any disease had been named, only that she had used the word 'growth' and had said that it periodically caused Edwin bouts of severe pain.

Adelaide told Dyson that at one time she had consulted Dr Nichols about her husband's mysterious illness. The doctor, she claimed, had given an alarming prognosis, without even examining the patient, saying that Edwin would probably not live 'more than a year.'

The effect she was having on young George Dyson seems to have softened his brain, for he appears to have accepted her improbable tale without question.

Whilst enjoying her tutorial sessions with Dyson during the day, Adelaide dedicated her evenings to persuading Edwin to move house once more. By coincidence, the lease of The Cottage was due to expire in September of that year, and although they seemed to have been happy there, for some reason Edwin decided not to renew it.

On the last day of August, before they left Merton, the Bartletts and Dyson dined together. During the evening Adelaide announced that they planned to take a holiday in Dover, and they both begged the preacher to join them there. Unfortunately, his pastoral duties interfered with the pleasant prospect of a couple of weeks by the sea, but he promised to visit them whenever he could. He pointed out, however, that as he was obliged to live on his stipend of a hundred pounds a year, money was rather short. Hearing this, Edwin, with great generosity, swept aside any financial difficulties by insisting on paying for George Dyson's train fares to and from Dover.

For her part, Adelaide must have felt confident that Dyson would eventually join them in Dover for she had already booked the accommodation – a drawing-room, a double bedroom and a single bedroom, the latter presumably reserved for the young preacher. Nor was she disappointed, for Dyson managed to spend the first week of September walking the chalk cliffs with her instead of counting his new flock in Putney. Edwin, in the meantime, conscientious as ever, continued to work in his shop in Herne Hill as usual.

Then something prompted Edwin to make a new will. On the afternoon of 3rd September he asked two of his assistants to sign a document which was 'folded so as to leave only the narrow portion of the lower half visible'; thus it was that they both witnessed Edwin's signature without knowing the nature of the document before them.

There is nothing remarkable about a man not wishing to reveal the wording of his will to his employees; it was unusual, however, that Edwin's solicitor, Mr Wood, knew nothing about it, especially as he had drawn up both the marriage contract and the original will in 1875. In fact, the first Mr Wood heard of the new will was when Adelaide handed it to him the day after Edwin died.

It was a simple document that read as follows:

> I, Edwin Bartlett, will and bequeath all my property and everything I am possessed of to my wife, Adelaide, for her sole use, and appoint George Dyson, BA, Wesleyan Minister, and Edward Wood, Esquire, Solicitor, 66 Gresham Street, to be my executors.

With Adelaide's future thus assured and the prospect of Edwin's likely demise under discussion, was it more than coincidence that after October 1886 George Dyson would have completed his final probationary year of service in the ministry and, the following year, be free to marry?

CHAPTER 4

A Change of Air

Having changed his will leaving all he possessed to Adelaide, whether she married again or not, Edwin actively encouraged the friendship between his wife and the young preacher – or so it seemed, for he set himself a punishing routine apparently devised for the sole purpose of leaving them alone together as much as possible during the Dover holiday.

Every morning he caught the three o'clock train to London and did not return to Dover until half-past ten at night. This gruelling timetable was quite unnecessary as far as his business affairs were concerned; in fact, his partner Mr Baxter, remarked that Edwin was arriving in London so early that he had to walk the streets for a couple of hours, waiting for a reasonable time to open the shop. He gave Baxter no explanation for this bizarre behaviour.

On about 8th September, George Dyson left Dover to return to his ministerial work and, on 19th September, Edwin paid him a surprise visit at his new lodgings in Putney. He at once told him that he had made a new will naming him as an executor. He then complimented Dyson on the fine quality of his preaching, saying that Adelaide found it most uplifting. He showed Dyson one of her devotional letters, written from the Belgian convent, and expressed the hope that Dyson's influence and inspired teaching would lead her once more into a similarly devout frame of mind.

Dyson then confessed his emotional involvement and suggested that they discontinue the friendship as his fondness for Adelaide was beginning to affect his work.

This was hardly the sort of confidence a man might expect from a preacher, yet Edwin showed neither surprise nor chagrin; he merely said that he saw no reason for their friendship to end and went on to suggest that Dyson write to Adelaide in Dover, as he felt sure this would please her.

Apparently content at this stage to continue the liaison, George Dyson wrote to her the following day, Sunday, 20th September. The effect of his letter was evidently inspiring, for Edwin felt moved to reply:

> 14, St James Street
> Dover
>
> Monday
>
> Dear George
>
> Permit me to say I feel great pleasure in thus addressing you for the first time. To me it is a privilege to think that I am allowed to feel towards you as a brother and I hope our friendship will ripen as time goes on, without anything to mar its future brightness. Would that I could find words to express my thankfulness to you for the very loving letter you sent Adelaide today. It would have done anybody good to see her overflowing with joy as she read it whilst walking along the street, and afterwards as she read it to me. I felt my heart going out to you. I long to tell you how proud I feel at the thought I should soon be able to clasp the hand of the man who from his heart could pen such noble thoughts. Who can help loving you? I felt that I must say two words, 'Thank you', and my desire to do so is my excuse for troubling you with this.
>
> Looking towards the future with joyfulness,
>
> I am,
>
> > Yours affectionately,
> > Edwin

George Dyson's answer to this ambiguous and highly sentimental letter, written from his lodgings in Putney, arrived in Dover on 24th September:

> My dear Edwin,
>
> Thank you very much for the brotherly letter you sent me yesterday.

I am sure I respond from my heart to your wish that our friendship may ripen with the lapse of time, and I do so with confidence, for I feel that our friendship is founded on a firm, abiding basis – trust and esteem.

I have, from a boy, been ever longing for the confidence and trust of others. I have never been so perfectly happy as when in possession of this. It is in this respect, among many others, that you have shown yourself a true friend.

You have thanked me, and now I thank you, yet I ought to confess that I read your warm and generous letter with a kind of half fear – a fear lest you should ever be disappointed in me and find me a far more prosy, matter-of-fact creature than you expected.

Thank you, moreover, for the telegram;[9] it was very considerate to send it. I am looking forward with much pleasure to next week. Thus far I have been able to stave off any work, and trust to be able to keep it clear.

Dear old Dover, it will ever possess a pleasant memory for me in my mind and a warm place in my heart.

      With kind regards, believe me,
      Yours affectionately
   George

Attempts have been made to analyse these letters in the hope that they might provide a valuable insight into the strange relationship that existed between Edwin, Adelaide and George Dyson. Certainly, the style of the letters is verbose and the wording sentimental, yet they were couched in terms that were perfectly acceptable in the context of the period and do not necessarily in themselves indicate anything unusual.

In the last week of September George Dyson managed to spend a few more days in Dover as he had promised, happy to keep Adelaide company during her husband's absence. On 1st October, the last day of the holiday, Edwin went off to work as usual, leaving Dyson to escort Adelaide back to London, where rooms had been reserved at a hotel in the Strand. Once he had seen that she was comfortably settled, he returned to his own lodgings in Putney.

9   Edwin had sent Dyson a telegram containing the return fare to Dover.

During the next couple of days, while Edwin attended to his business, Adelaide was kept busy searching for a suitable flat.

It may seem strange to the modern reader, accustomed to equating material and social success with the acquisition of property, to learn that Edwin Bartlett, whilst owning several properties with living accommodation attached, should have chosen to lease a flat rather than buy a house. Leasing was widely practised in the late Victorian period and was by no means indicative of stringency or lack of social standing. Florence Bravo, for instance, an extremely wealthy women, leased, rather than owned, the Priory at Balham, the scene of the famous Charles Bravo poisoning. Likewise, Major Herbert Rowse Armstrong, convicted of killing his wife with arsenic, and the only British solicitor to be hanged for murder, leased, rather than owned his country villa, Mayfield, in the Herefordshire border town of Hay, though financially he was able to buy a house had he so wished.

It is possible that the Bartletts felt that a move across the river was a step up the social ladder, where the accommodation would be superior to the small South London flats they were used to. Whatever their reason for moving, Adelaide eventually found an apartment in a house in Claverton Street, in the St George's district of Pimlico – a very pleasant residential area, a few minutes' walk from the Embankment. No 85 was a recently-built terraced house, in a style typical of the day, with three floors and basement, and steps leading up to the front door, above which was a portico supported by two functional, rather than decorative columns.[10]

Mr Frederick Doggett, a Registrar of Births and Deaths, was the owner or leaseholder of the house, he, his wife Caroline and their son occupied the rooms on the ground and second floors, whilst the first floor was reserved for letting. It was certainly the best part of the house, with French windows leading onto the portico. The flat consisted of two rooms, separated by folding doors, though both rooms had access doors to the landing and stairs.

The Doggetts employed just one servant, a general maid called

---

10 Built about 1840 – now demolished.

Alice Fulcher, who slept in the attic under the eaves.

Mrs Doggett's first impression of Adelaide was not favourable – not only was she a foreigner but she had come to enquire about the flat unaccompanied. Nor was she too pleased when Adelaide made it clear that she would expect her new landlady to do all the shopping, provide Edwin with a substantial breakfast each morning, and, of course, prepare the evening meal. Once this was agreed, she made another stipulation, one which must have surprised and annoyed Mrs Doggett even more. Adelaide said that her husband suffered from dyspepsia, which gave rise to restlessness at night; she requested, therefore, that a separate bed be provided for him, suggesting that the existing double bed be replaced by two single ones.

Mrs Doggett protested, saying that she did not have a single bed to spare. In that case, said Adelaide, the double bed would have to stay, as long as Mrs Doggett could provide a folding camp bed instead which would be suitable for her husband. At this, Mrs Doggett warned that she was far too busy to go out and buy a folding bed immediately. Obviously displeased, Adelaide conceded that they would have to make do with the double bed, at least for the time being.

This was an unfortunate start to their acquaintance, but any initial misgivings Mrs Doggett may have had were at once dispelled when she was introduced to Edwin Bartlett that evening. At six-thirty he and Adelaide called at Claverton Street to finalise the letting arrangements, and his friendly manner and wholesome appearance eased the situation considerably.

At no time did Edwin mention his dyspepsia to Mrs Doggett or make any reference to the sleeping arrangements stipulated by his wife that morning. He told her that a gentleman would be dining with them 'once a week.' To this, Adelaide remarked that 'it was only a clergyman', thereby giving no hint of the importance that George Dyson had already assumed in their lives. Either she was affecting a casual attitude for Edwin's benefit or she rightly assumed that the likes of Mrs Doggett could not possibly understand the complex nature of their relationship with the young preacher.

After all, the Doggetts kept a very respectable, middle-class household where the slightest impropriety would be quickly noticed and frowned upon.

Adelaide may have dismissed George Dyson as 'just a clergyman', but it soon became clear that his visits to Claverton Street were to be more frequent than, as Edwin had put it, 'once a week.' Not only that, Mrs Doggett noticed that Adelaide kept a blue serge lounge coat and a pair of slippers in the flat for the use of *Georgius Rex*, as they called him, so that he could feel more comfortable, physically at least, during his tutorial visits.

It did not take long for Mrs Doggett and the maid, Alice, to realise that there was an unusual degree of intimacy between Mrs Bartlett and the young preacher: the lace curtains in the ground floor drawing-room at 85 Claverton Street must have provided the perfect screen for the landlady's surveillance. She noticed that George Dyson sometimes stayed all day, taking dinner with the Bartletts in the evening, while at other times Adelaide and George Dyson lunched at the flat and afterwards walked out together.

The carrying of dishes and cleaning of rooms was Alice Fulcher's job, so Mrs Doggett had little occasion to enter the Bartletts' flat on the first floor. The maid, however, was able to glean further details of the scandalous affair. On several occasions she found Adelaide and George Dyson alone together, sometimes 'sitting on the sofa', and once 'Mrs Bartlett sitting on the floor with her head on Mr Dyson's knee.' She also reported, mischievously, that Mr Dyson never seemed to be carrying any books when he came to the house.

This was certainly odd, for according to Dyson Edwin had given him a season ticket from Putney to Waterloo so that he could 'continue to supervise Mrs Bartlett's studies.'

'For that purpose,' he later explained, 'I went to Claverton Street two or three times a week, usually in the afternoons.'

At Adelaide's subsequent trial, Mr Justice Wills, clearly giving little credence to George Dyson's story, was scathing in his condemnation:

'It is not a pleasant spectacle that of a Christian minister steadily taking advantage of the husband's weakness, increasing the frequency of his visits under the guise of giving lessons (as to which, however, there is scarcely a trace of corroborative evidence) passing hour after hour – twice, three times, or four times a week – with the woman.'

It was during one of these intimate moments, with her head on George Dyson's shoulder, that Adelaide confided further details of Edwin's serious internal complaint. She told him that it was getting worse and was causing him 'great pain' and that to soothe him she had been accustomed to using chloroform. She told Dyson that she had not consulted any other doctor after Dr Nichols's prognosis because Edwin was 'very sensitive about his affliction.' Nurse Annie Walker had tried to help, she explained, by supplying the chloroform with which to soothe him.

Dyson, however, had not noticed anything seriously amiss with Edwin's health, although he said 'he appeared to have a severe pain in his left side' which Edwin had said was dyspepsia. This was especially troublesome after a large meal or too much wine; other than that, he seemed perfectly healthy.

But as Mr Justice Wills later remarked: 'When a young wife and a younger male friend get to discussing, whether in the presence of the husband or out of his presence, the probability of his decease within a measurable time, and the possibility of the friend succeeding to the husband's place, according to all ordinary experience of human life, that husband's life is not one that an insurance office would like to take out any premium.'

Perhaps the judge in all his wisdom was right. Was Edwin a victim of misguided trust in George Dyson's integrity and his young wife's loyalty? Alice Fulcher testified that when she had entered the room and saw Adelaide sitting with her head on the preacher's knee, neither of them seemed to be embarrassed in any way and 'still sat as they were.'

This blatant flaunting of convention, especially in the presence of servants, would indicate that the lovers felt it to be quite in order for them to openly display their affection for one another. When questioned after Edwin's death both of them said that Edwin was perfectly aware of their intimacy and had given them his blessing.

But did Edwin *really* know the extent of his wife's intimacy with George Dyson – or was Adelaide going her own sweet way, whether her husband liked it or not?

CHAPTER 5

Edwin's Mysterious Illness

During October 1885, Edwin's usually robust health began to fail. The onset of his symptoms was gradual and insidious. With hindsight, the illness so clearly suggests the effects of slow poisoning that it seems extraordinary that his doctor failed to suspect it. It must be said, however, that few doctors can expect to come across many cases of criminal poisoning in everyday practice, and when they do, must sometimes take them to be the result of bacteria, innocently consumed in food, for instance.

Edwin became weary and depressed, showing signs of physical and mental exhaustion. He also suffered from excessive salivation and complained of a metallic taste in his mouth, accompanied by twitching of the limbs. But the most distressing symptom of all was the swollen and spongy state of his gums. They eventually became so bad that he found it unbearable to wear his dental plate, yet still his morbid fear of dentists made him refuse to seek help.

Naturally, he tried to treat the condition himself by rinsing his mouth with Condy's fluid, a patent oral antiseptic, but this brought little relief. The poor man found that the twitching of his limbs prevented sound sleep and he also complained that the light sometimes hurt his eyes, so much so that he soon developed the habit of half-closing his eyes to protect them.

Despite this alarming array of symptoms (described by the doctor they eventually called), neither Edwin or Adelaide mentioned the illness to anyone, not even Edwin's father. Though feeling most unwell, Edwin did not seem unduly concerned about his condition, as though he fully expected to feel his old self in a matter of days.

But his health did not improve. Instead it became steadily worse, and in the second week of November he suffered a bad attack of nausea and diarrhoea. Yet with all the discomfort and debilitating effect of this and further attacks, he continued to go to work each day. The period before Christmas was, of course, a particularly busy time in the grocery trade and, despite his illness, he worked himself as hard as ever.

In the little spare time he had, he was busily preparing two of his best dogs for a show scheduled for 9th December. It is not known exactly where the dogs were housed after they left The Cottage at Merton, although they appear to have been somewhere near or perhaps behind the shop at Herne Hill. They were certainly not kept at 85 Claverton Street, for Mrs Doggett, when enumerating Adelaide's additional requirements on renting the flat, made no mention of providing for animals as well.

Edwin was looking forward to the dog show and on 4th December he washed and groomed the dogs in readiness. Four days later, however, he was feeling so ill that he left work early. Back at Claverton Street he suffered further bouts of diarrhoea but these attacks eased later in the day and he spent the evening on the sofa in the front room, warmly wrapped in his quilted dressing gown.

At nine-thirty the next morning, George Dyson arrived at Claverton Street to accompany the Bartletts to the dog show. He was concerned at Edwin's appearance and learned that he was still having bouts of vomiting and was clearly unwell. Despite this, Edwin insisted on proceeding with their proposed trip and the three, not in the best of spirits, made their way to the show.

Soon after they arrived, however, Edwin complained of intense pain in his stomach and seemed on the verge of collapse. There was little alternative but to return home as quickly as possible. Back at Claverton Street the pain and sickness continued, and Adelaide was prompted to call a doctor at last. However, instead of asking Mrs Doggett to recommend a good local physician, which would have been the most natural thing to do, she decided to walk round the district in search of one.

She selected Dr Alfred Leach, in Charlwood Street, apparently at random though later events were to prove it was a fortunate choice. He was young, newly qualified and a little naive; never having met the Bartletts before, he knew nothing of their medical history and could not know whether Edwin's symptoms were psychosomatic or due to a physical disorder.

Having found a doctor, Adelaide gave him an account of her husband's symptoms, at the same time suggesting that he was a bit of a hypochondriac. He even *imagined*, she said, that he was the victim of an incurable disease!

Dr Leach had no reason to doubt her and so called on his new patient with a preconceived idea about the nature of his illness. He was later to describe his first meeting with Edwin Bartlett in an article in *The Lancet*:[11]

> About 10am on December 10th at 85 Claverton Street, I first saw Mr E. Bartlett, aged 40. He was a rather short, muscular man, in appearance not over 30, of fair complexion, with blue eyes and a light brown beard. He was somewhat pale and looked timid and anxious and nervous. His limbs were a little shaky. It was difficult to 'catch his eye' but it could be arrested momentarily by direct reference to his bodily ailments. He was not much inclined to speak and turned to his wife for answers. His pupils were very contracted – this condition of the pupil was very persistent until death. The pulse was poor and small and slight. He was in a very bad state.

Despite this impression, Dr Leach considered that 'the physical state of the man was not seriously impaired.' Clearly, he favoured the opinion that Edwin's symptoms, though distressing, were primarily caused by his highly nervous state – as Adelaide had already suggested.

At the end of his examination, Leach diagnosed sub-acute gastritis and prescribed a concoction of bismuth, cinchona and tincture of nux-vomica.

In the doctor's opinion, the blue line that had recently appeared

---

11 *The Lancet*, 22nd May 1886.

around the edge of his patient's gums was by far the most disturbing symptom of all. This, and the excessive salivation, suggested to him that Edwin had been taking doses of mercury.

Keen to delve further into the matter, Leach hurried back to his consulting room to study the subject of mercurialism. Returning to Claverton Street in triumph he examined his patient 'very carefully for signs of the reason for taking mercury – in other words, syphilis.'

To his surprise he found no sign of the disease but told Edwin that he was suffering, not from gastritis, as he had originally diagnosed, but from mercurial poisoning. Having said this, he expected Edwin to confess that he had been dosing himself with mercury to cure syphilis, real or imagined.

He was mistaken; Edwin vehemently denied taking anything that contained mercury – for any reason whatsoever.

This left Dr Leach perplexed and unable to cope with the possibility that his diagnosis was wrong. Lacking in experience, he clung resolutely to his textbooks and so may have misconstrued the significance of the symptoms presented to him.

However, that same evening, Edwin suddenly admitted to swallowing 'a blue pill' that he had found in a drawer in his desk at work. Salesmen were always giving him pills to sample, he explained, and as he had been feeling unwell recently, he had taken one of them.

Dr Leach seemed to accept this explanation and launched enthusiastically into a further investigation, eventually coming up with the following theory:

> This man years ago was badly used by some dentists, some teeth that should have been drawn were filed off. He could not clean his teeth and his mouth became foul, and sulphides were naturally among the products of decomposition. Having got a dose of mercury into the system, the sulphides seized upon all that circulated through the margin in the gums, and formed a deposit in their edges of black sulphide of mercury. The general mercurial symptoms I accounted for by supposing him to have an idiosyncrasy (an allergic reaction) for that drug. I communicated this argument to him and his wife and it seemed to be acceptable to both.

Adelaide was happy to accept this long-winded theory, whilst Edwin seemed content to lie back and let his wife handle Dr Leach and the whys and wherefores of his illness.

So sure was Leach that he had solved the mystery of the blue line that even after the subsequent post-mortem report showed that traces of lead, not mercury, had been found in Edwin's jaw, he continued to offer his own theory of mercurialism. Although Adelaide conscientiously preserved specimens of her husband's excreta, urine and vomit during his illness, Dr Leach declined to make an analysis as he was quite satisfied that his diagnosis was the correct one.

From 10th December, until Edwin's death on the last day of the year, the doctor called almost daily at Claverton Street, sometimes making as many as three visits in one day. In all that time, he found Adelaide to be a devoted and kindly nurse – if anything, he thought that she was over-anxious about her husband's health and made the comment that she 'petted him too much.'

She certainly did everything she could to make him as comfortable as possible. She rearranged the furniture, bringing the camp bed into the front room and placing it at right angles to the fireplace. She also pushed the heavy sofa against the folding doors, insisting that it was no bother to go into the back bedroom by way of the landing whenever necessary. As it happened, she had to make this journey quite often, for, in an attempt to make the front room look as cheerful as possible, she had moved all the medicine bottles and lotions into the other room, out of sight.

At the same time she assumed full responsibility for nursing her husband and Dr Leach entrusted her with the administration of all the medicines he prescribed.

Taking her duties seriously, she discouraged visitors from the start of Edwin's illness, saying that he needed peace and quiet – even those who were allowed to call had their times arranged beforehand. It was noted, too, that Adelaide always stayed by her husband's side during visiting times and as Dr Leach observed, answered the questions that were put to him as though he were incapable of speaking for himself.

As for Mrs Doggett, she seems to have gone out of her way to make things easier for her tenants, even giving Adelaide the use of the little smoking room downstairs as a reception area. Alice Fulcher was instructed to show all visitors into the smoking room where they were obliged to wait until Adelaide came downstairs to greet them. She even insisted that Dr Leach observe the same rule when he came to see his patient.

On 11th December Edward Baxter arrived to see Edwin. He had just received a letter from him in which he said that he was 'indisposed' but expected to be 'over it within a few days.' He was shown into the smoking room by the maid, and when Adelaide eventually came down she told him that the doctor had ordered Edwin to be quiet and 'not to see anyone to do with business.' She refused to allow Mr Baxter to go upstairs but suggested that 'if he called at six o'clock the following Sunday she thought that Edwin might be well enough to see him for a short time.'

With that, Edwin's friend and business partner was shown the door. Within minutes of his departure however, old Mr Bartlett arrived, having called at the shop to see his son. Hearing that he was ill, he had come straight round to see him, and was therefore surprised and annoyed when the maid showed him into the smoking room as though he were a stranger. As Adelaide kept him waiting for several minutes before coming downstairs to greet him, the old man took this as an added insult and was most displeased. She gave him Dr Leach's diagnosis but did not refer to the doctor by name. Old Mr Bartlett said later that Adelaide had 'seemed reluctant to say much about the doctor', merely saying that he was 'from up the street.'

Edwin's father was far from happy with all this and complained bitterly about the visiting arrangements. Seeing how angry he was, Adelaide went back upstairs, saying that she would ask Edwin if he wished to see his father. When she returned, she led the way up to the front room where, according to the old man, Edwin was 'lying on a sort of chair bed and was partially undressed. He said the doctor had told him he was suffering from mercurial poisoning. He said he could not remember taking any mercury. He appeared rather dazed. He looked ill.'

That was to be the last of the old man's unscheduled visits. The following day he received a letter from his daughter-in-law:

> Dear Father,
>
> The doctor was very angry that I had permitted Edwin to see visitors last night, as it caused his head to be so bad; and he says no one is to be admitted unless he gives permission. Edwin is slightly better this morning. I will write to you every day and let you know how Edwin is. I can see myself how necessary it is that he should be kept calm.
>
> With love,
> Yours, Adelaide

This letter leaves no doubt that Adelaide's feelings towards her father-in-law were extremely cool, and that she was no longer concerned to hide them; it was her intention to treat the old man in the same way as any other visitor to the sick-room.

Dr Leach continued to visit Claverton Street, treating Edwin with various concoctions. He noted, however, that whilst his patient's physical condition showed some improvement, his spirits did not. The blue line along Edwin's gums had gradually disappeared and only a 'grey sloughing' was left, but he was still suffering from insomnia and on Sunday, 13th December, Dr Leach gave him a dose of bromide as a sedative.

Edward Baxter, however, failed to notice any great improvement in Edwin's condition when he called that Sunday evening as arranged. On the contrary, he thought that his friend looked very ill, finding him 'scarcely able to speak.' That same day Leach had called three times, and as Edwin was still sleeping badly he resorted to injecting morphia. This may have had the desired effect, for another injection was given the following day.

Over the next couple of weeks Dr Leach came to know Adelaide Bartlett quite well. At first, he called every morning in an official capacity, but as the days went by he started to pop in around four o'clock in the afternoon. He seemed to be much taken with her and gallantly declined to make any charge for these solicitous afternoon calls. Having secured the doctor's confidence Adelaide soon dispensed with conventional drawing-room chatter and ventured on more intimate matters, and Leach, feeling himself to be a man of the world, listened intently to her account of her marriage to Edwin.

She told him, for instance, that night after night she was obliged to sit in a chair by her husband's bed – holding his toe! Surprised by this bizarre revelation, young Leach protested that she should take more rest at night lest she make herself ill. But to this she replied:

> What would be the good, doctor? He would walk about all night. He will not sleep unless I sit and hold his toe.

Intrigued rather than amused by this strange behaviour, Dr Leach began to wonder whether his patient was insane; yet his concern was mainly for Adelaide – she was petite, delicate even, with an appealing accent, a combination that engendered concern and a desire to protect. So it was that Dr Leach begged her to consider employing a professional nurse to relieve her of the more arduous and unpleasant tasks in the sick-room. Adelaide, however, declined, saying:

> 'Edwin likes *me* to attend to him.'

The next visitor to Claverton Street was George Matthews, Edwin's old friend from East Dulwich. He arrived on Monday, 14th December, and was told by Adelaide that Edwin was suffering from slight mercurial poisoning and also from verdigris. She said he might possibly have got the poison from moving things in the warehouse, as he had been hunting rats. She took Matthews upstairs, but he found Edwin 'very prostrated' and did not stay long.

Although the condition of Edwin's mouth had improved a little, on 16th December Dr Leach decided to bring Thomas Roberts, a local dentist, to Claverton Street, to see if there was anything more to be done. Roberts was introduced to Adelaide on the landing outside the door and asked her if her husband was in the habit of taking mercury in any form.

'I do not know,' she replied.

Roberts examined Edwin's mouth and looked at his gums. Like

Leach, he judged that he was suffering from mercurial poisoning.

The dentist decided to extract two roots there and then and returned the following day to extract a further eleven. Four days later he went back to Claverton Street to extract four teeth, using a solution of cocaine on the gums. At that time he thought that 'the signs of mercurial poison had lessened.'

This protracted treatment must have been torturous for Edwin with his inordinate fear of dentists, but being given the 'new drug' cocaine seemed to make him much more cheerful about the whole thing. Very pleased with the way things had gone, he told Mrs Doggett that he had felt no pain at all, which he thought was 'wonderful.'

Clearly, Edwin was improving at last, although Adelaide still discouraged spontaneous visits from family and friends. In order to keep Mr Baxter at bay she wrote him a daily bulletin on Edwin's progress and promised him a visit the following Sunday at six o'clock. This arrangement seemed to satisfy Edward Baxter, but Edwin's father was not so easy to handle. Naturally, he wanted to see his son whenever he wished and thereby monitor his progress for himself, but Adelaide treated him disdainfully, refusing to make any concessions at all. After his first visit on 11th December, he called six or seven times before he was allowed to see his son, and each time he was sent away with a message from Adelaide that she could not leave Edwin. In all, he saw his son only three times during his illness. The fourth time he was lying dead.

He had arrived at Claverton Street on 17th December, whilst Mr Roberts was upstairs attending to Edwin's teeth. Despite the fact that he had obviously called at an inconvenient time and was told that he could not see his son, he went away worried and disgruntled.

The following day he received this letter from Adelaide:

Dear Mr Bartlett,

Edwin is up; he seems to have stood his tooth-drawing very well. Please do not trouble to come all this distance; it is not right to have visitors in a sick-room and I don't feel it right to leave Edwin so long alone while I was downstairs talking to you. When he wishes to see you I will write and let you know.   Yours, Adelaide

The old man was furious. He immediately arranged a meeting with the rest of the Bartlett family, a gathering which presumably included Edwin's sister, Caroline, who was living in Croydon. On hearing Mr Bartlett senior's version of the events surrounding Edwin's illness and of Adelaide's hostile attitude towards him, they too, were unhappy with the situation. It was decided, therefore, to engage another doctor to examine Edwin and give them the benefit of a second opinion.

This agreed, Edwin's father went straight round to Claverton Street to 'have it out' with his daughter-in-law. When she eventually came down to the smoking room he told her:

> I wish to bring a physician of my own choosing to Edwin as he does not seem to be getting any better.

To this, Adelaide replied that they could not afford to call another doctor. The old man retaliated by saying: 'Nonsense, Adelaide! Not afford it, indeed!'

'Well,' she said. 'We cannot.'

'You had better,' retorted the old man.

After he had left the house, Dr Leach made his usual morning call and was told by Adelaide that the Bartlett family wanted a second opinion. Asked if this was true, Edwin seemed embarrassed and apologised to Dr Leach, saying that his family 'were not friends' with his wife. Adelaide retaliated by saying that 'they were never content' with what she did for Edwin.

Turning to Dr Leach she made a remarkably accurate prediction:

'If he should get worse, or die,' she said, 'Mr Bartlett's friends would accuse me of poisoning him.'

With this in mind, Edwin eventually agreed to see another doctor, but one chosen, he stipulated, by Dr Leach, not by his family. He emphasised that he was only agreeing to a second opinion 'for the protection of my wife.'

The next morning, while she was waiting for Dr Leach and another physician to arrive, Adelaide wrote again to Edwin's father.

Edwin's Mysterious Illness

Dear Father

Edwin seems slightly better, and has passed a restful night. I am expecting another doctor, so you must excuse this note.

Yours sincerely,
Adelaide

She also wrote a similar note to Edward Baxter but favoured him with this addition: 'Edwin will be pleased to see you on Sunday 20th between six and eight.'

Clearly, Adelaide was not prepared to tolerate any interference from old Mr Bartlett. Edward Baxter, though, was a different matter – he obeyed her instructions, accepted her opinion and did not ask awkward questions. She saw no harm, therefore, in allowing him to call on Edwin every now and then. As for Edwin's father, he was obviously suspicious of the treatment his son was receiving and was proving very difficult indeed.

CHAPTER 6

Signs of Hysteria

The man chosen to give a second opinion on Edwin's malaise was Dr John Dudley. On Saturday, 19th December, he went with Dr Leach to Claverton Street, and, having examined Edwin very thoroughly, found 'no physical signs of disease whatsoever.' The alarming symptoms which Dr Leach had previously attributed to mercurial poisoning had by now disappeared and there was no longer any sign of sub-acute gastritis.

'I saw no blue line,' Dr Dudley stated in evidence, 'and was not informed by Dr Leach that it was a case of poisoning. I noticed the sponginess of the gums which Mrs Bartlett attributed to a pill he had taken.'

'He had a depressed mental appearance and seemed disinclined to change his position or even raise his eyelids. He told me he had been overworked and required rest and sleep; that he had not slept well for a considerable time and scarcely at all the last few nights.

'After I had examined him I told him that he was a sound man, and that he ought to sit up and go out for a walk or a drive daily. I do not think he made any reply.

'Mrs Bartlett was present throughout the interview. She replied to several questions I put to her and took part in the conversation generally. With regard to his previous health and habits, her answers were all favourable; that his habits were temperate and his general health had been previously good. Mrs Bartlett seemed attentive and anxious.'

Dr Dudley prescribed various medications containing small

amounts of bromide and morphia to calm Edwin, and when he left Claverton Street that day he was convinced that his patient was well on the way to recovery and would soon be fit to resume work. Certainly, Edwin appeared to be more cheerful after the doctors' visit, and he was delighted when Mrs Doggett brought up a plate of hot buttered toast for his tea. Surprisingly, his hearty appetite had not been impaired by his illness and, turning to his landlady, he declared that it was 'wonderful that he could eat!'

Having munched his way through afternoon tea, the invalid was apparently too ill to receive his father when he called later that evening. All the old man was told by Adelaide was that another doctor had examined Edwin earlier in the day. He was not allowed to go upstairs and was obliged, yet again, to leave Claverton Street without seeing his son.

The next day, Sunday, 20th December, Edward Baxter arrived promptly as arranged and was taken up to the sick-room to see Edwin – though, as usual, Adelaide stayed by her husband's side the whole time. It is possible that during this visit Baxter, acting as mediator, ventured to offer a plea on old Mr Bartlett's behalf, for after he had left the flat that evening Adelaide wrote this note to her father-in-law:

> Dear Mr Bartlett,
> Edwin will be very pleased to see you on Monday evening from six to eight. He is still very weak, and cannot bear visitors for long at a time.

The next day was Monday, 21st December. During the morning George Dyson called at Claverton Street to say goodbye to the Bartletts before going to spend Christmas with his family in Poole. Left in Pimlico with only a sickly husband for company, Adelaide must have watched her lover's departure with despair.

Later in the day, Mr Roberts, the dentist, returned with Dr Leach to extract Edwin's last two rotten stumps and four decaying teeth. As before, he used cocaine for the operation and Edwin said that he felt no pain and that it was more bearable than any previous dental treatment he had received.

In the Interests of Science: Adelaide Bartlett and The Pimlico Poisoning

That evening his father called again as arranged. He thought his son was looking rather depressed but Adelaide explained that he had had more teeth drawn earlier in the day. Once again, she remained in the room the whole time father and son were together, giving them no chance to talk to one another privately, had they so wished.

Yet, despite his misgivings, Edwin's father had to admit that his son was looking a little better, physically at least. His mental condition, however, had deteriorated: prior to his illness, he had been 'an optimistic sort of fellow, energetic and full of fun'. He was certainly none of these things now.

Dr Leach, writing in *The Lancet*,[12] described Edwin's state of mind thus:

> He was depressed by trifles, but never angered by anything. He was passive under treatment and did what he was told, provided it involved no great effort. He gave the impression of suffering from partial paralysis of the will and emotional ataxy. His wife remarked in his presence, 'You would never think, seeing him now, that he rules a staff of employees, kindly and considerately, but with unequalled firmness.'

By all accounts this was perfectly true.

Edwin's physical health, however, continued to improve, and by 22nd December his recovery was almost complete. Mentally, though, he had deteriorated still further and it was clear that there was something drastically wrong with him, something he could not explain.

To quote again from *The Lancet*,[13] Dr Leach gave this description of his patient's demeanour:

> I could not cajole him into a resolution to go out of doors, but he managed to get out of bed and potter about the room. His wife, on several occasions, told me before him, 'He still talks about dying and not recovering.' He would not explain his reasons. She also said that he slept a great deal better than he thought he did. He consented

12   *The Lancet*, 22nd May, 1886.
13   *The Lancet*, op. cit.

to go to Torquay but postponed his departure. He and his wife both protested against a diminution of professional visits, declaring that he 'derived strength' from them and felt weak in the intervals.

I was desirous of removing him from both his wife and myself, but he persisted that strangers would not understand his complaint. He would not have a nurse. His wife still sat up all night and took short sleeps on the sofa, or in the armchair by his bed, and when remonstrated with she declared that he would not compose himself or rest unless she sat close by holding his foot; and when she was absent from her post he would leave his bed and wander about. By day he showed no such inclination.

He was now obtaining some sleep; had lost no flesh; his muscles were firm and his countenance more cheerful. One morning he told me that, being unable to sleep and feeling exhausted, he had risen from his bed and stood for two hours with his arms outstretched over his sleeping wife and felt her vital energy entering his fingertips, after which he slept.

No wonder Leach felt that Adelaide needed a break from her demanding and demented husband. Having persuaded Edwin to spend some time in Torquay after Christmas, the doctor offered to accompany him on the journey and to introduce him to a local physician when they got there.

'What would have done him good,' he said, 'would have been a trip with no one to nurse him or hold his toe and that sort of nonsense.' To this he added that Edwin was, at that time, 'practically hysterical.'

During Dr Leach's visit that evening it was decided that Edwin should travel to Torquay on Boxing Day. Adelaide, however, was not happy with this arrangement, saying that her husband was still too weak to make such a long journey. She begged him to wait until the New Year but her objections were overruled.

When Dr Leach arrived the next morning, Adelaide had an unpleasant surprise for him. Edwin, she announced, had 'passed a lumbricoid worm.'[14]

This was an unexpected and distasteful turn of events, but in the

---

14 An intestinal parasite found in both humans and dogs but slightly larger in the human bowel.

days before refrigeration many people suffered various degrees of worm infestation at some time in their lives. The doctor himself admitted that he had previously fallen foul of worms yet Edwin reacted violently to the appearance of the parasite – it seemed to worry him deeply and disproportionately so that his depression increased. Dr Leach recorded that 'Mr Bartlett was very much perturbed. He was shocked. He was in such a condition about it that I put off treatment for a couple of days, partly to see if any more worms were present, and partly to let him gather pluck and spirit.'

To calm his distraught patient without giving any actual medication, Leach, unknown to Adelaide, gave Edwin a placebo during this period. Poor Edwin was so convinced that he was crawling with worms that he told his father he could 'feel them in his throat'. On another occasion, depressed and tormented, he cried:

'Can anyone be as bad as I am and yet survive?'

The fact that the appearance of the worm affected him so badly was strange; it was a morbid and hysterical reaction, for he had treated his dogs for worm infestation on numerous occasions and knew quite well that it was relatively simple to get rid of them. Being in a highly nervous state, the presence of the worm had triggered off other hidden fears within him and, of course, any plans for the trip to Torquay were immediately forgotten.

In the meantime, Dr Leach did his best to placate his patient and prescribed two large doses of Epsom Salts to dislodge any other worms that might be lurking in his bowel.

The next morning the doctor arrived at Claverton Street expecting to find that the laxative treatment he had prescribed had produced some positive results. He was very surprised, therefore, when he was shown a 'single motion of normal consistency and containing no trace of worms.'

Suspecting that Edwin had not, in fact, taken the Epsom Salts as prescribed, but had craftily, 'done away with them', Dr Leach decided to supervise the next purging session himself. He wrote a prescription for various volatile purgatives and asked Adelaide to get them from the chemist in readiness for the following day.

So depressing was the atmosphere at the Bartletts' flat that day, it was difficult to believe that it was Christmas Eve. Edwin was in a state of nervous collapse on his bed, eyes closed, body prostrate, and, in his mind at least, hovering between life and death. As for Adelaide, her pretty face had begun to show signs of strain after a fortnight's continuous nursing with very little sleep. Dr Leach was right. She was exhausted, and Christmas 1885 promised to be, for the Bartletts at least, a far from festive time.

Dr Leach called round for a few moments on Christmas morning, but whereas other people were exchanging brightly wrapped presents and tokens of good cheer, Adelaide presented him with the collection of purgatives she had collected from the chemist. Dr Leach then instructed her to ensure that Edwin had nothing at all to eat from midnight onwards.

This was especially hard on Edwin, for eating seemed to be the only worldly pleasure he had left. Leach was adamant, however, and promised to call round the next day to supervise the evacuation of his patient's bowel.

With this unpleasant prospect before him, young Leach hurried home to enjoy his Christmas fare as best he could in the circumstances.

CHAPTER 7

The Reluctant Worm

At three o'clock on Boxing Day, Dr Leach arrived at Claverton Street, ready for action. He was not the only visitor, for George Dyson was already there, having just returned from spending Christmas with his family. It is doubtful whether poor Edwin really appreciated having an audience at such a time but without further ado he was given some croton oil and a dose of santonine, a mixture that was lethal to worms.

Shortly afterwards, Alice Fulcher came upstairs with afternoon tea and, while Edwin lay prostrate on his camp bed, Adelaide, Dr Leach and George Dyson enjoyed some hot buttered toast and a plate of cakes. Excluded from such mouth-watering treats, the weary patient lay back on his pillows and waited. Nothing happened. George Dyson took his leave about eight o'clock, at which time Dr Leach decided to administer the first purgative to flush out the santonine and, hopefully, the dead worms.

Confident that his treatment would ensure rapid results, Leach and Adelaide sat by the fire and waited. Still nothing happened.

At nine o'clock the maid came in to lay the supper things. Adelaide and the doctor then proceeded to consume a tasty meal while poor Edwin lay immobile, empty and thoroughly miserable.

Soon after eleven Alice returned to replenish the coal scuttle and bank up the fire for the night. When she had finished, she bade them goodnight and went upstairs to bed. Adelaide was by now growing tired, Leach had begun to look puzzled, and the patient lay still and said nothing.

But Leach had no intention of giving up his vigil and Adelaide seemed quite happy to sit by the fire and wait. At one point during the evening they began to discuss various medical subjects which seemed to have a rallying effect on Edwin. Coming out of his trance-like state, he became livelier and showed signs of wanting to 'engage in conversation.' Leach, however, was having none of this – his mind was on action, not words, and he was losing patience. When twelve o'clock passed without any positive result he was mystified and utterly deflated.

He ordered Adelaide to ply Edwin with numerous cups of hot tea and coffee to stimulate the sluggish movement of his bowel – but still nothing happened. Finally, Leach records, 'at about 3.30am, he said he was feeling a bit tired and wanted some solid food, so with a humiliating sense of defeat I left, telling him that the resources of civilisation were at an end. Six hours later than usual matutinal evacuation occurred'.

This puzzled Dr Leach even more; naive as he was, he began to wonder if Edwin had again somehow managed to avoid taking the purgatives. He wondered, too, whether the santonine had ever reached the patient's stomach. According to the textbooks, after so long in his system it should have produced the most alarming symptoms – green vision and vomiting – yet when asked how he felt Edwin merely said that the medicine had been comforting to his stomach.

It must have crossed the doctor's mind, therefore, that Edwin, with Adelaide's connivance, had taken something that *looked* like santonine but was, in fact, some innocuous concoction, for no man could have withstood such a violent purging without more positive results.

But why should the Bartletts indulge in such a silly charade, one that served no purpose, except to leave Edwin bored but no better and Dr Leach speechless with frustration?

Had the wretched worm really come from Edwin or had it, perhaps, come from one of the dogs?

Adelaide was worming them at the time, and it would have been quite simple to deposit one of the dog worms into Edwin's chamber pot and so increase his hysteria that the trip to Torquay had to be cancelled. If so, it was an ingenious trick and one that fooled Edwin and Dr Leach, yet it seemed odd that she should contrive to keep Edwin at home when she clearly needed a break from nursing him.

While they were waiting for the treatment to take effect, Edwin started to talk enthusiastically about mesmerism, and asked the doctor if he would mesmerise him. Leach declined and asked Edwin whether he thought he was under mesmeric control of some sort. Edwin said that a friend had visited them the previous summer and mesmerised him.

At this, Adelaide broke in.

'Oh, Edwin, how absurd you are! He does get some strange ideas into his head nowadays, doctor!'

'I think he mesmerised me through my wife,' Edwin went on. 'Is that a possibility?'

To this Dr Leach replied that he did not know but asked why Edwin should feel he was under some kind of mesmeric control. The patient's only reply was that 'they were doing things that were unusual and contrary to common sense.'

Leach then asked Edwin how long he had continued to do strange things, to which he replied, 'I am still doing them.'

'But what are they? asked the doctor.

'Well, perhaps I should not be here if it were not for the influence.'

'Where would you be?' enquired Leach.

'Elsewhere; perhaps at the seaside; perhaps abroad,' he said.

At this Leach began to wonder whether his patient might really be in terror of somebody who had acquired ascendancy over him. 'Do you feel a sinking or depression when you hear him coming, or do you shudder when he approaches?' he asked.

'No, not at all,' answered Edwin. 'I like him.'

Then, despairing of making head or tail of his patient's mental condition, Leach put a final question:

'Do you feel positive that your supposed friend is really a friend, and not trying to work out his own ends through his influence over you, mesmeric or otherwise?'

Edwin said he was sure this was not the case. Leach appealed to Adelaide for her opinion, but she merely replied, 'Edwin and he are the best of friends and he is a true friend to both of us.' Leach later repeated the question to her in private and received the same reply.

To keep faith with his patient, Leach later consulted a distinguished student of things mystical, asking the latter if he believed it within the bounds of possibility that any dominant idea could be made to possess a man in Edwin's state and, if not, how he could best be restored to his right senses again. When he next visited Edwin he assured him that his delusions had been very carefully considered, and was able to argue convincingly that they were no more than that. Edwin seemed to accept what he was told.

We cannot know whether the mysterious friend was George Dyson or some other acquaintance of the Bartletts, but clearly Edwin was convinced that he was under some sort of mesmeric control. Whether or not these feelings were engendered by his weak mental state is difficult to assess, but it seems likely, from the complexity of his symptoms, that he was suffering from a nervous breakdown.

Almost deranged through lack of sleep and totally dependent on his wife, delusions of being mesmerised tortured his mind, making him especially susceptible to any suggestion Adelaide might make. His well-being was entirely in her hands and he was fast losing touch with reality.

Even Dr Leach realised that Edwin had become mentally unbalanced, yet it did not occur to him that the sudden appearance of the worm might have been one of the 'strange things' his patient had mentioned. Edwin may have known that all the doctor's efforts to flush out more worms would fail. He may have realised, too, that Adelaide had planted the worm to prevent him from going to Torquay and then exchanged Leach's santonine for some other substance from her medicine chest. Edwin had told Leach that they were both doing things they would not normally do but he was obviously in no state to question the logic of his wife's behaviour.

Yet Edwin's hysterical reaction to the appearance of the lumbricoid worm suggests that he was not party to the deception and really thought he was infested with worms, with the result that his depression was further exaggerated and his morbid fancies began to run riot. The poor man obviously felt that he was so riddled with worms that he was literally rotting away. He told Dr Leach on one occasion, 'We call them snakes,' which would indicate that Adelaide chose to make light of Edwin's pitiful delusion when they were alone, instead of trying to reassure him that it was merely a product of his imagination.

Whatever her reason for tormenting her husband in this way, she knew that Edwin was afraid to leave her and was terrified of the trip to Torquay. It was probably on these grounds, therefore, that she justified her deception, for the appearance of the worm had effectively quashed all plans for Edwin to go away – at least for a while.

Having retired shortly after three o'clock that morning, young Leach returned to Claverton Street at noon the next day, labouring under a 'humiliating sense of failure'.

By this time, Edwin was looking much better. Adelaide, however, was exhausted, and at this stage Dr Leach was more concerned for her health than for Edwin's. He told her once more that she must try to get more sleep and put an end to the habit of holding her husband's foot all night. The conversation led Leach back to the subject of Torquay, and he managed to persuade Adelaide to agree to a tentative date of 5th January. In the meantime, he suggested that she should try to get Edwin to leave the house occasionally – to go for a drive or a walk instead of lying in bed all day, prey to his morbid fancies.

But Adelaide was adamant that he would not go out and 'still talked of dying', saying it would 'kill him to go out.' Hearing this, Dr Leach went away to think things over, hoping to come up with a solution to his patient's unusual problem.

That evening Edward Baxter called at six o'clock as arranged.

Edwin was looking better but told his visitor that he had passed a worm and could feel more of them 'wriggling up his throat.' He also mentioned that his father was far from happy with the restrictions Adelaide had placed on his visits. Although sensing that the old man's discontent might lead to complications, Adelaide had written to him making it plain that she had no intention of being intimidated:

> Dear Mr Bartlett,
>
> I hear that you are a little disturbed because Edwin has been too ill to see you. I wish, if possible, to be friends with you, but you must place yourself on the same footing as other persons – that is to say, you are welcome here when I invite you, and at no other time. You seem to forget that I have not been in bed for thirteen days, and consequently am too tired to speak to visitors.
>
> I am sorry to speak so plainly, but I wish you to understand that I have neither forgotten nor forgiven the past.
>
> Edwin will be pleased to see you on Monday evening any time after six.
>
> Adelaide

Warmly wrapped against the cold night air, Adelaide was on her way downstairs to post this note when the maid answered the front door bell. It was George Dyson, who was expected at nine o'clock that evening. As he was a little early Adelaide asked him to walk with her to the letter-box, and after she had posted her letter they took the opportunity of strolling along the Embankment. Adelaide had a proposition to make to Dyson and was glad of the chance to speak to him alone.

One wonders if any passer-by noticed the young clergy-man in his black serge overcoat and his pretty, dark-eyed companion, as they leaned over the parapet to watch the dank, still waters of the Thames, their heads together, deep in conversation.

Adelaide was reminding Dyson about Edwin's previous illness when, as now, she had nursed him for weeks and had felt herself breaking down through want of sleep. On that occasion she had used chloroform externally to quiet him, and she now wanted to do so again; but Nurse Annie Walker, who had obtained it for her then, had gone to America, and she know no way of getting it except with Dyson's help.

The young preacher already knew, from their previous conversations, that Adelaide had nursed her husband without a doctor in attendance in three former illnesses, and that she had a medicine chest and a very considerable knowledge of drugs. Edwin himself had endorsed this more than once. Adelaide now went on to say that when her husband had one of his attacks he sometimes became delirious and violent. There were signs that an attack was coming on, and she would need the chloroform to sedate him. Dyson asked her how much she would need. He had better get a medicine draught bottle full, she said, as it was very volatile and rapidly evaporated. Dyson said that he would try to get the chloroform in the neighbourhood where he lived.

Having made these arrangements, Adelaide gave Dyson a gold sovereign and told him to meet her, with the chloroform, at eleven o'clock the next morning.

Their stroll to the post-box that evening had taken much longer than they had anticipated, for when they reached Claverton Street it was ten-thirty. George Dyson went straight upstairs to see Edwin for a while but said nothing about the chloroform. Nor, of course, did Adelaide.

However, when he returned to his lodgings that evening, Dyson began to think more clearly about Adelaide's request. Realising that the purchase of such a large quantity of chloroform was likely to be extremely difficult, he decided to write to a friend, Theodore Styles, who was a medical student at Bristol, and ask him to send the required amount through the post.

The next morning he went to meet Adelaide at eleven o'clock as planned. However, far from being pleased that he had been cautious enough to send for the chloroform instead of buying it over the counter, she was furious at the delay, and made him send a telegram to his friend cancelling the order. Then she sent him off again, this time to buy the chloroform as originally planned.

He called first on Mr Humble, a chemist in the Upper Richmond

Road. Humble recognised him immediately, for Dyson's chapel was just up the road from the shop. The preacher arrived at twelve-thirty and asked for a bottle of pure chloroform. The chemist showed him a half-ounce bottle, but Dyson said that he needed a larger size. Humble then showed him a one ounce bottle and he said that would do.

It was unusual for an ordinary member of the public to buy chloroform, and Mr Humble enquired discreetly what it was wanted for. Dyson at once asked if he was right in thinking it was a good thing to use for removing grease spots from a jacket. The chemist ultimately give him one ounce of methylated chloroform in a bottle labelled *Chloroform – Poison*. Despite his misgivings about dispensing such a large quantity of the drug without a prescription, he reassured himself with the thought that he knew the preacher well by sight. His clerical attire gave confidence and, after all, his name was on the notice board outside his chapel.

From Putney, Dyson travelled to Wimbledon and at about one o'clock entered a shop run by Mr T. Penrose. The chemist had been a member of George Dyson's congregation at the chapel in Merton and therefore recognised him at once. From the account he gave of the meeting, the preacher was obviously far from honest with him.

'I want you to let me have some chloroform for cleaning purposes,' he said. 'I have been in the country for a week and you know what clothes get like there.'

Dyson asked for two ounces of chloroform in two separate bottles as it was 'so very volatile.' This chemist, too, thought it rather a large amount for someone to buy without a prescription. He gave it to him, however, after carefully sticking a label marked *Poison* on each of the bottles.

From there Dyson made his way to another chemist in Wimbledon, Mr Mellin. Once again, he asked for two ounces of pure chloroform, saying that he needed it to remove grease stains. Mr Mellin suggested that he use turpentine or ammonia instead, but Dyson said that he preferred chloroform as 'turpentine had such a smell.' On this occasion, too, the chemist only agreed to complete the sale because

George Dyson was a churchman and well-known in the area. He sold him the chloroform in a two-ounce blue fluted bottle – the word *Poison* was clearly marked in raised glass letters.

This purchase completed Dyson's mission and he noted with satisfaction that he had managed to buy five ounces of chloroform for nine shillings and sixpence. He felt sure that Adelaide would be pleased with his efforts and glad, too, to have some change from her sovereign.

When he got back to his lodgings, he borrowed an eight-ounce bottle from his landlady into which he poured the contents of the smaller bottles. This done, he added a label marked *Chloroform – Poison* and put all the bottles into a cupboard until the following day. With that, he was obliged to attend to his ministerial duties, having spend the best part of the day running around at Adelaide's bidding.

While Adelaide had been out of the house that morning, remonstrating with George Dyson for not getting the chloroform quickly enough, Dr Leach had called at 85 Claverton Street, and, finding Edwin alone, had managed to prise his defenceless patient from his bed and force him out of the house. Leach recalled the event with evident relish:

> On the 28th, I took him by surprise and insisted on his going for a drive with me when I went on my rounds. It was genuine alarm and misgiving he showed as, muffled up from head to foot, he was assisted downstairs by two people.[15] On his return he ran upstairs quite lightly.

When Edwin's father was shown into the smoking room that evening, Adelaide surprised him by coming downstairs immediately, having previously made a point of keeping him waiting. Even more out of character, she leaned forward to kiss him and then, without hesitation, led him straight upstairs. Though puzzled by his daughter-in-law's friendly manner, especially after her nasty letter,

---

15 Probably Mrs Doggett and the maid, Alice.

the old man was heartened by his son's appearance.

'He seemed much better and stronger,' he said later. 'He got up and walked about the room. He said he was getting much better. He talked a great deal more than he had done before. He spoke of going away to the seaside and getting back to business and enjoying the evenings as we had before. He said he would go away on Tuesday.'

During the visit they discussed the mysterious cause of his illness, and Edwin said he could not imagine where he could have got any mercury into his system; on the other hand, he said, if he was suffering from *lead* poisoning this could be easily explained, for he had been unloading lead-lined tea chests at work and could have become contaminated. He did not say whether Adelaide thought this was the answer to the mystery, but it was an ingenious explanation for the traces of lead that were later found in his body.

Later, at the Old Bailey, Edwin's father was to be questioned at some length about the conversation he had with his son that evening. When asked if Edwin had talked of dying or had expressed any morbid thoughts, he replied:

'Never. Never mentioned. Never the least idea of it.'

He left the house sometime between half-past eight and nine o'clock, satisfied that his son 'seemed much better in his spirits.' He actually parted from Adelaide 'on the best of terms', kissing her and shaking hands with her before he wished her good-night. 'I then went away and that was the last time I saw my son alive.'

Clearly, when Mr Bartlett, senior, left the house that evening Edwin's health had greatly improved, and even the tense relationship with Adelaide had eased a little. That same evening Adelaide wrote this note to Edward Baxter at the shop:

> Dear Sir
>
> With the other things will you please send a bottle of brandy called Lord's Extra, a bottle of Colonel Skinner's Mango Chutney, a bottle of walnuts, and a nice fruit cake? I know these things are not fit for Edwin to eat, but he fancies them. You can see Edwin on Wednesday. A very happy New Year.
>
>   Yours truly,
>   Adelaide Bartlett

In the Interests of Science: Adelaide Bartlett and The Pimlico Poisoning

Adelaide was apparently feeling a little more optimistic than she had been of late. Festive even, ordering tasty treats for Edwin to enjoy: a bottle of best brandy and choice nuts to celebrate the New Year – perhaps even a new beginning for both of them after so much illness and despondency.

Was there a special reason why she chose brandy to seal their happiness? We have no evidence to suggest that it was Edwin's favourite tipple. It was, however, according to Adelaide's hefty medical book,[16] an excellent solvent for that most deadly and capricious of drugs, *chloroform*.

---

16 She kept a copy of Squire's *Companion to the British Pharmacopoeia* and was often seen to study it.

Part Two

'Murders by poison are not committed, like crimes of sudden passion, often in the light of day. They are necessarily mysterious and hidden in their operation.'

Sir Charles Russell: Speech for the Crown

CHAPTER 8

On the Stroke of Twelve

On the following day Edwin plucked up enough courage to accompany Adelaide on a drive along the Embankment. His spirits had been lifted a little and his 'spin' with Dr Leach, although against his will, had at least restored some of his confidence. He even talked about his proposed trip to Torquay without too many qualms and much of his recent nervousness had gone.

Dr Leach, who called soon after the Bartletts returned from their drive, was so pleased with his patient's progress that he saw no reason to call again. But whenever he suggested that house calls were to longer strictly necessary, Edwin became very upset, so much so that Adelaide took the doctor to one side, saying:

'You had better come, doctor, or he will be anxious.'

Leach saw that his patient was upsetting himself, and agreed to call again on December 31st to see how he was bearing up.

Lunch that day was interrupted by the arrival of George Dyson. Adelaide, guessing that he had brought the chloroform with him, quickly suggested that they take a stroll together after lunch. Dyson was to say in evidence that he did not give Adelaide the chloroform when he arrived at the flat because Edwin had another visitor at the time – a Mr Hackett. It must be said, though, that this gentleman's involvement in the case is rather nebulous and he was not called as a witness, either at the inquest or at the trial. If Hackett *was* there with Edwin that day, then Dyson's reticence was perfectly understandable. If, on the other hand, the presence of the other man was a fabrication, then this cloak-and-dagger behaviour might well be construed as sinister.

During their stroll by the river Dyson gave Adelaide the bottle of chloroform, but neither of them mentioned it when they returned to Claverton Street – even though the mysterious Mr Hackett had gone.

Dyson, however, was far from happy with the situation. Having just handed over a lethal quantity of chloroform, certain doubts began to creep into his mind - doubts that were barely formulated yet made him uneasy. He felt he had to broach the subject with Adelaide that same afternoon.

'I advised her,' he testified, 'to get a nurse to assist her, consequent upon her telling me that the friends were saying unkind things about her... I told her that it would be better in the eyes of the world if she were to have a nurse with her – meaning that that would stop them talking. She was offended, and said that I suspected or did not trust her. I told her that I trusted her thoroughly, and Mr Bartlett overheard. He did not hear the whole of the conversation. But he heard that exclamation... He said, "Oh yes, you may trust her. If you had twelve years' experience of her as I have, you would know you could trust her."'

Notwithstanding her husband's unquestioning support, Adelaide took George Dyson's remarks very much to heart and they parted that evening on decidedly frosty terms.

The next morning a repentant George Dyson arrived at Claverton Street, begging Adelaide to forgive him. Whatever transpired between them appears to have mended the rift, superficially at least, but she began to lose faith in him from that day and their friendship was irrevocably weakened by his ungentlemanly, though understandable, lapse into scepticism.

That same evening, Edward Baxter called to see Edwin as arranged.

'He seemed quite cheerful,' recalled Baxter, 'very much better – getting on nicely. I stayed about two hours... There was something said about his going to the seaside, hoping that the change of air would prove beneficial, and that he would be able in the course of a week or two to resume business.'

According to both Dr Leach and Mr Baxter Edwin's health

was nearly back to normal and there was little wrong with him physically; to corroborate this, both Mrs Doggett and Alice said that he displayed a very hearty appetite for man supposed to be so ill. On 31st December, the day after Baxter's visit, Edwin lunched on half-a-dozen oysters with bread and butter, followed by tea and a slice of cake. Less than three hours later, Alice Fulcher brought him a delicious meal of jugged hare, and Edwin scoffed the lot.

It was while the ravenous invalid was finishing this meal that George Dyson arrived to see him. He noted that Edwin seemed 'nervous and was in great pain with his teeth. He said he was expecting the doctor and asked me to call and tell him to come. I went for Dr Leach but did not see him and left a message. I returned to Claverton Street and found Dr Leach there.'

Earlier that day, Leach and Adelaide had arranged between themselves for Edwin to visit the dentist at five o'clock that afternoon. He needed to have another tooth extracted – an operation that would entail the use of gas, so that a visit to the dental surgery was essential. Knowing how neurotic Edwin was, they had decided to keep the appointment a secret until the last minute. Dr Leach arrived about three o'clock to prepare Edwin for his ordeal and to assist Adelaide in getting him out of doors.

Whatever they said to Edwin had a miraculous effect, for they had no trouble persuading him to get into the doctor's carriage; his manner was more carefree than it had been for some time and Adelaide was in a positively flirtatious mood as they drove to the surgery. Dr Leach was to testify that she always tried to be cheerful and to lift Edwin's spirits. During the journey she even went as far as to tell the doctor that she wished she and Edwin were not already married, so that they might have the pleasure of marrying all over again! Edwin's answer to this absurd piece of sentimentality was lost as he buried himself more deeply in his woolly scarf. When Dr Leach made the observation that Adelaide's remark came as a great compliment to him, Edwin said something to the effect that 'they suited each other' – nothing more romantic than that.

At the surgery, Dr Leach prepared to administer nitrous oxide gas which, unlike ether or chloroform, is not a true anaesthetic in that it does not cause the patient to lose consciousness. It does, however, deaden the sensation of pain, allowing medical treatment to progress without too much resistance. Leach noticed that it took rather longer than usual for Edwin to lose sensitivity to pain and, unfortunately, he was still sufficiently aware to hear the doctor and dentist discussing the condition of his jaw. During the conversation that followed the word 'necrosis' was mentioned, but in Edwin's case, although the gums were covered with a fungoid growth, there was nothing seriously wrong. The necrosis was only just commencing and although it was unpleasant and potentially dangerous, it was not sufficiently advanced to constitute any threat to life.

Returning to Claverton Street that evening, Edwin seemed satisfied that the tooth extraction had gone well. It is possible that the remark about necrosis of the jaw preyed on his mind and that he became depressed by the implications, but this seems unlikely, for he did not mention the subject to anyone, nor did he seem in any way upset by the treatment he had received.

Intent on celebrating the New Year in the traditional way, the Doggetts were expecting guests that evening and Mrs Doggett and the maid were busy with the preparations. The landlady still found time, however, to waylay the Bartletts in the hall on their return and to ask about Edwin's visit to the dentist. Recalling their conversation she said:

> He told me he thought the worst was over, and he would get better. He told me that Dr Leach had given him orders to go to the seaside for a change. Mrs Bartlett said that she thought the journey would be too long. He also said that the mornings were getting lighter and he should get up an hour earlier the next day.

Mrs Doggett remembered that Adelaide asked her if she had ever taken chloroform:

> I said that I had years ago. She then asked me whether it was a nice or a pleasant feeling. I said I did not think I knew very much about it. Mrs Bartlett said that Mr Bartlett was in the habit of taking some sleeping drops; ten was a strong dose, but she should not, or did not,

hesitate in giving him twelve. She told me what the drops were, but I do not remember the name.

She recalled that Edwin thanked her for his dinner and said he had enjoyed it. 'He said that he had eaten all that was sent up, and he had so enjoyed it that he could eat three dinners a day,' Mrs Doggett later served Edwin a tea-supper at about nine o'clock consisting of another half-dozen oysters, and bread and butter, and cake.

At ten o'clock Alice Fulcher went upstairs to clear away the supper things. Edwin was walking about the room again but seemed cheerful – in fact, he told the maid that he wanted a large haddock for his breakfast the next morning and that he would 'get up an hour earlier at the thought of having it.'

Twenty-five minutes later, Alice went back upstairs with some coals for the night. Adelaide told her to take in the coals, 'and put her finger up and told me not to go into the room again. She told me to take a basin up for the beef tea, and to put it on the table outside on the stair landing.' When she took the coals in Edwin was in bed; she did not think he was asleep, but he did not speak to her. She put the basin on the table on the landing and did not go into the room again. Some time after twelve she went to bed: 'The basin I put on the table was empty. Mrs Bartlett had Liebig's essence (a concentrated beef extract) in the room.' When she went up to bed she noticed that the basin was still there, and it was still untouched next morning.

It had been a long day for Alice Fulcher, for the party that evening had meant a lot of extra work. When she went wearily to bed, Mr and Mrs Doggett were still downstairs entertaining their friends, and it was well past twelve-thirty when they, too, climbed the stairs to bed.

The moment she crawled into bed that night Alice fell into a deep slumber, but her peace was short-lived. A few hours later she was woken by Adelaide, who was shaking her vigorously and shouting at her to get up.

'Alice,' she cried, 'I want you to go for Dr Leach. I think Mr Bartlett is dead.'

It was four o'clock in the morning. Tired and reluctant to rouse herself, the maid dressed and ran to fetch the doctor from Charlwood Street. She was not too sleepy, however to notice that Adelaide had changed out of the dress she had been wearing the night before. She was now wearing a blue afternoon frock and, far from looking shocked and distraught, she was neatly groomed and quite composed, not a bit like a woman who had woken in the middle of the night to find her husband dead.

It struck Alice as odd that Adelaide should have apparently washed and changed *before* raising the alarm. Wouldn't it have been more natural to call for help as soon as she woke up, still wearing the dress she had been wearing the night before, crumpled from being worn so long? And wouldn't her hair have been dishevelled and in need of attention? Her calm, tidy appearance aroused the maid's suspicions.

As Alice left the house, Adelaide made her way to the room on the second floor where the Doggetts were fast asleep. She shook them awake and asked them to come downstairs. 'I think Mr Bartlett is dead,' she told them.

Still bleary-eyed from the night's celebrations, Mr Doggett pulled on his dressing-gown and followed her down to the first floor flat. As he went into the room he noticed a strong smell, like chloric ether. Edwin was on the bed in its usual place in the corner by the fireplace, lying on his back. His nightshirt was open and his left hand was across his chest. Mr Doggett touched him and found him 'perfectly cold'.

'Do you think he's dead?' Adelaide asked.

'Yes,' he answered. 'He must have been dead some two or three hours.'

Still relatively calm, Adelaide began to explain what had happened during the night.

'I had fallen off to sleep with my hand round his foot, and I woke up with a pain in my arm and found him lying on his face. I put him in the position in which you see him, and tried to pour brandy down his throat – nearly half a pint.'

At least part of this explanation seemed reasonable to Mr Doggett, for he could undoubtedly smell brandy on the body, but it puzzled him how a woman of Adelaide's small build would have had sufficient strength to lift and turn a hefty man like Edwin. Stranger still, the body was reclining in a natural, relaxed pose, the eyes closed as though he had drifted gently from sleep into death. He commented on this, and Adelaide hastily said that she had closed her husband's eyes when she realised that he was dead - although Doggett remembered that when she had fetched him from upstairs she had said that she *thought* he was dead. Furthermore, the bedclothes were smooth and unruffled, showing no sign of the disturbance that would have been involved in lifting and turning a dead weight.

Doggett noticed that there was a wine glass on the mantelshelf just above the bed, about three-quarters full of some liquid the colour of brandy. He sniffed at it and thought that although it did indeed smell of brandy there was another smell mixed with it, some drug like ether or paregoric.

By this time Mrs Doggett had come downstairs to join her husband. Thinking that Edwin was merely in a deep sleep she inadvertently uttered one of the most poignant *faux pas* in criminal history.

'Did you give him those drops?' she asked, turning to Adelaide.

'I have given him nothing,' snapped the other.

Like her husband, the landlady looked keenly about the room and noticed that it was extremely hot and stuffy. The fire, which she would have expected to have burnt right down during the four hours Adelaide said she had been sleeping with her arm around her husband's foot, to her surprise was banked up high and burning brightly. Was it conceivable that Adelaide had stopped to make up the fire before climbing the stairs to seek help?

CHAPTER 9

A Strong Smell of Chloroform

Meanwhile, Alice Fulcher had run all the way to Dr Leach's house, but had to knock several times before she could get any answer. When the doctor eventually opened the door and heard what had happened, he and the maid hurried to Claverton Street, taking a hansom cab to save time – although at this stage he rather suspected that the whole thing was a false alarm.

When they arrived, Mrs Doggett opened the door to them and led them upstairs to the first floor flat where her husband and Adelaide were waiting. Afraid that Adelaide might get upset while the doctor examined her husband's body, the landlady suggested that she join her downstairs for a cup of tea. Surprisingly, however, Adelaide refused to leave the room, saying that she preferred to stay – indeed, she watched intently while the body was being examined and even helped Dr Leach and Mr Doggett to straighten and tie the legs with a piece of wide tape from her work-basket.

As soon as he'd entered the room Dr Leach had realised that Edwin was dead. He examined him carefully, noting a smell of brandy on the chest but no odour on the mouth. There was nothing to suggest that death had come other than naturally and peacefully, and he was completely mystified. When Adelaide asked him what he thought had been the cause of death he said he was not sure, although the rupture of a small blood vessel near the heart might account for it. Having said this, however, he began to search the room, evidently hoping to find something else to account for his patient's sudden demise.

> I certainly looked for anything that could throw light on the subject I had in hand. There was a little lock-up next to the fireplace which I examined along with Mr Doggett. There was nothing of a suspicious nature in it.[17]

The doctor's attention then fell on a large bottle of chlorodyne which stood on top of the cupboard. He seized it, firmly convinced that an excessive dose of chlorodyne must be the cause of Edwin's death. Dismissing any further search as unnecessary, he did not even bother to inspect the back bedroom where, it must be remembered, Adelaide mixed all the medicines.

Triumphantly clutching the bottle, he asked Adelaide what Edwin had used it for. Not surprisingly, she said that he had used it to rinse his mouth, as he, the doctor, had prescribed.

'Rinse his mouth?' Leach exclaimed. 'Then he must have swallowed some!'

'No, he only rubbed his gums with it …' protested Adelaide.

Disregarding her last comment, Dr Leach bent down to peer into the chamber pot, hoping to find evidence of chlorodyne expelled from Edwin's mouth – but there was none. At this point, he felt obliged to admit that, whereas chlorodyne had a strong smell, he had not detected any odour of it on Edwin's mouth. However, he was still prepared to favour his chlorodyne theory. As little as a drachm of chlorodyne had been known to kill, he told her, and they both knew that Edwin's reaction to certain drugs was peculiar.

Clearly, both Doggett and Leach were uneasy about the circumstances of Edwin's death. They found it impossible, however, to voice their suspicions in front of Adelaide, and as she seemed determined to stay near the body they were obliged to keep their thoughts to themselves. Doggett, having made his own search of the room, was even more anxious to have a word with the doctor, but he was in a corner with Adelaide who was talking to him earnestly. Tired of waiting for a chance to interrupt them, Doggett went downstairs, intending to catch the doctor in the hallway as he was leaving the house.

17   Statement from Leach's evidence at Adelaide's trial.

In the Interests of Science: Adelaide Bartlett and The Pimlico Poisoning

According to Dr Leach, the moment Mr Doggett left the room Adelaide burst into tears, showing for the first time any display of shock or grief. Leach did his best to comfort her and, attempting to ascertain the cause of death, asked her if Edwin could have got hold of any poison. Her reply was spontaneous and quite emphatic:

'No, he could have no poison without my knowing it,' she said. 'He could have got no poison without my knowledge.'

Perhaps, by saying this, Adelaide had hoped to convince the doctor that Edwin had died from some natural but hidden disease or malfunction. However, by making such a statement she plainly laid herself open to suspicion if poison *was* subsequently found to be the cause of her husband's death. Had she known that her landlord, Mr Doggett, was a Registrar of Births and Deaths, she might well have spoken more cautiously, for she was saying, in fact, that if her husband had taken poison, *she* must have given it to him, or, through an act of negligence on her part, allowed him access to it. However, when Dr Leach told her there would have to be a post-mortem, she offered no objection; on the contrary, if the doctor is to be believed, she 'expressed the utmost anxiety that the examination should take place as soon as possible.'

Mr Doggett, too, had realised that a post-mortem would be necessary. He waylaid Dr Leach as he was leaving the house at six-thirty, obliged to hurry back for his surgery at nine. Drawing the doctor to one side, he admitted that he was unhappy about Edwin Bartlett's death and was certainly not prepared to register it in the usual way.

Perturbed by all that had happened, Leach hurried back to his house, cancelled his morning surgery, and was back at Claverton Street by seven-thirty.

No sooner had Mr Leach left Claverton Street than Adelaide sent a message to the local undertakers. They promptly sent along a Mrs Ann Boulter who, though a charwoman by profession, helped to lay out the dead in her spare time. She arrived between seven and eight in the morning, and proceeded to wash and lay out the body with Adelaide's assistance. She noticed that the legs were tied.

'Did he have a fit?' she asked.

'Why do you ask that?' enquired Adelaide.

'I thought he might have struggled as his legs were tied,' replied the charwoman.[18]

'No, poor dear,' said Adelaide, 'he suffered very much with his head, also his teeth for some time.' She then remarked that it was curious that he should have made a will a day or two previous to his death,[19] and when Mrs Boulter asked her if the will was in her favour she replied that it was.

It was during this conversation that the maid brought up a letter that had just been delivered in the morning post. Adelaide, on reading the contents, cried out, 'Oh, how cruel!' When Mrs Boulter asked her why she was so upset she said that the letter was from Mr Bartlett's brother in America, wishing him a happy New Year. The arrival of Frederick's letter was, indeed, badly timed, and Adelaide's reaction to it was puzzling. Evidently, the letter announced that Frederick was on his way back to England. If, during the previous ten years, she had been hoping for his return, her response to the news would have been one of spontaneous excitement. The fact that the prospect of a reunion with her former lover was clearly upsetting to her seems to indicate that it did not feature in her future plans. Frederick, apparently, had left it too late.

Frederick Bartlett did return to England as he promised in the letter, arriving at Claverton Street five days after Edwin's death – but by that time Adelaide had already gone to stay with George and Alice Matthews in East Dulwich, and the first floor flat at Claverton Street was empty.

Both Frederick's letter and his subsequent appearance in London added a new dimension to the situation, for the fact that his return coincided very neatly with Adelaide's sudden bereavement was only

---

18 The legs had been tied by Dr Leach as rigor mortis had set in.
19 Edwin wrote his will on 3rd September, 1885, nearly *four months* before his death, not two days.

too obvious – nor was it overlooked by old Mr Bartlett and the rest of the family, who were still mindful of Adelaide's scandalous flight with Frederick several years before.

When she had recovered from the initial shock of the letter, however, Adelaide could not allow herself to dwell on Frederick's intentions for long – she had far more pressing problems on hand. She finished helping Mrs Boulter strip the camp bed and ordered Mrs Doggett to have the sheets and pillowcases washed immediately, with the result that, at the post-mortem, none of Edwin's bed linen was available for examination.

After Mrs Boulter had left, the undertaker himself arrived to take measurements and arrange the burial, but as a death certificate had not yet been issued, Adelaide was unable to finalise the funeral instructions. Instead, she asked for Edwin's body to be placed in a coffin and taken into the back bedroom.

When the undertaker had gone to order the coffin, Adelaide went into the bedroom to write some letters and telegrams. At nine o'clock she asked Mr Doggett to dispatch them for her. He recalled taking three telegrams – one to Edwin's father, one to Alice Matthews, and the other to Edward Baxter. She had also written letters to her solicitor, Mr Wood, and to George Dyson, in which she told them of Edwin's sudden death and asked them both to call at the house the next day.

Later that morning arrangements were made for the post-mortem. Dr Leach suggested that they contact Dr Thomas Green, a very experienced pathologist at Charing Cross Hospital, asking him to perform the operation. Although at the time the doctor did not seem to think that Adelaide appeared unduly nervous about the prospect, he was later to say that she seemed 'not only grieved but very much alarmed – very much scared.'

With Adelaide's agreement, Dr Leach sent a telegram to Dr Green, asking him to perform the post-mortem that afternoon at Claverton Street. This done, he went about his medical practice, promising to return when he had received a reply.

Adelaide spent the rest of the morning in the back bedroom while Edwin's body still lay on the little camp bed at the front. Eleven o'clock came and went and Mrs Doggett, growing concerned about her, decided to go up to the flat to see if there was anything she could do. She asked Adelaide if she would come downstairs and have a little breakfast but Adelaide declined, remarking how strange it was that Edwin had not long made his will.

'Are you thinking about money?' asked Mrs Doggett.

'It is necessary,' Adelaide replied.

By way of explanation, she told Mrs Doggett that she had no money of her own as all her assets had been invested in her husband's business; it was fortunate, therefore, she said, that Edwin had left her his money, for without the new will the money paid by her father's agents would have remained in the business and been lost to her forever.

During this rather mercenary conversation Mrs Matthews arrived from East Dulwich. Naturally, she had been shocked by the news of Edwin's sudden death and had set out at once. They met in the smoking room and went upstairs to the room where the body was; here Adelaide gave her friend the same account of the tragedy she had already given to Frederick Doggett when the body was found. She told her that it was 'after twelve o'clock before she had gone to sleep, because she heard the people downstairs wishing each other a happy New Year.' When Alice Matthews asked her what had caused her husband's death she said, 'We don't know. There must be a post-mortem.'

While the two women were talking in the front room, Mr Baxter also arrived in response to Adelaide's telegram. He was grieved and highly shocked by the news, for Edwin, as well as being a business partner, had been a close friend for many years – in fact, Baxter was so upset that he was unable later to recall to anything that was said when he arrived at Claverton Street that morning.

Knowing what a terrible shock Edwin's death would be to old Mr Bartlett, Baxter was anxious to find him and break the news in private as soon as possible. He went straight to Berkeley Square, where he knew the old man was working, and told him that his son was dead. They returned to his cottage to find Adelaide's telegram which had arrived after he had left for work that morning. The wording was cold and the message clear, untarnished by any sentiment or concern for the old man's feelings. Posted at 9.36am that morning, it read: *'Edwin is dead. Come at once. Bartlett.'*

Edwin's father must have been glad of Edward Baxter's support as they hurried over to Claverton Street. Not surprisingly, as soon as they entered the room, he masked his overwhelming grief with an act of open hostility. Going over to the bed, he bent and kissed his son on the forehead, at the same time smelling his lips in the belief that he might have been poisoned by prussic acid. However, he could detect no smell of that kind. Dr Leach was there and Mr Bartlett said to him, 'We must have a post-mortem examination; this cannot pass.' Leach replied that he would not give a certificate without one, and again mentioned Dr Green, who would have Dr Montague Murray, also from Charing Cross Hospital, to assist him. He and Dr Dudley would also attend the post-mortem. Even so, the old man was not satisfied and insisted on yet another doctor being present. When Leach said he would get him one he was told: 'No, I will get *you* one – not one that was in the case or the neighbourhood.'

After further discussion it was decided that they should approach Dr Cheyne, of Mandeville Place, to assist Drs Green and Murray. This settled, Dr Leach and Mr Bartlett rose to leave the room. As they did so the latter turned to Adelaide, remarking bitterly:

'You are not to have him put in his coffin until after the post-mortem.'

Adelaide retaliated to this hostile remark with equal venom:

'Dr Leach has to see to that; it has nothing to do with me or you.'

The old man's reply has not been recorded.

By mid-day the post-mortem had still not been arranged, for Dr Green had sent a telegram to say that he could not perform the operation that day. When Adelaide heard this she became very agitated, begging Leach to contact Dr Green again, this time offering more money. He promptly sent another telegram, offering a larger fee on condition that the post-mortem was performed the following morning.

At this the doctor suddenly found that his other commitments were not quite so pressing, and he agreed to come to Claverton Street to operate at 2.15pm the next day. At the time it was quite common for post-mortems to be carried out at the home of the deceased. So, too, was the practice of allowing the corpse to lie in an open coffin in the front parlour so that mourners might pay their respects.

The fact that Adelaide was so anxious to have the post-mortem done quickly, despite the cost involved, was later taken to be indicative of her innocence. It was certainly a point in her favour that she did nothing whatsoever to obstruct the investigation into her husband's death.

On the contrary, she seemed to welcome it.

After Mr Bartlett and Dr Leach had departed that afternoon, the undertakers arrived to place the body in the coffin , which was then carried into the back bedroom and lowered onto coffin stools. As soon as they had gone Adelaide started to rearrange the furniture in the front room. Once the camp bed had been removed the room looked much the same as it had on the day the Bartletts had moved in; there was no longer any evidence of Edwin's recent illness and death.

Having already attended to her correspondence that morning, Adelaide decided to go with Alice Matthews to Jay's Emporium in Oxford Street, to select her widow's weeds. On their return, soon after four-thirty, Mr Matthews called to collect his wife and offer his condolences. He joined the two ladies for tea by the fire and they talked for several hours about the tragedy. They suggested to Adelaide that, once the funeral was over, she should come and stay with them in East Dulwich, and she accepted gratefully.

George and Alice Matthews took their leave at nine o'clock that evening. Their departure was closely followed by the arrival of Dr Leach, and Edwin's father also returned to the house during the course of the evening. He became upset when he saw his son's body already in the coffin, protesting that the post-mortem should have been done first. However, later that evening he and Adelaide fell to remembering Edwin's good and gentle nature and the hostility between them temporarily subsided.

Fond though her memories may have been, Adelaide chose to sleep on the sofa in the front room that night, while Edwin lay in his coffin on the other side of the folding doors. One cannot help wondering which lay more at peace that night – the corpse of the husband or the body of the wife?

The first that George Dyson heard of Edwin's death was in the letter Adelaide sent him on 1st January. When he arrived at Claverton Street the following day, Adelaide gave him a detailed version of the tragic events, relaying Dr Leach's suggestion that a small blood vessel may have broken near the heart, causing sudden death.

Dyson was still there when Drs Dudley, Green, Cheyne, Murray and Leach arrived to perform the post-mortem operation. Adelaide's solicitor, Edward Wood, had also arrived, and it was decided that he, Dyson and Adelaide should wait downstairs. So it was that the three of them sat by the fire in the smoking room while the doctors began their gruesome task in the flat above.

Edwin's father, however, remained outside.

He had watched the arrival of the doctors but refused to enter the house, preferring to pace the street, despite the bitterly cold weather. It was not until about four o'clock, when Dr Green had driven away in his brougham, followed by Drs Murray and Cheyne, that the old man rang the front door bell. Alice Fulcher let him in and showed him into the smoking room where the others were still sitting.

The atmosphere in the room must have been tense as they waited for the summons from the room upstairs. It was made even more uncomfortable when Edwin's grieving father joined the company. They sat for a further twenty minutes but there was little conversation.

When they were eventually summoned to hear the doctors' verdict, they knew as soon as they entered the room that there was something seriously wrong. Dr Dudley, his face grave, stepped forward and, putting his hand on Mr Bartlett's shoulder, said:

'Your son has no business to be lying in there – a strong man like that.'

The doctor went on to explain that as they had found no pathological cause of death the contents of the stomach would have to be preserved - these contents, he confirmed, were suspicious and would need to be examined further.

Dr Dudley's next statement must have come as a profound shock to everyone, especially Adelaide. He announced that both rooms in the Bartletts' flat were to be locked, sealed and held under the jurisdiction of the District Coroner. 'In the meantime,' he added ominously, 'nothing whatever must be removed from them. Mrs Bartlett must not pack anything in a bag or take anything away with her.'

The implications were only too clear, yet surprisingly, Mr Bartlett spoke up for his daughter-in-law.

'Adelaide may take her cloak,' he said. 'There are no pockets in it. I will be answerable for that.'

Despite the fact that Adelaide said that she did not want to take her cloak, the old man insisted. This gallant gesture was not quite what it seemed, however, for his words confirmed that he had already checked Adelaide's cloak for pockets and found none.

And so, feeling confident that Adelaide had no means of concealment on her dress, he said goodbye to her in a civilised manner and even kissed her on the cheek before leaving – little knowing that there were other pockets and hiding places in a woman's attire that even he would dare not probe.

When old Mr Bartlett and Dr Dudley had left the flat, Mrs Doggett who, it must be said, turned out to be an exemplary landlady, rose to the occasion extremely well. Notwithstanding that she had been obliged to accommodate first a death and then a post-mortem in her house, and to stage-manage the comings and goings of all the medical men and mourners, she graciously provided refreshments for Adelaide, George Dyson, Mr Wood and Dr Leach. And it was while they were sipping their tea that Dr Leach rather unprofessionally announced that when Dr Green had opened Edwin's stomach, there had been a *very strong smell of chloroform.*

This observation must have nearly choked poor Dyson, despite Leach's attempt to defuse the situation by suggesting that Dr Green's diagnosis was incorrect and that the smell was probably chlorodyne. This can have been of little comfort to Dyson, and he must have been desperate to speak to Adelaide alone so that he could ask her outright whether she had given her husband any of the chloroform he had procured for her. Unfortunately, the presence of the doctor and the solicitor forced him to remain silent a while longer.

The immediate problem, now that the flat was to be sealed, was to find a temporary home for Adelaide, and it soon became clear that she had few close friends. Although Edward Baxter lived but a short distance away, in Deronda Road, Herne Hill, it seems likely that he was a bachelor and therefore unable to offer Adelaide a refuge. That left only George and Alice Matthews in East Dulwich. It was decided, therefore, that George Dyson should escort Adelaide to the Matthews' home, although at this stage he knew nothing about them, nor they him.

They were on the point of leaving the flat when Adelaide refused to go without her hat. Giving her keys to Dr Leach, she asked him to bring her hat from the back bedroom where Edwin's body lay. Not knowing which hat she wanted to wear, Leach brought the whole drawer from the clothes chest so that she could make her choice. This done, he returned the drawer to the back room and locked the door behind him.

Adelaide was to maintain that the large bottle of chloroform, unopened, was lying in a drawer of the clothes chest when Dr Leach went to fetch it, even though he failed to notice it, and that it was still there when she left the flat that day; however, it is possible that it was in the second drawer, which the doctor did not touch. Neither drawer was examined by the Coroner's officer when he visited the flat two days later.[20]

Adelaide also said that she had taken nothing with her when she left Claverton Street – no bag, no spare clothes – nothing. But had she stealthily concealed the incriminating bottle somewhere on her person before leaving the flat? It can be assumed that the three gentlemen present would automatically have averted their eyes had Adelaide begun to adjust her underskirts – a thought that obviously occurred to the judge at her subsequent trial, for he was to say: 'That bottle may have been either in the drawer or in her pocket, and exactly where it was no human being can tell.'

George Dyson and Adelaide went to Victoria Station by hansom cab. The tension between them was mounting, for the mention of chloroform in Edwin's stomach had confirmed the preacher's worst fears. As soon as they were seated on the train to East Dulwich he demanded to know what she had done with the chloroform he had given her. She denied that she had had reason to use it at all. Dyson, however, felt that she was lying, and begged her to say what she had done with the bottle.

Irritated by his nervous interrogation, Adelaide stubbornly refused to discuss it any further. Their fondness for each other had diminished at the first sign of trouble. Dyson sensed that he had been tricked into supplying Adelaide with the poison that had killed her husband. That in itself had come as a profound shock; more disturbing still was her sudden change in temperament. She was no longer the charming, amiable woman he had admired so much; she was now cold and preoccupied, and seemed to lack any feeling for him, his state of mind or his precarious position.

Adelaide could not tolerate weakness and George Dyson's was beginning to show.

20 In its report of the trial, *The Penny Illustrated Paper* of 24th April 1886, noted: 'He [the judge] marvelled at the action of the Coroner's officer, who, sent to the house on Jan 4 to assist in the search after the truth, did not search the drawers for the missing chloroform bottle. He neglected to do so, and yet he was a grown-up policeman.'

CHAPTER 10

Preacher in a Panic

Despite their invitation of the previous day, it is debatable whether George and Alice Matthews were exactly overjoyed when Adelaide and a young preacher appeared without warning on their doorstep that evening, for it was getting late and they had another guest staying with them. George Dyson was plainly ill at ease, and once the introductions had been made and the situation explained, he wasted no time in returning to his lodgings in Putney.

The Matthewses, as old friends of Edwin, had little choice but to open their doors to his widow, but the presence of their other guest left little opportunity to evaluate the crisis – nor was there any chance to discuss the post-mortem findings in any detail, though Adelaide did briefly mention that Dr Leach thought chlorodyne was the cause of death.

Meanwhile, George Dyson had returned to Putney feeling very troubled indeed. He was acutely aware of the gravity of the situation, and his possession of the four small chloroform bottles had become a terrible burden on his conscience.

The next day, after a night in which to consider the possible repercussions of keeping the bottles, he decided to throw them away as soon as possible. He was due to preach in Tooting that Sunday morning and so, whilst crossing Wandsworth Common on his way to church, he threw the bottles into some bushes. His action would, he hoped, absolve him from the whole unfortunate affair.

But he was still worried. Very early the next morning, Monday, 4th January, he arrived on Dr Leach's doorstep, asking for details of the post-mortem. Leach proceeded to show a complete lack of professional restraint, for he should not have discussed the findings with anyone outside the medical profession – particularly with Dyson, who as a frequent visitor to the deceased, would undoubtedly be called to give evidence at the forthcoming inquest. Not only did he answer all his questions, he even showed him some of the notes he had taken during the operation – notes which made it perfectly clear that Dr Green considered chloroform to be the cause of Edwin Bartlett's death.

George Dyson was mortified. Unable to still his anxiety, he decided to confront Adelaide with the post-mortem findings. Clearly, he now suspected that she had deliberately used the chloroform not to soothe, but to poison, her husband. Not only that, the post-mortem had revealed that Edwin had been perfectly healthy, with no sign of disease, so the story Adelaide had told him about Edwin having a serious illness was a complete fabrication. Dyson realised, moreover, that his purchase of the chloroform had been made under a misconception, and a very treacherous one.

Little wonder that he hurried from Dr Leach's house and went directly to East Dulwich. The journey must have been fraught with anxiety as his precarious position became clearer to him – and more horrifying. By the time he reached Friern Road Adelaide had gone out, but Mrs Matthews showed him into the drawing-room to await her return. It was here that they met a little later. Alice Matthews left them alone for a minute or two, and then heard a sound like someone stamping.

'I went into the room, and I saw Mrs Bartlett stamping around the room. I asked her what was the matter. It was some time before she said anything. She was very out of temper. She then said that Mr Dyson was bothering her about a piece of paper. At that moment my little boy fell and cried. I left the room and returned in a few minutes. I then heard Mr Dyson saying to Mrs Bartlett:

'"You did tell me that Edwin was to die soon!"

'"No, I did not!" she shouted.

'"Oh, my God!" the minister cried, his head on the piano.

One can imagine Alice Matthews's reaction to such dramatic scenes. She was shocked to witness a man of the cloth holding his head and moaning that he was a ruined man, whilst her guest rampaged about the room, stamping her feet in the most alarming way. Fearing that further scenes might follow, she ordered Dyson to leave her house at once.

Later, she asked Adelaide what the paper was, and was told it was a piece of poetry which Dyson had written to her and which he now wanted her to return. It was a puerile little piece,[21] hardly worth fighting over, one would have thought. Adelaide did, in fact, return the poem a few days later, but not before she had taken a copy – an act of sneakiness that the preacher, not entirely conversant with the ways of women, had not anticipated.

Dyson's version of Adelaide's tantrum helps to fill out the details:

> She was alone when I first saw her and I asked her what she had done with the chloroform. She got in a great rage, stamping about the room, and said:
>
> "'Oh, *damn* the chloroform!"[22]
>
> Mrs Matthews came in and Mrs Bartlett became calmer. When Mrs Matthews left the room again Mrs Bartlett asked me if anything had been found in the stomach of the deceased. I replied that the doctor said a few drops of chlorodyne or cholorform. She asked me which of the two had been found. I told her I was not sure, that I confused the two. She asked me to repeat the doctor's words exactly. I said I could not remember. Then I emphasised the fact that she had told me her husband was suffering from an internal complaint:
>
> "'You *did* tell me that Edwin was to die shortly!"
>
> "'No, I did not!" she said.

---

21 A sample verse from the poem, entitled '*My Birdie*':
 Who is it that has burst the door,
 Unclosed the heart that shut before,
 And set her queen-like on the throne
 And made its homage all her own?
 My Birdie
22 The word '*damn*' was omitted from the account in *The Times*.

Obviously, George Dyson's anguish was entirely on his own account but his alarm was perfectly understandable. There was little doubt that, if it was subsequently proved that Edwin had died from chloroform poisoning, Dyson's career in the church would be ruined. His interest in Adelaide and his desire to protect her had swiftly waned and from that time he thought only of himself. She was not longer an object of desire but one of fear and revulsion as the possibility of her involvement in Edwin's death became only too clear to him.

Adelaide, for her part, had anticipated the adverse reaction of her meagre bunch of friends. That morning she had wisely contacted her solicitor, Mr Wood, and enlisted his services. Strengthened by his support, she could afford to look on George Dyson's panic with scorn. He, meanwhile, returned to Putney in a state of intense agitation.

But he was in for an even greater shock, confirming his worst fears: waiting for him at his lodgings was a summons to appear before the Deputy Coroner of Westminster, at the inquest into Edwin's death, on Thursday, 7th January, where he would be called upon to give evidence.

Now almost frantic with worry, Dyson raced back to East Dulwich and again demanded to know what Adelaide had done with the bottle of chloroform. Her answer was short:

'Do not mention the chloroform to me.'

Faced with her infuriating refusal even to discuss the matter, Dyson threatened to tell the Coroner not only about the chloroform, but also about the lies she had told him concerning the state of Edwin's health. Adelaide retaliated by asking point blank if he suspected her of poisoning her husband. He did not answer directly but repeated his intention to 'make a clean breast of it' at the inquest.

At this point they must have known that the rift between them was complete. As though to emphasise this, the preacher laid four sovereigns on the table, money which Edwin had given him to cover the Dover expenses; next to these he placed Edwin's watch which Adelaide had given him the day after her husband had died. Clearly, this was a vain attempt on his part to disassociate himself from the whole affair, yet even he must have realised that he had no hope of avoiding the scandal that was sure to follow.

With that, the young man left the house in East Dulwich, turning his back on his *'Birdie'*, only too anxious to free himself from a woman he now considered not merely deceitful, but positively dangerous to know.

Adelaide wasted no time in consolidating the support and sympathy of her new champions. Early the next morning she went back to see her solicitor who introduced her to Edward Beal, a young lawyer who had been assigned to attend the coming inquest and watch the proceedings on her behalf. This was an unusual move, for it must be remembered that at this stage Adelaide had not been charged with any offence relating to her husband's death. Evidently, Mr Wood felt there was a possibility that Adelaide would eventually fall under suspicion and wished to have her represented as a cautionary measure should a charge be made against her. Before leaving his office, Adelaide was told that the police had completed their search of the flat in Claverton Street and that the keys were with Dr Leach; this meant that she was now at liberty to remove her belongings whenever she wished.

The following day, 6th January, accompanied by Alice Matthews, she went to Claverton Street to sort out her things. Before they set out a letter had arrived from Dr Leach making an appointment for Adelaide to see him at three o'clock that afternoon, and telling her she could have the keys to the flat. He indicated that he wished to discuss the coming inquest in the hope that she could help him recall various details relating to Edwin's illness and death.

While the two ladies were preparing for their journey, George Dyson arrived with some of Edwin's business letters which Mr Baxter had found amongst the papers in the office. He had given them to Mr Wood, the solicitor, who had asked Dyson to deliver them to Adelaide.

At this stage, at least in company, Dyson and Adelaide were still attempting to disguise their antipathy towards one another with a thin veneer of civility. It was snowing heavily as they left the house, so the young minister ordered a hansom cab to take them to Peckham Rye railway station. From there, the three travelled to Victoria together, deliberately avoiding any reference to the source of contention that was hanging over them.

The weather was particularly harsh that January, and as the train passed Peckham Rye Pond Alice Matthews noticed that it had frozen over, affording great delight to a group of youngsters who were happily risking life and limb by skating from one side to the other.

There is some confusion in the accounts of what happened when they reached Victoria. The ladies appear to have gone straight to Charlwood Street to pick up the keys to the flat, while Dyson went off to buy some cord to tie up Adelaide's boxes. However, when Dyson later arrived at Charlwood Street, he was given the keys by Dr Leach who had been out when the ladies called – not surprisingly since it had been well before three o'clock, the time when he was expecting them – and was told that they had proceeded to Claverton Street. Presumably Dyson found them there, waiting in the smoking room downstairs, and handed over keys and cord – after which Adelaide told him to go away until it was time for her appointment with Dr Leach.

Once inside the flat, the ladies began to sort and pack Adelaide's belongings, and at three o'clock Dyson duly returned to escort them to Dr Leach's house as planned. When they arrived the maid showed them into the drawing-room and then brought them tea while they waited for Leach to appear. A little later, Adelaide was shown into the doctor's consulting room and there they discussed Edwin's death and the inquest the following day. Although chloroform was obviously mentioned during their conversation, Leach later admitted that 'on this occasion chlorodyne was again referred to because, unfortunately, I continued to harp on the subject.'

Of course, as the contents of Edwin's stomach had not yet been analysed, Leach was still able to indulge in his obsessive speculation.

The specimen jars, each covered with brown paper and labelled, had been left at the Bartletts' flat until 4th January, at which time the Coroner ordered them to be taken to the mortuary at Millbank. But it was not until 11th January that they were finally transferred to Guy's Hospital where they were examined by Dr Thomas Stevenson on behalf of the Home Office.

While Adelaide sat with Dr Leach recalling the night Edwin died and listening once more to his chlorodyne theory, George Dyson remained in the drawing-room with Alice Matthews. Unable to contain his anxiety any longer and having a sympathetic listener to hand, he launched into a harrowing account of his impending ruin. He proclaimed that Adelaide had duped him, told him lies and made him believe that Edwin was suffering from a serious complaint from which he would soon die.

Clutching at straws, he asked Alice Matthews if she had ever known Edwin Bartlett to be seriously ill. Her reply was not very reassuring. He had been unwell a few years back, she said, but his general health had always been extremely good. Despair seized Dyson. He began to babble – about the long weeks of nursing, the delirium and violence, and the chloroform that had been used with such soothing effect.

Alice Matthews stared at him, mystified, and her obvious perplexity stimulated him to unburden himself completely. In a few minutes he had relayed the whole of the whispered conversation that had sounded so convincing that night on the Embankment. As he described Adelaide's plight now that Annie Walker had gone to America, and her plea that he should obtain chloroform for her, the enormity of what he had done overwhelmed him. 'She asked me to get it for her – and I did,' he finished on a wail.

The relief at having at last confessed his purchase of the chloroform calmed Dyson down. He asked Mrs Matthews if she thought he should tell all he know at the inquest the next day. Aware of the extreme gravity of his situation, she wisely advised him to return to East Dulwich with her and Adelaide, and talk things over with her husband before making any decision. Dyson agreed to this, glad that he no longer had to bear the burden of his conscience alone.

A few minutes later Adelaide joined them in the drawing-room. The three then walked back to Claverton Street where, to their surprise, Adelaide bade them goodbye, saying that she would take a later train to East Dulwich when she had finished her packing.

It was impossible for Dyson to confide in George Matthews during the evening at Friern Road. When the minister left, however, Matthews walked with him to the station and they talked the matter over. Matthews later described Dyson as 'panic-stricken.' The preacher admitted that he had bought the chloroform for Adelaide, believing it would be used to soothe Edwin during one of his violent spells. He also insisted that Edwin was partly to blame for having 'thrown Mrs Bartlett so much in his company so that he was attacked on his weakest side, with the result that he had been duped by a wicked woman'. George Matthews advised him to 'keep silent until the report of the Home Office analyst had been received.' For, as he pointed out, no one could be sure that it *was* chloroform that had killed Edwin. It might have been something else.

As things stood, therefore, there seemed little point in confessing to anything – yet.

CHAPTER 11
Adelaide Stands Alone

The inquest on Edwin Bartlett's death was opened the following day, 7th January. It was held in the parochial boardroom in Buckingham Palace Road, before the Deputy Coroner of Westminster, Mr Braxton Hicks, and a jury of twelve.

Adelaide appeared in court dressed in fashionable mourning, complete with veil, an ensemble which accentuated her small frame and pale complexion. Throughout the hearing she sat between her lawyer, Edward Beal, and her solicitor, Edward Wood. The public benches were empty, for at this stage in the story the case was considered to be of little importance. Only a couple of reporters had bothered to attend, and even they could not have imagined that the death of a South London grocer was likely to become headline news.

They were mistaken, however, for by the time the case reached the Central Criminal Court at the Old Bailey, it has become one of the most celebrated cases of the 1880s – so much so that the name of Adelaide Bartlett appeared on the front page of every newspaper in London and street vendors were selling her photograph by the thousand.

The proceedings that day began with the calling of Mr Bartlett, senior, as the first witness and he made it clear to the Coroner that, until his last illness, his son had been a strong, healthy man. Having said this, the old man took the opportunity of publicly complaining about Adelaide's visiting restrictions during the last few weeks of Edwin's life. As he spoke, his bitterness and animosity towards his daughter-in-law were apparent to everyone in the court. Consumed with anger and grief, Mr Bartlett stepped down and Adelaide was called to give evidence.

To the great surprise of the spectators, she at once made it clear that her delicate appearance was misleading; far from dabbing her eyes with a lace handkerchief, she tossed back her veil and charged her father-in-law with being vindictive and meddlesome. She also proclaimed that he had always disliked her because she was a foreigner and a Roman Catholic.

Rather taken aback by this unexpected outburst, the Coroner intervened, saying that 'these family matters could not be gone into.' He then adjourned the proceedings until 4th February, by which time, he said, Dr Stevenson, the Home Office analyst, would have submitted his report on his findings.

This assumption was precipitate, however, for, unknown to him, the contents of Edwin's stomach were still bottled up and waiting to be examined at Millbank mortuary.

Adelaide's fiery tirade in the witness-box was her first and, so far as is known, her last call to give evidence in a court of law. Her lawyer, Edward Beal, refused to let her give evidence again and, judging by her assertive performance that day, this was undoubtedly a wise precaution. Yet her spirited attack on her father-in-law offers an illuminating glimpse of her true character and one can see that she was by no means the passive, suburban housewife some writers have imagined her to be. She was, in fact, aggressive, outspoken and perfectly capable of speaking up for herself – in public, if necessary.

As soon as the court had adjourned she hurried from the building, having previously arranged to meet George Dyson 'for dinner together in a private room at Mrs Stewart's the confectioner's shop' near Victoria. According to Dyson, this last-minute rendezvous was for the purpose of discussing as he put it, 'the recent events which had happened, the post-mortem, and my having bought the chloroform, and so forth...'

Over the meal, fearing that George Dyson's panic would lead him into making a premature confession that would, in turn, implicate her, Adelaide tried to calm him down by reminding him that Dr

In the Interests of Science: Adelaide Bartlett and The Pimlico Poisoning

Leach was still convinced that Edwin had swallowed chlorodyne, accidentally. She emphasised that until the Home Office analysts had sent in their report there was absolutely no proof that Edwin's death had been caused by chloroform. Finally, she suggested that Dyson was worrying unnecessarily. He, however, was not so easily pacified.

'I have reason to be alarmed!' he retorted. 'My position is perilous. I am not afraid to stand by the truth when it affects me.'

From this last remark, Adelaide could see that the preacher in George Dyson was reasserting himself and this worried her. Fully aware that her influence on him had irrevocably weakened since Edwin's death, she felt threatened by his sanctimonious attitude and tried to bargain with him: 'If you do not incriminate yourself, I shall not incriminate you.'

In other words, she was warning Dyson to keep quiet about the chloroform, or they would both be in trouble. Dyson's conscience, however, still troubled him. Refusing to be cajoled into silence, he demanded again to know what Adelaide had done with the bottle of chloroform. She refused to answer him. Clearly, she had no intention of telling him anything. As she rose to leave the shop he tried once more.

'If you don't tell me,' he warned, 'I shall persist in my intention of making a full and complete statement.'

Still refusing to answer him, she walked towards the door. Dyson, however, caught hold of her arm. Hoping to frighten her into telling the truth, he said that George and Alice Matthews already knew about the chloroform. To this she made no reply while her expression registered nothing but contempt. She left the shop without a word. The friendship between Adelaide Bartlett and George Dyson was now dead.

The following day, at Edwin's funeral, they stood together by the graveside but neither a look nor a word passed between them as those mourning Edwin Bartlett struggled privately with their grief.

Clearly, Adelaide had finally dismissed George Dyson as an unreliable and potentially damaging ally. She must also have sensed that she could no longer rely on the friendship of George and Alice Matthews. They knew about the chloroform and they, too, were beginning to have doubts about her honesty. Indeed, Alice Matthews was later to say that by this time she had begun to feel uncomfortable with Adelaide 'because she told such lies.'

Realising that she no longer had any guarantee of their good will, or their silence, Adelaide turned instead to Mr Wood and Edward Beal for support, making another appointment to see them on the morning of Saturday, 9th January. About the same time, George Dyson, still worried about the chloroform, went back to East Dulwich to see George Matthews. Unfortunately, he was at work, but his wife suggested that Dyson meet him at his office in the City. As it was a Saturday, she said, her husband would finish work at two o'clock, so if Dyson met him at the office shortly before that time they could talk things over on the journey back to East Dulwich.

Gratefully accepting this advice, Dyson hurried straight back to George Matthews's office in town, arriving at eleven o'clock. Not surprisingly, he was asked to come back at two, but it was still only one o'clock when he returned, and he was obliged to wait in the lobby outside, in a frenzy of anxiety, until Matthews was ready to leave.

One can imagine George Dyson's dismay when he looked up to see Adelaide coming through the doorway! Her surprise at seeing him must have equalled his own, for she had come straight from her meeting with her solicitor, hoping to persuade George Matthews to keep quiet about the chloroform. The situation was extremely awkward for both of them, for neither felt able to broach the subject foremost in their minds. When George Matthews eventually left his office that afternoon, he, Adelaide and the preacher made their way back to East Dulwich – Adelaide and Dyson each frustrated by the other's presence while poor Matthews was inadvertently wedged between the two of them.

The train journey must have been an uncomfortable one, for the animosity between Adelaide and Dyson intensified, so much so that when they finally reached the Matthews' home, George Dyson lost control, demanding to know yet again what Adelaide had done with the chloroform.

'I must know,' he wailed, 'or I am a ruined man.'

George Matthews, embarrassed by this confrontation and possible anticipating a full-blown row, intervened by suggesting that Dyson was possibly exaggerating the seriousness of his predicament. The preacher, however, would not be consoled.

'It is no exaggeration,' he said. 'Whatever happens I am a ruined man so far as my prospects in the ministry are concerned if the slightest breath of this reaches the ears of my superintendent.'

Unable to divert the approaching storm, Matthews remained silent while Dyson turned on Adelaide once more.

'I bought the chloroform at your request because you told me lies about Edwin's state,' he shouted. 'The contents of the stomach are being analysed... supposing that it turns out...'

At this point, Adelaide interrupted and, giving full rein to her scorn and resentment, challenged him to come out with it and accuse her directly of poisoning her husband. At this, Dyson backed down a little but still persisted in his harassment of her.

'Supposing it was discovered that you gave him chloroform, and I gave it to you, what would be the opinion of the world? How should I come out in such a case?'

Adelaide remained unruffled:

> I told you before that I never opened the bottle,' she asserted. 'I left it behind when I left Claverton Street – in a drawer in the bedroom. When I went there on the 6th – after the police had made a search – I found it in the same drawer. I put it in my bag. Coming back here that evening, when I was on the train, I opened the window, pouring the chloroform away on the line, and threw the bottle into Peckham Rye Pond.

This totally implausible explanation left them speechless. Alice Matthews, of course, knew it to be a complete fabrication, for at the time when Adelaide alleged that she had thrown the bottle into the pond, the water had been frozen solid with youngsters skating over it.

At this point, Adelaide must have known that her flat had been searched by the police - it is surprising, therefore, that she should imagine they would have overlooked a large bottle of chloroform when examining the rooms of a man who had just died in suspicious circumstances, and whose stomach, when opened, had smelt like a freshly opened bottle of chloroform! George Dyson's patience was spent. He simply 'flung up his arms and left the house immediately.' There was little else he could do, faced with Adelaide's infuriating resistance to reality.

Nothing more was said about the chloroform bottle after George Dyson's departure, but there was no denying that Alice Matthews was curious to know the post-mortem result and, having avoided the subject while her other guest was present, could curb her curiosity no longer. She asked Adelaide directly what the doctors had found and then asked her why she had told George Dyson so many lies about Edwin's health.

Adelaide, however, stood her ground, insisting that Dyson had misunderstood her for she had said, in fact, that during Edwin's illness he had *thought* he was going to die. She did admit, however, that she had asked Dyson to get some chloroform to calm her husband, at the same time assuring Alice Matthews that she had had no occasion to use it.

This explanation seemed reasonable enough, yet knowing Adelaide's tendency to bend the truth, Alice still felt inclined to disbelieve her.

The following Monday, 11th January, was a day of departures all round. George Dyson, still at odds with his conscience, travelled to Poole to discuss his predicament with his father. This must have been a particularly difficult decision to make, for his father was also a church minister. To confess his involvement with a married woman was bad enough, but he also had to admit that he had been duped into providing the poison that had probably killed the husband. Dyson's journey to Poole, therefore, must have been undertaken with great trepidation.

Adelaide was also on the move that day. While Dyson was preparing to face his father's wrath, she was settling into new lodgings in Weymouth Street, Portland Place. It was not exactly clear why she left Friern Road, but it would be a fair assumption that she was asked to leave. The angry scenes between Adelaide and George Dyson had been scandalous, for such displays of temper were unseemly between a woman recently widowed and a minister of religion. It must be remembered, too, that Alice Matthews had at least one young child in the house to consider, and possibly more; furthermore, Adelaide had arrived on her doorstep on the day of the post- mortem, unexpectedly. It was a difficult situation for all concerned, and Adelaide had proved to be a far from satisfactory guest.

However, the explanation Adelaide gave later for her sudden departure from East Dulwich was that Alice Matthews had refused to accept any payment for her lodgings and so, not wishing to feel beholden to anyone for her keep, she had sought rooms elsewhere.

While all these dramas were going on, the contents of Edwin's stomach remained on the shelf in the mortuary at Millbank. It was not until the day after Adelaide left East Dulwich that Dr Stevenson made his analysis for the Home Office.

Anxious to keep abreast of the findings, Adelaide visited Dr Leach at his surgery on the 14th, 18th and 26th days of January, confident that the doctor would furnish her with all she wanted to know. Leach certainly saw a great deal of Adelaide during this period, admitting later that, besides her visits to his surgery, he had also called at her lodgings on 'two or three occasions, as she had not been very well.'

Adelaide obviously knew how to handle Leach and her delicate health was not the only topic of conversation during their frequent meetings. By 20th January Leach had discussed further details of the post-mortem with her, saying that as far as he knew Edwin had not died from inhaling chloroform as he had seen no change in the structure of the brain. It was certainly incautious of Leach to be so open with Adelaide; however, this lack of caution enabled her to monitor the progress of the investigation into Edwin's death without any trouble at all. Faced with her expert interrogation it appears that the doctor had little control over his reckless and garrulous tongue.

On Wednesday, 13th January, George Dyson returned to London accompanied by his father who, from the time his son confessed his involvement in the case, gave him every possible support. Encouraged by his father's good sense, Dyson obtained legal advice before making his confession to the Council of the Ministry, the governing body of the Wesleyan Church. This done, he disassociated himself from Adelaide Bartlett and all that had existed between them. To underline his intention he went back to Friern Road on 18th January and told Alice Matthews that he would be giving evidence against Adelaide when the Coroner's inquest was resumed. He begged her to do the same if, as he feared, chloroform was found to be the cause of Edwin Bartlett's death.

Alice Matthews, however, seems to have been a kindly woman with a keen sense of loyalty, for she was reluctant at first to incriminate Edwin's widow and her former friend. But George Dyson went on to urge her to consider her duty and pleaded with her to give evidence at the inquest. She eventually agreed but only, she said later, because of the preacher's earnest request that she do so.

CHAPTER 12

An Ingenious Tale

In the meantime, Adelaide must have been worried. She knew that George Dyson had confessed to the Wesleyan authorities and that her possession of chloroform would be revealed when the inquest was resumed on 4th February. Nor could she count on the continued silence of George and Alice Matthews, for they were bound to divulge the angry scenes they had witnessed in Friern Road shortly after Edwin's death.

She must also have been very angry with herself, for her story about throwing the chloroform bottle into the pond at Peckham Rye had been a foolish mistake. Perhaps she had been too preoccupied that day to notice that the pond was frozen; perhaps she had simply forgotten; in any event, she had been caught out in a lie, with the result that her former friends had grown suspicious and had lost all faith in her.

What is more, having disposed of the bottle she had no way of proving that she had *not* used the chloroform. Yet, by the same token, she realised that no one could prove that she *had* used it either...

The fact that she had destroyed the evidence must have suggested to all but the most naive that her act was that of a guilty person – but then, George Dyson had done the same thing, so did that make him guilty of murder? Or was he justifiably panic-stricken and acting on impulse? If this was so, the same could be said of Adelaide.

Unfortunately, her position became even more precarious when, on 26th January, Dr Leach told her that the Home Office had completed the analysis of Edwin's stomach and confirmed that chloroform *was* the cause of his death. She knew that this statement, when presented at the inquest alongside George Dyson's confession, would be her downfall.

Dr Leach, however, having told her the result of the Home Office analysis, thought that she would be relieved, for chloroform had never been associated with murder.

'That should set your mind at rest,' he assured her. 'Had it been one of the secret poisons given in small amounts, and which could be administered without the patient knowing it, you would have most certainly been very seriously accused of poisoning him.'

Being at this stage totally ignorant of Adelaide's secret acquisition of chloroform, he was surprised by her strange reply:

> I'm afraid, doctor, it is too true. I wish anything but chloroform had been found.

Realising that she had to present a quick and plausible reason for possessing chloroform, Adelaide immediately launched into an account of her marriage which was certain to awaken a flow of chivalrous indignation in the heart of the young Dr Leach. It was an imaginative piece, carefully constructed to rationalise her possession of a large bottle of deadly poison. Leach made careful notes of their extraordinary conversation:

> She began by giving a preface containing a sketch of her married life. The sketch was simply this, that, being married young, she had been induced to enter into a marriage compact, scarcely understanding the meaning of its terms; and this marriage compact was that the marital relations of the pair were, in deference to certain peculiar views held by her husband, to be of an entirely platonic nature; sexual intercourse was not to occur.
>
> The terms of this compact were adhered to with a solitary exception, when a breach of the terms was permitted in consequence of her fondness for children and her anxiety to become a mother. After her confinement the former terms – that is to say, those of a platonic nature –were resumed, she being indifferent on the matter.
>
> Her husband was kind to her. They were affectionate and each strove in every way to fulfil each other's wishes, and succeeded in living

> upon the most amicable terms, the happiness of which was on one occasion, disturbed by her husband's father. She then entered into some family details which really have quite slipped my memory... Her husband's brother was not referred to. She told me she had consented to her husband's father living with them but he made her life miserable by his constant insults; and when she appealed to her husband to resent those insults, he, in his mild way, did not act upon her suggestion with the zeal that she thought the occasion demanded. She consequently left her husband's house and hid herself from him – I think in the house of her aunt – I forget for how long; and she only consented to return upon an ample apology being made...
>
> She then said that her position had not been an easy one: it might almost be called cruel, for her husband, though meaning no cruelty, put her in a very difficult position for a woman to maintain. No female friends or relations were ever invited to the house, but he had always liked to surround her with male acquaintances. She said, "He thought me clever; he wished to make me more clever; and the more attention and admiration I gained from these male acquaintances the more delighted did he appear. Their attention to me gave him pleasure....
>
> "We became acquainted with Mr Dyson. My husband threw us together. He requested us to kiss in his presence, and he seemed to enjoy it." She gave me to understand – in fact, she used these words, "He had given me to Mr Dyson."

Dr Leach was clearly amazed by Adelaide's story, and she surprised him still further by saying that, just before his death, Edwin, having more or less promised her to George Dyson, had begun to show signs of desire – as though he wished, after all, to claim his marital rights. This had offended Adelaide's fine sense of morality and she had managed to dissuade him by saying:

> Edwin, you know you have given me to Mr Dyson; it is not right that you should do now what during all the married years of our life you have not done.

Apparently, this remonstration cooled Edwin's ardour for a while at least but then, late in December, when his health was improving, he began to show the same distasteful inclination towards his wife. Adelaide, therefore, felt perfectly justified in using chloroform on him to persuade him to abandon any passionate pursuits.

> She said that her object was to sprinkle some of the chloroform upon a handkerchief and wave it in his face every time it was necessary, thinking that thereby he would go peacefully to sleep.

Even young Leach, however, was unable to accept his explanation without comment and he rebuked her smartly:

> Trying to put chloroform upon your handkerchief and waving it in the face of your husband, he would have resisted it, a struggle would have ensued, the bottle would have capsized and chloroformed the pair of you!

But Adelaide countered his horrified reproof with a pious reply:

> I never kept a secret from Edwin, and the presence of the chloroform in my drawer troubled my mind. And I was also troubled with some scruples as to whether putting my plan into practice would have been right. On the last day of the year, when he was in bed, I brought the chloroform to him, and gave it to him, and informed him of my intention. He was not cross; we talked amicably and seriously, and he turned round on his side, and pretended to go to sleep, or to sulk.

Prior to this, according to Adelaide, Edwin had looked at the bottle for a moment before putting it on the mantleshelf above his head. Adelaide had then settled herself on the chair next to the bed, with her hand, as usual, on her husband's foot.

When Dr Leach had considered this incredible story he ventured to ask who had got the chloroform for her, but she merely said that 'someone had got it for her', and seemed reluctant to say more. Surprisingly, the doctor made no further enquiry on that point; he was more concerned with the whereabouts of the bottle.

He inquired what she had done with the bottle of chloroform, and she was positive that it had remained on the mantelpiece throughout the night and early morning. She had put it away in her drawer about breakfast time. She had taken the bottle from the flat on 6th January and thrown it into Peckham Rye Pond. The lie, once told, could not be abandoned.

Yet there were parts of her story that began to puzzle Dr Leach.

For one thing, he was absolutely sure that there had been no bottle of chloroform on the mantelpiece when he had searched the room in the early hours of 1st January. Nor had she left the room at any time while he and Mr Doggett were searching it. She must either have put the bottle in her drawer before rousing the maid, or secreted it about her person until she was alone again.

The whereabouts of the chloroform bottle at four o'clock on the morning of Edwin Bartlett's death was a mystery as far as Leach was concerned – he was even more perplexed when he heard Alice Matthews testify that Peckham Rye Pond was frozen over on 6th January.

Poor Leach, what a confusing start to his medical career!

By the time the inquest was resumed on 4th February, the press had somehow sensed that the death of Edwin Bartlett was not, as it had first appeared to be, a mundane domestic tragedy. Already there were whispers of murder and intrigue and 'the large room in which the investigation was held was crowded with interested persons.' Members of the press were there in force. *The Times* and various other newspapers reported daily on the proceedings, involving their readers in the story they now referred to as *The Pimlico Mystery*.

Once the court officials were assembled and the spectators settled into the public benches, the Coroner called on Adelaide Bartlett to give evidence. At this point, however, her lawyer, Mr Beal, asked that her examination be postponed until after Dr Stevenson had given the results of his analysis. The Coroner obviously objected to this change in the usual procedure and again called her to the witness box. Mr Beal rose to protest, saying that 'it was idle to pretend that she was not under a considerable amount of suspicion, and questions of an incriminating character might not improbably be put to her in the course of her examination.'

The Coroner replied that whereas he 'could not compel her to come forward, her counsel should understand that the jury would draw an unfavourable inference from her refusal.'

This said, he called upon Dr Stevenson to read the results of his analysis, which were diligently noted by the reporter from *The Times*:

> The stomach had apparently been acted upon by some irritant during life and shortly before death. There was no other poison present beside chloroform in the stomach. The stomach fluid was fairly acid and contained nearly five per cent of chloroform. Everything pointed to the administration of a large and fatal dose of chloroform. The post-mortem appearances were consistent with it – probably over an ounce had been taken. Nothing could take away the hot and fiery taste of chloroform, but it might be greatly mitigated by mixing with a bland fluid. Brandy would act as a solvent.[23]

Having read his report, Dr Stevenson emphasised that, despite many years of scientific experience, he had never heard of chloroform being used in a case of murder. It was, he told the court, more usually found in cases of suicide or accidental death.

Caroline Doggett was called next and offered a detailed account of the night Edwin Bartlett had died. Her husband, Frederick, followed her and reminded the court that he had smelt paregoric or ether as soon as he had entered the sick-room. He had noticed, too, that the wine glass which was standing on the mantelpiece above the bed had a similar smell.

'Unfortunately,' he added, 'in the confusion after the death, the wine glass which smelt so powerfully, and other things, had been taken downstairs and washed by the servant.'

Then came Dr Alfred Leach with a resumé of Edwin's medical treatment during his last illness. He managed to convey these details reasonably well, but when asked about the various conversations he had had with Adelaide Bartlett since her husband's death, he became hopelessly confused. Apologising to the Coroner, he said that he could not remember her exact words without 'applying his mind to it and refreshing his memory.' He felt that he would find it much more constructive to write down his recollections at his leisure. At this, the Coroner dismissed him, suggesting that he

---

23 *The Times*, 6th February, 1886

remove himself from the court and start writing. Dr Leach did as he was told, promising to have his report ready by 11th February, when the court would reassemble.

Inspector Marshall of the Metropolitan Police was the next witness. He had brought into court a copy of Squire's *Companion to the British Pharmacopoeia*, which he had found during his search of the Bartlett's flat. He handed the book to the Coroner who, on receiving it, 'drew the attention of the jury to the significant fact that it appeared to open naturally on the very page on which the drug *chloroform* was described.'

This observation caused a number of raised eyebrows and knowing looks among a spectators in court. It also confirmed the suspicions of the jostling reporters that the Pimlico Mystery would, after all, provide them with a very good story indeed.

CHAPTER 13

A Charge of Murder

During the week that the inquest was adjourned, *The Times* gave The Pimlico Mystery considerable coverage. It seemed to have the makings of an irresistible piece of melodrama, with all the essential ingredients – a chloroformed corpse, a beautiful widow, the chilling presence of poison and, most riveting of all, a lapsed man of God lurking in the wings!

Little wonder that the case was beginning to attract so much public interest, and the more scandalous details the newspapers revealed, the more that interest was fired, fanned still further by the surge of rumour and speculation that inevitably followed.

When the inquest was resumed on 11th February, the courtroom was packed with spectators; members of the press were there in force, and Adelaide, as the *femme fatale* of the piece, found herself the centre of avid attention. Nevertheless, she sat in court looking quite composed, almost detached from the whole affair, surveying the scene as though she, too, were merely a spectator. Throughout the proceedings she sat in close proximity to George Dyson – but, as at Edwin's funeral on 8th January, not a glance passed between them.

George Dyson was surrounded by a posse of reverend gentlemen, grim-faced and soberly dressed for the occasion. Now that his involvement in the Pimlico affair had been made public he had become, to some at least, a figure of fun, to others an object of scorn. Bereft of the respect generally given to his calling he was, as he had predicted, a ruined man and one who could expect little sympathy from the crowd.

The proceedings that day began with the reading of Dr Leach's written statement. Having been given time to collect his thoughts he had allowed his pen to flow freely, and consequently the statement was long and laboured. This was followed by the evidence of the three chemists from whom George Dyson had purchased the chloroform.

The dye was cast when George Dyson himself rose to speak. It undoubtedly eased his conscience to confess his unwitting part in the tragedy but, with every word he uttered, Adelaide's credibility was inevitably diminished.

The Coroner, acutely aware of her perilous position, again asked her to give evidence, but still her lawyer, Edward Beal, resisted the request on her behalf.

The situation was extremely grave. After further reference to the evidence of George Dyson and the three chemists, the foreman of the jury announced that 'they were all of the opinion that Mrs Bartlett should not longer be left at liberty.'

The Coroner accepted their decision.

'As you have expressed that opinion, gentleman,' he declared, 'I see no reason why she should not be taken into custody. She will be charged before a magistrate. It is for this reason I asked her just now if she would give evidence. I wanted to give her a last chance.'[24]

Turning to the court, he said:

> The police are here and have heard the statement as to the opinion of the jury, who do not say they are ready to give their verdict but they think there is evidence enough to charge Mrs Bartlett.

With that, the Coroner made out the necessary warrant for her arrest, whereupon Inspector Marshall of the Metropolitan Police took Adelaide into custody, there and then in full view of the assembly. She was escorted into a side room and charged with the murder of her husband; when cautioned, she replied, 'I have nothing

---

24 The Coroner was anxious that Adelaide should have a chance to speak as, at the time, a person on trial for murder was not allowed to give evidence in his or her defence. The law was changed in 1898.

to say.'

From there she was driven to Rochester Row Police Station and the following day, 12th February, came before the magistrate, Mr Partridge, at Westminster Police Court. She was charged with 'causing the death of Edwin Thomas Bartlett, by administering a poisonous dose of chloroform to him on or about midnight on the 31st December, 1885.'

Adelaide, who appeared in court 'dressed in deep mourning, and thickly veiled', was described in *The Penny Illustrated Paper* as a 'large-eyed young lady of attractive appearance.' When asked if she had anything to say why she should not be remanded on the charge, her solicitor, Edward Wood, spoke for her, saying 'No, sir.'

Thereupon, Adelaide was remanded in custody and taken to Clerkenwell Prison.

Meanwhile the inquest was adjourned until 18th February, by which time the case had become the talking point of the day. The illicit relationship between Adelaide and the young preacher had caught the imagination of the public; people were shocked yet fascinated, and more than ready to believe that Adelaide Bartlett was not only an adulteress but quite capable of murder. She was, after all, they whispered, a foreigner of dubious origin, whose moral standards were highly unconventional.

The resumption of the inquest drew enormous crowds. The clamour for seats, for standing room even, was so great that much resentment was felt by those who were turned away.

Those who were lucky enough to gain entrance hurried into the court expecting to hear further revelations, but they were disappointed, for the first two hours were spent in reading the depositions of the previous witnesses, allowing them the opportunity to make any adjustments or additions they felt necessary.

At one point during this tedious procedure, Mr Doggett was recalled to the witness box and testified once more that there had been no bottle of chloroform in the room when he and Dr Leach had made their search shortly after Edwin was found dead. On the strength of this evidence, the jury had to decide whether Adelaide was mistaken or lying when she said that the bottle was still on the mantelpiece that morning.

Dr Stevenson, the Home Office analyst, was recalled next and asked about the nature of chloroform and its effects. He considered that it would be 'quite possible to make a person partially insensible by the inhalation of chloroform, and then pouring more of the drug down his throat, the person so operated upon being in such a state as to be oblivious of the pain this would cause. People could be chloroformed during sleep, he said, but as a rule, when chloroform was inhaled or taken in a large quantity, it produced vomiting. It was exceptional not to vomit. Medically speaking, a very large quantity of the drug had been swallowed.

The court was told that when Dr Leach examined Edwin Bartlett's body on the morning of 1st January, he had not noticed any signs of vomiting. Had he wished to inspect the bed linen more closely later, he would have found that the bed had already been stripped and the sheets and pillowcases laundered.

Summing up the proceedings that day, the Coroner asked the jury to decide whether or not George Dyson's evidence, 'voluntarily and fully given, amounted to an exculpation of his conduct, or whether he was open to so much suspicion that he should be sent for trial on the charge of being an accessory before the fact of Mr Bartlett's death.'

The jurors, needing time to consider their verdict, retired to another room, returning to the court some forty minutes later.

George Dyson sat quaking in the midst of his clerical friends, a look of dread on his flushed face. His horror and shame were complete as the jury delivered its verdict:

> The jury are of the opinion that the deceased, Edwin Thomas Bartlett, died from chloroform administered by his wife, Adelaide Bartlett, for the purpose of taking his life, and that the Reverend George Dyson was an accessory before the fact.

The Coroner went on to inform the assembly that 'in the eyes of the law an accessory before the fact was equal to the principal on the first degree. This,' continued Mr Braxton Hicks, 'is a verdict of wilful murder against Mrs Bartlett and Mr Dyson.'

The gravity of his words hung heavily over the court. *The Times* reporter noted:

> A very painful scene took place in the crowded court on the verdict being delivered. The Reverend George Dyson sank into his chair, almost fainting, and cried. His Wesleyan friends, particularly several ministers, were standing round him in a sad and sympathetic manner. After a lapse of a few minutes Mr Dyson became calmer and he was taken into custody by Detective Inspector Marshall who received the Coroner's warrant.[25]

For both Adelaide and George Dyson the situation was grim. However, 20th February, two days later, was to mark the turning point in Adelaide's fortunes. Prompted by the urgency of her predicament, her anonymous father came to the rescue, ordering Mr Wood to instruct Messrs Lewis & Lewis[26] of Ely Place to engage the services of the most promising lawyer in the country for her defence.

His name was Edward Clarke. His brief was simple: *to save Adelaide Bartlett from the gallows*. The substantial fee he received must have come from her natural father – it could hardly have come from anyone else for she was without friends and penniless; nor could she rely on inheriting the money from Edwin's will, for old Mr Bartlett had already started proceedings to contest it.

A week later, on 27th February, both the accused were taken to the Westminster Police Court for further examination before the magistrate, Mr Partridge.

Not for Adelaide, however, the indignity of the Black Maria. She had complained so vehemently about the discomfort of the police

---

25 *The Times*, 19th February, 1886.
26 Sir George Lewis, described by Georgina Battiscombe in Queen Alexandra (Constable, 1969) as 'the famous solicitor who knew more than any man about the scandalous secrets of Victorian society...'

van, saying that it made her 'sick and giddy', that she was allowed to travel to and from the court in a privately hired hansom cab. This concession was sanctioned by the magistrate himself, on account, he said, of her 'delicate health', and was the first sign of her preferential treatment following Edward Clarke's acceptance of her case.

George Dyson, however, without any such influential support, was forced to suffer the misery and ignominy of the Black Maria, much to the satisfaction of the jeering crowds gathered at the gates to witness his shame.

Once inside the court, Adelaide and Dyson were obliged to sit together in the dock, but each ignored the presence of the other as though they were complete strangers. The centre of attention that day was undoubtedly Adelaide, described by one reporter as 'a lady of considerable personal attractions'. Sitting on a wooden bench, she was 'attired in deep mourning, draped in crape.' She had 'long black hair and dark hazel eyes, with lashes of the same colour. She wore a long widow's veil, which she kept down, and appeared to be suffering from weakness, a female being allowed to be in attendance on her.'

Seated with only a grim-faced gaoler between them was the Reverend George Dyson, described as a 'young man of medium height, with dark hair, heavy moustache, close-cut whiskers, and a heavy jaw; he was dressed in clerical attire. Although very pale, he appeared composed.'

Adelaide remained outwardly calm throughout the proceedings, though a little pale, whereas Dyson's initial composure soon crumbled. His fear and shame became only too apparent to the spectators. At one point, whilst listening to Dr Leach's evidence, he became very agitated, jumped out of his chair and shouted:

> I won't sit here and listen to such lies! Look at his face – is there no protection?

This outburst brought a sharp remonstration from the magistrate, after which Dyson 'fell back in his chair as though resigned to his fate.'

A Charge of Murder

There were several adjournments in the days that followed, but as the inquiry progressed a wealth of medical evidence was offered to the court. On Saturday, 20th March, Dr Stevenson stated that whilst making his analysis he had looked for metallic poisons and found traces of lead and copper in part of Edwin Bartlett's lower jaw. His next comment underlined Dr Leach's lack of medical experience and his tendency to adhere to his initial diagnosis:

> In lead poisoning there is a characteristic blue line round the gums. Mercurial poisoning does not exhibit quite such a characteristic line.

In fairness to Dr Leach, it must be said that the dentist, Thomas Roberts, also believed the blue line round Edwin's gum to be the result of mercurial poisoning.

Dr Stevenson conceded, however, that to make a thorough search for mercury in Edwin's body, the liver and other organs would have to be analysed as well. This was never carried out, as no exhumation order was ever made.

'It was obvious to the eye,' went on the doctor, 'that the deceased's stomach had been acted upon by an irritant but the post-mortem appearance did not, in itself, suggest that chloroform, in particular, was responsible.'

It was the subsequent analysis of the contents of the stomach, however, that had confirmed that death was due to the swallowing of liquid chloroform.

With this evidence in mind, and George Dyson's confession fresh in his memory, the magistrate ruled that there was a *prima facie* case against both Adelaide Bartlett and George Dyson. Following this decision, they were charged jointly with the wilful murder of Edwin Bartlett and committed for trial at the Old Bailey. The application for bail on George Dyson's behalf was refused.

Adelaide Bartlett with the short hair which so outraged female spectators at the Old Bailey
© *Hulton Archive / Getty Images*

Below:
Croydon Parish Church, where Edwin Bartlett married Adelaide de la Tremoille on 6th April 1875

Above:
Edwin Bartlett
from Police News, 6th March 1886

Left:
The double shop at Station Road, Herne Hill. The Bartletts lived in the flat above
from Police News, 20th February 1886

Wesleyan Church, Putney, where the Rev George Dyson preached

The Rev George Dyson

The Cottage, Merton Abbey, where the Bartletts were living when they made the acquaintance of the Rev George Dyson
from Police News, 6th March 1886

Above: *Edwin Bartlett Senior*
from Police News, 6th March 1886

Below: *Dr Leach - young, inexperienced, gullible*
from Police News, 27th March 1886

85 CLAVERTON STREET

The Bartlett's last home together: 85 Claverton Street, Pimlico. Built in the 1840s, the street runs down to the Embankment from Lupus Street. Number 85 has since been demolished
from Police News, 20th February 1886

The Police News gave cartoon serial treatment to its coverage of the evidence given in the magistrate's court on 13th March (top) and 20th March. Every hint of scandal was ruthlessly exploited, and the artist allowed his imagination to run riot in suggesting Mr Dyson's choice of text for Latin study. His spelling was equally imaginative.

*The scene in court as Edward Clarke makes his speech for the defence
from the Penny Illustrated Paper, 24th April 1886*

Sir Charles Russell,
Attorney General in 1886,
Counsel for the Prosecution
© Hulton Archive / Getty Images

Mr Edward Clarke QC,
Counsel for the Defence
Courtesy The Mansell Collection

Mr Justice Wills

Mr Edward Clarke cross-examines Edwin Bartlett senior
Courtesy The Mansell Collection

*Adelaide Bartlett listens as the jury deliver their verdict on the last day of the trial
from Police News, 24th April 1886*

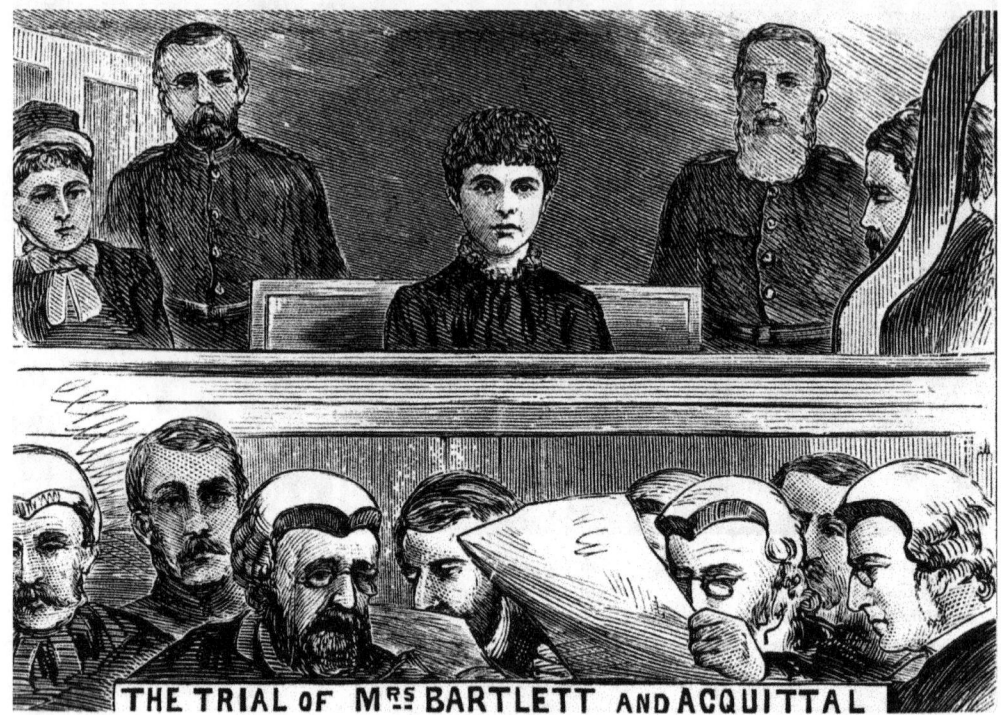

*First page of a letter from Sir Edward Clarke to Viscount Knutsford discussing the fate of Adelaide Bartlett following her acquittal
Courtesy Mark Ripper*

*Inscription by Edward Clarke to his son Percival in a copy of The Trial of Adelaide Bartlett (1886)
Courtesy Mark Ripper*

Morgan.

C/

27 Dec.

85 Claverton St
S.W.
Sunday night

Dear Mr. Bartlett
I hear that you are a little disturbed, because Edwin has been too ill to see you.
I wish, if possible, to be friends with you, but, you must place yourself on the same footing

Letter from Adelaide Bartlett to her father-in-law Edwin Bartlett senior, dated 27th December 1885
© The National Archives

Left:
Lord Alfred Paget - Adelaide's father?
© *National Portrait Gallery*

Below:
Lord Paget (centre) in 1857, two years after Adelaide's birth, flanked by Earl Carlisle and Isambard Kingdom Brunel
© *National Portrait Gallery*

Part Three

'We have had certainly strange incidents. I do not speak now of the remarkable relations which appear to have existed between Mr Bartlett and his wife – relations which would be almost inconceivable if they had not been proved to be true.'
Edward Clarke – Speech for the Defence

CHAPTER 14

Trial at the Old Bailey

Monday, 12th April, 1886, was the date set for the trial of Adelaide Bartlett and the Reverend George Dyson at the Central Criminal Court, scene of so many sensational British murder trials. Some thirty years later, the tragic figure of Edith Thompson would stand accused in the same sombre surroundings and ultimately pay the terrible penalty for committing her romantic fantasies to paper and unwittingly, to posterity. So, too, would Alma Rattenbury and Ruth Ellis who, like Edith Thompson, were tried for offending public morality as much as for murder.

Many more were to occupy the same dock in the years that followed Adelaide's appearance, among them names that have become synonymous with the most evil of crimes – Dr Harvey Crippen, Neville Heath, John Reginald Christie and, more recently, that chilling loner, Dennis Nilsen.

However, of the four most celebrated poison cases of the nineteenth century, only Adelaide faced trial at the Old Bailey. Madeleine Smith's case was heard in Edinburgh and Florence Maybrick's in Liverpool, whereas Florence Bravo, although never charged with murder, was, nonetheless, mercilessly interrogated during the inquest at Balham, following police enquiries into her husband's death.

It must be remembered that, in cases of murder, until the abolition of capital punishment in December 1965, a verdict of guilty carried with it the sentence of death. The tension during a murder trial was therefore tremendous: the life of the accused hung in the balance, and miscarriages of justice did occasionally occur. The law is, after all, fallible, and the scales of justice have been known to slip under the influence of a fervent political or moral climate.

It was fortunate, therefore, that Adelaide had the support of a wealthy father, for the case against her was overwhelming: fortunate, too, that the current political tensions were, indirectly, in her favour, for there was bitter contention at Westminster at the time, following Mr Gladstone's first reading of the Home Rule Bill on 8th April, 1886.

As Attorney General, Sir Charles Russell[27] was committed to lead the prosecution for the Crown at Adelaide's trial. Naturally Russell, along with many other prominent Liberals, was very much against the Bill, whereas the Conservatives were raring for battle on such an explosive issue – there was even talk of a General Election. In the circumstances, Sir Charles viewed the possibility of the Government's defeat with some pessimism, for if the Tories gained power he stood to lose his prestigious and lucrative position. He attended many late night sittings at the House of Commons and was involved in all the current debates. At the time of the trial, his thoughts may have been centred on pressing parliamentary issues rather than on poisoned grocers. He was, moreover, also involved in the defence of Sir Charles Dilke, a political colleague, in the throes of an extremely complicated divorce case.

It would therefore be fair to say that Sir Charles came to Adelaide's trial preoccupied and perhaps less than fully primed for battle. Though astute in his assessment of the facts, his approach to the case lacked the vigour necessary to match Edward Clarke's manipulative oratory and complete mastery of the crucial medical evidence.

In contrast, Edward Clarke had but one brief on his mind when he entered the court that day – to free Adelaide Bartlett from a charge of murder – and he set out to achieve his objective with a dogged professionalism that ran circles round his adversaries. Unlike Sir Charles, he absented himself from the House to study Adelaide's

---

27 Sir Charles Russell, 1832-1900. Attorney General 1885 and 1892. In his memoirs Edward Clarke describes him as having 'a commanding presence, a full resonant voice, a flashing eye and imperious gesture, which often bore down opposition, and unnerved the witness he was cross-examining, or a young counsel – and sometimes even the judge.'

case. He wrote later:

> As early as 20th February, I had been retained by Mr Wood for the defence of Mrs Bartlett, and I had, of course, carefully studied the evidence given before the coroner and the police magistrate, which was fully reported in the newspapers. My brief was delivered on Monday, April 5th.[28]

In his memoirs, he described his single-minded approach more fully:

> It was evident that questions of medical science would be of supreme importance, so I postponed some cases and returned other briefs, and spend a week or ten days in studying at the British Museum or in my own library all that was known about the qualities and effects of chloroform and the methods of its administration.
>
> During the week of the trial I read nothing but the papers in the case and the medical books. I drove down to the Old Bailey every morning, and when the Court rose in the afternoon drove straight back to Russell Square; then went for an hour's walk round the Regent's Park or up to Hampstead or Highgate; and then, after a light dinner, spent the evening in preparing the cross-examination or speech for the following day.[29]

Dedication such as this was exceptional, common to only a few of the great defence lawyers. Unusual, too, were the scenes at the Old Bailey, which Clarke also described in his book:

> The public interest in the case rose to an extraordinary pitch. The claims or solicitations for admissions to the court were so many that one of the principal doors was blocked up by rows of seats, and special tickets of admission were issued by the sheriffs. On the morning of April 12th, every seat was filled and crowds were vainly seeking admission.

Clearly, there was something about Adelaide Bartlett that had fired the imagination of the crowd, and as the newspapers had given detailed accounts of her story during the inquest, the case has

---

28 From 'Leaves from a Lawyer's Casebook, The Pimlico Mystery' by Sir Edward Clarke. *The Cornhill Magazine*, December 1920.
29 From *The Story of My Life* by Sir Edward Clarke. John Murray, 1918 p.249.

become a *cause célébre* even before the trial had begun.

Her air of defiant isolation seemed to hold a particular fascination for members of her own sex, for crowds of women gathered outside the gates of the Old Bailey to catch a glimpse of her. Many must have wondered how this grocer's wife had managed to raise the money to pay for one of the best lawyers in the country. It was inevitable, therefore, that rumours concerning the presence of a wealthy benefactor spread rapidly, inspired in part by the illustrious gathering of legal gentlemen assembled for the trial.

The case came before Mr Justice Wills, and assisting the Attorney General were Mr Harry Poland, QC, Mr Robert Wright and Mr Moloney. All three were subsequently knighted, and in 1894 Sir Charles Russell was raised to the peerage as Lord Russell of Killowen and made Lord Chief Justice; Mr Wright later became a High Court judge. The Reverend George Dyson was defended by Mr Francis Lockwood, QC, and Mr Charles Mathews, both of whom were also to receive knighthoods in due course.

But undeniably, the most prestigious figure of them all was that of Edward Clarke. Though small in stature and sombre of face, he had a powerful and compelling presence. A deeply religious man, a member of the Anglican Church, he was also a Freemason who took his Masonic duties very seriously and was much respected by his associates.[30] Though of humble origin, he was ambitious and through determination and hard work had soon risen in his chosen profession. At the time of Adelaide's trial he was at the height of his powers as an advocate, earning as much as £10,000 a year.[31] His defence of Patrick Staunton in 1877, whilst failing to secure an acquittal, had been much admired by his colleagues and brought his name to the public notice. In the same year he had secured an

---

30 In 1875, he was Master of the Caledonian Lodge.
31 This would be well over half a million in today's currency. Clarke's wealth may be fully understood when one remembers that a young barrister like Charles Bravo was only earning £200 a year, Edwin Bartlett about £300 from his business, and someone like the maid, Alice Fulcher, would make no more than £12-£15 a year.

acquittal for Chief Inspector George Clarke,[32] in the Bribery of the Detective case, and likewise for Esther Pay, accused of child-murder, when he defended her in 1882. All three cases were heard at the Old Bailey, attracting a great deal of attention and establishing Clarke's reputation as a dedicated defender of the underdog – though he later admitted that his reputation at the Bar was greatly enhanced by his successful defence of Adelaide Bartlett.

He went on to acquire considerable wealth and achieved further acclaim throughout his long career, culminating in his appointment as Solicitor General in the same year as Adelaide's trial, a post he held until 1890. In 1892, he received a knighthood.

His life was not without disappointments, however. He had hoped for a second career in politics and although he won the Southwark seat for the Conservatives in 1880, he never attained high office and his political ambitions were largely unfulfilled.

He also failed in his defence of Oscar Wilde in 1895, in one of the most sensational trials ever held at the Old Bailey – at which Mr Justice Wills again presided. It must be said however, that the odds against an acquittal for Wilde were formidable, despite Clarke's brilliant advocacy on behalf of his recalcitrant client. He could never have won the case whilst Her Imperial Majesty was still on the throne and the populace clung to the hypocritical dogma about sex and morality prevalent during her reign. Certainly, if anyone could have succeeded in the case it would have been Edward Clarke, and many must have thought that Adelaide was lucky indeed to have a man of such eminence defending her.

Once the jostling spectators had taken a good look round the courtroom and peered into the empty dock, they settled themselves in their much coveted but uncomfortable positions on the narrow wooden benches provided for them.

After a few minutes the legal gentlemen began to file into court, imposing figures in their black robes and curled wigs; with calm

---

32 Chief Inspector George Clarke was the Metropolitan Police Officer who had investigated the death of Charles Bravo in 1876, the year before his trial, accused of bribery and corruption. The other detectives were found guilty as charged.

efficiency they took their places amongst the files and papers piled high on the bench before them. Despite the quiet formality of the scene there was an air of expectancy, excitement even, as members of the public talked amongst themselves. But the low hum of conversation stopped immediately when, in response to a command from the usher, everyone rose to their feet as the judge entered, stern-faced, bewigged and resplendent in his crimson and black robes.

As the case was formally opened the atmosphere became tense. The prisoners, waiting in the cells below, were summoned. A few moments to wait. No one stirred. 'All eyes were turned to the dock,' wrote the reporter from the *Daily News*, 'from whose rear, without further delay, the first of the prisoners came to the front – the Reverend George Dyson.'

Then, at last, the lady at the centre of this dramatic tableau appeared. According to the *Daily News*:[33]

> After a brief interval came Mrs Bartlett, conducted by two female warders. The prisoners were placed wide apart, almost at the extremities of the front, the woman to the left, the man to the right, facing the judge. Both looked very ill. Mrs Bartlett's eyes were drooping and she stood motionless, with arms straight down the sides – a small figure, conspicuous by the great shock of short black hair surmounting a somewhat broad and sallow face.

In 1886, it would have been considered outrageous for Adelaide to enter the court bareheaded – she was the only female present to do so – but more shocking still was the fact that her hair had been cut unusually short, worn at a length that did not find favour with most decent women of the period. The whole effect caused a tremendous stir and many present must have felt that her decision to flaunt convention still further by forsaking her widow's weeds for a 'well-fitting black silk dress, with layers of white lace at the neck', was singularly inappropriate on such a momentous occasion and in such tragic circumstances.

---

33 *Daily News*, 13th April, 1886.

Two reporters, one from the *Daily Telegraph*[34] and one from the *Daily News*,[35] gave very different accounts of Adelaide's demeanour that day. One said that she sat 'very still, listening intently to all that was said, and appeared to scrutinise each member of the court in turn, as though her interest in the proceedings were entirely objective.' The other said she had the look of 'a person stupefied by grief or pain and only half conscious of what was going on around.'

But both agreed about the composure of George Dyson, saying he 'looked grave and sorrowful but keenly on the alert.' In fact, it was noted that as the jurors took their places on the jury bench and were sworn in, Dyson made a point of gazing intently at each man. One of them, indeed, declared himself a personal friend of the minister and was replaced by another.

Immediately, the case took an unusual turn. Mr Lockwood, for George Dyson, rose to request that the two prisoners be tried separately. Far from objecting to this last-minute change, Edward Clarke, for Adelaide, expressed his 'complete concurrence' with the suggestion. Both prisoners were then arraigned and, according to the *Daily News* reporter, when asked whether she pleaded '*Guilty*' or '*Not Guilty*' to a charge of murder, 'Mrs Bartlett's lips moved but no sound was heard'. But, he went on, 'Mr Dyson's "*Not Guilty*" was distinctly audible. After this formality, Mrs Bartlett's hitherto downcast eyes seemed to be closed, and so she remained, her head on one side and apparently heeding nothing.'

Then, to everyone's astonishment, the Attorney General declared that he had decided that 'there was no case to be submitted to the jury upon which he could properly ask them to convict George Dyson.' At this, the judge turned to the jury and announced:

> Gentlemen, the Attorney General, having thoroughly considered the matter, has decided that the proper course to be followed in this case is to offer no evidence on the part of the Crown against Mr Dyson. Therefore your duty is to say at once that he is not guilty.

---

34 *Daily Telegraph*, 13th April, 1886.
35 *Daily News,* op. cit.

Having merely commented that he thought it 'proper not to express an opinion one way or another on the matter', he then proceeded to instruct the jury to hear the case against Adelaide Bartlett 'on the principle that Mr Dyson is innocent.'

It must have been a very relieved young man who walked free from the dock that morning, leaving Adelaide to face the charge of murder alone.

But she had her trump card and it was a brilliant one. Edward Clarke possessed the ability to turn a disaster such as this into an advantage. Some thirty years later he was to recall the situation in court that day:

> The advantage to me was obvious. Having admitted that Dyson was innocent, the Attorney General could not help calling him as a witness, and so offering him to my cross-examination. That would not be hostile, but friendly and sympathetic, for the more closely I could associate his actions with those of Mrs Bartlett, the more I could strengthen the reluctance of the jury to send her to the hangman's cord while he passed unrebuked to freedom.[36]

This was a retaliatory masterstroke. By dismissing Dyson, Russell had unwittingly played into Edward Clarke's hands and the battle for Adelaide Bartlett's life had begun with an unforeseen, but most welcome, advantage.

Sir Charles gave the court a detailed account of Adelaide's marriage and the events leading to Edwin Bartlett's death. To conclude, he drew the jury's attention to what he called 'the real question in this case':

> You will probably have no difficulty in coming to the conclusion that the deceased died from the effects of chloroform. How did it get there? So far as I know there are only three ways in which it could have got there. The first of those ways is that the deceased himself should have intentionally taken it with the view of destroying his life. I submit, when you have heard the facts, that you will find nothing in the circumstances of the case to support that suggestion. He was in returning health, in improved spirits, and, as I have told you, he had gone to his bed on that night having made arrangements as to what

---

36 Sir Edward Clarke, 'Leaves from a Lawyer's Casebook'. Op.cit.

he should desire for breakfast next morning.

As to the second possible suggestion – that he took it accidentally – you will be told by those who know the qualities of chloroform that it is in the highest degree improbable that a man, if he accidentally poured out into a glass or tumbler this liquid, would not at once perceive the mistake he had made even before it was raised to his lips. He could not fail to notice that it was something which he ought not to take.'

The pain of drinking would, he thought, be so intense that the person would scream out and 'could not have failed to attract attention.'

Thirdly, he suggested that the chloroform might have been administered by another person – the inevitable resistance being minimised by first lulling the victim into a stupor by applying chloroform externally. This done, more chloroform 'could be conveyed to the stomach without it being followed by circumstances and occurrences which must have attracted attention.'

Charles Russell then warned the jurors to dismiss from their minds anything they had previously heard about the case and urged them to apply their minds to the 'candid consideration' of the evidence to be put before them. 'You ought not to find the prisoner guilty,' he exhorted them, 'unless the evidence against her, dispassionately weighed, dispassionately considered, brings home to your minds the conviction of guilt beyond any reasonable doubt.'

Once these laboured formalities had been completed the court prepared to hear the evidence of Mr Bartlett, senior. He took his place in the witness box, a be-whiskered, middle-aged man with rather a dour expression on his face, not unlike Edward Clarke in countenance.

Questioned by Harry Poland, he described how his son had first met the prisoner, while she was staying with his brother Charles in Kingston. At the time, he said, she called herself not Adelaide, but Blanche. Throughout the time he had lived with the young couple in their flat above the shop in Station Road, Herne Hill, they had, he said, 'lived together as man and wife, occupying the same room and the same bed.'

He then told the court of Adelaide's unfortunate confinement, its tragic outcome, and the couple's subsequent move to the smaller flat in Lordship Lane, East Dulwich.

'They were there about twelve months,' he said, 'and I believe they lived in the same way there. I visited them once or twice.' After they had removed to The Cottage at Merton, he 'visited them frequently. They were living together then in the ordinary way as man and wife', and he believed that they had continued to do so after their move to Claverton Street: they had been 'on affectionate terms, as far as I know; I know nothing to the contrary.'

At this point, however, he began to speak of disharmony in the family, complaining bitterly, as he had done at the inquest, about Adelaide's visiting restrictions during Edwin's illness, and allowing her letters to be read out to the court. He remembered that, during his last visit, on 28th December, Edwin had talked of having worms and had told him: 'A good job she [Adelaide] has doctored the dogs to clear away the worms, because she knew I had worms.'

The old man appeared sceptical about the will made on 3rd September – in fact, he admitted that he had already taken legal advice on the matter and proceedings were underway to contest its authenticity.[37] He refused to confirm or deny that the signature on it was that of his son, and in order to clarify the situation, Mr Poland called the two assistants who had witnessed Edwin Bartlett's signature. Both affirmed that this was the document they had signed, although they had not known it was a will.

Old Mr Bartlett was asked again to verify the signature but he was clearly determined not to admit that the will was that of his dead son. 'I have seen him often write in several different hands,' he hedged. 'You could never depend on his writing to be the same a second time.'

---

37 In this he was unsuccessful. The will was proved on 12 June 1886. The value of Edwin's estate was £3,858. 16s. 6d. and Adelaide was the sole beneficiary. In today's money this sum would equate to more than a quarter of a million pounds.

When the court reassembled after a short adjournment, Mr Bartlett came face to face with Edward Clarke who immediately asked him if he had approved of his son's marriage to Adelaide Bartlett. The old man replied that he 'was not asked whether I thought she was suitable or not', adding, rather naively, that he had not been asked to the wedding as 'they knew I was busy'. He even told the court that during the time the three of them were at the flat in Station Road they had lived on 'most friendly terms together.'

Within minutes, however, this bubble of domestic bliss was well and truly burst when, under fire from Edward Clarke, the old man admitted that he had at one time made detrimental remarks about his daughter-in-law – with the result that his son had made him sign an apology, albeit with reluctance.

'Did you know of your son's having any exceptional ideas on this subject of married life?' enquired Clarke.

'No,' replied the old man. 'He used to chaff and joke about such things – that was all. I never knew him to have any solid ideas about anything different to other people.'

'What used he to say?' urged Clarke.

'He said one ought to have two wives, one to take out and one to do the work.'

Having said this, however, he insisted that he had only once heard his son make that particular remark, although he often joked about marriage for he was a 'very merry man'.

He was equally emphatic when asked if Edwin had been a believer in mesmerism. As far as he knew he was not, and he had never heard his son talk of mesmerism or of being mesmerised, or anything of that sort. Edwin had talked mainly about the grocery trade for 'he was wrapped up in his business.'

Edward Clarke pressed Mr Bartlett to reveal his opinion of his son's state of mind during his illness. The old man thought that Edwin had seemed depressed and 'very averse to talking', although the last time he saw him he had 'talked more than he did before and he appeared stronger and better.' Before that, he had sometimes 'burst out crying' – much to his father's surprise, as he was usually so optimistic and full of life.

By this time it had become clear that Mr Bartlett disliked his daughter-in-law and bitterly resented her treatment of him during Edwin's last illness. Only once, he said, had she shown any affection towards him, and that was on the Saturday when the post-mortem had been completed. As they were going downstairs that evening Adelaide had, surprisingly, placed her arm around his neck, saying:

> My dear father, do not fret, it shall make no odds to you. I will see you never want. It shall be just the same as if Edwin was alive.

Next, Edward Clarke broached the delicate subject of Adelaide's earlier escapade with young Frederick Bartlett and the latter's departure for America. It must have come as a surprise, therefore, when Mr Bartlett announced that Frederick had recently returned:

> I heard he turned up on the 5th [January]. I sent him something to come home and his brother was going to give him a manager's place in one of the establishments.

There was even more surprise when he admitted that he still had not seen his youngest son, even though he had been back in London for four months. This was certainly odd, for the Bartletts were a close-knit family and the old man had kept in touch with Frederick by 'scores of letters' since he went to America. Old Mr Bartlett said that he had always hoped his son would come home eventually, and that once before, in 1879, he had sent him sixty pounds towards his passage.

It seems most likely that Frederick had returned to England with the promise of a job from Edwin and on arrival had gone straight to Claverton Street to see him. Maybe, the letter Adelaide received on the morning Edwin died had indicated that Edwin, generous and forgiving by nature, had arranged the reunion with his young brother. This would certainly explain Adelaide's exclamation, 'Oh, how cruel!'

But why was Frederick avoiding his father? He had arrived after his brother's death and so could not have been implicated in it.

Edward Clarke declined to probe the reason behind this strange behaviour, which leads one to believe that any revelation might well have damaged rather than strengthened Adelaide's case. Had there been the slightest advantage to be gained by exposing the truth, one can be sure that Clarke would have been the first to seize upon it.

The next witness was Edwin's business partner and friend, Edward Baxter. He, too, had noticed that Edwin had seemed 'very depressed and low' during his illness and at times was 'scarcely able to speak'. He insisted, however, that the had never heard Edwin mention anything about mesmerism or express any unusual ideas about marriage.

Mr Baxter was succeeded by Frederick Doggett, Adelaide's landlord, who told the court that although they had been his tenants, he was not familiar with either the prisoner or the deceased. He had, though, seen the Reverend Mr Dyson call at the house on several occasions.

In response to questions from Harry Poland, he described the events of 1st January and his mounting suspicions – the state of the body, the smell of the chloric ether in room, the wine glass with its unidentified contents, and the banked-up fire in the grate. He had not seen a bottle on the mantelpiece, or anywhere else in the room, but he thought that it would have been easy for someone lying in the camp bed to reach up and take a glass or bottle from the mantelpiece.

Mrs Caroline Doggett followed her husband into the witness box and wasted no time in telling the court about George Dyson's frequent visits to Claverton Street.

'He came twice and three times a week, and sometimes more. He came at all times. He has been as early as half past nine in the morning.'

She made great play of the clothes kept at Claverton Street for Dyson's use, which she had seen him wearing on two occasions, and of the fact that during Edwin's illness the preacher 'used to go up to his room on some occasions, but not always. When he called he would see Mrs Bartlett downstairs.'

What Mrs Doggett did not say was left to the imagination of the listeners, and they loved every minute of her evidence – surely delivered with telling emphasis through delicately pursed lips. Questioned by Edward Clarke about the fire that was burning in the front room on the night Edwin died, she confirmed her husband's statement that it was still banked up high at four o'clock that morning. She had noticed it as soon as she entered the room. 'The bed was so near the fire it would have been too hot for Mr Bartlett,' she declared, 'and the gas was alight.' Despite Clarke's attempts to make her admit that the state of the fire could have been achieved either by applying fresh coals or by stirring it up with a poker, she would not budge from her opinion – housewifely pride forced her to concede that the fire would have been well banked up the night before. 'It had been attended to,' she insisted. 'it hadn't burnt hollow at all... the coals were quite lighted.'

The body, however, was stone cold.

CHAPTER 15

Drawing-room Dramas

The second day of the trial brought a renewed rush for seats in the public gallery as crowds of Londoners – again mainly women – flocked to the Old Bailey. As soon as the judge and learned counsel were seated, Harry Poland, for the Crown, rose to examine the Doggetts' maid, Alice Fulcher. Within minutes, she too had told the court all about George Dyson's tutorial visits to Mrs Bartlett – and she readily confirmed Mrs Doggett's observation that a comfortable lounge coat and slippers were kept in the flat for the minister's use.

That was not all, she told the hushed court: she had seen Mr Dyson and Mrs Bartlett alone in the front room with the 'window curtains pulled together and then pinned', and she described the compromising intimacy in which she had found them. 'I do not remember when that was, nor could I say how long it was before Mr Bartlett's death. I never found the door locked.'

Under cross-examination, she admitted that the curtains would have hung close and covered the window whether they had been pinned or not.

Having recounted the events of New Year's Eve and the early hours of the next day – including the fact that Adelaide appeared to have changed her dress before summoning help – Alice recalled that she had gone back into the Bartlett's flat about half-past five or six o'clock that morning but did not remove the tray of glasses until later, when she took them downstairs. 'I noticed that one wine glass was about half-full of something which I thought was brandy, judging from the smell and the colour. I washed it away,' She had washed all the glasses except one, which she described as a 'tumbler containing some liquid with a bottle turned downwards in it. The Coroner's officer took charge of that,'[38] she said.

In his cross-examination, Edward Clarke was able to emphasise the concern Adelaide had shown towards her husband during his illness. He also sought to introduce an element of doubt into Alice's assertion that Adelaide had changed her dress, although the maid remained sure that the colour was lighter. Most important of all, he ascertained that Mr Doggett had seen the tray of glasses downstairs before they were washed. Why, one wonders, did he not remove the incriminating wine glass for the Coroner's attention?

After Alice Fulcher had left the witness box Mrs Ann Boulter was called to describe the laying out of Edwin Bartlett's body, and then Dr William Clapton, medical officer to the British Equitable Insurance Company, testified to Edwin's excellent state of health five years earlier. There was a pause in the proceedings. Spectators in the public gallery shifted in their seats and talked amongst themselves, eagerly awaiting a glimpse of the Reverend George Dyson who, it was whispered, was due to give evidence next. This was what everyone was waiting for: there was no doubt that his involvement in the case had engendered much of its notoriety and everyone present was anxious to see him and hear his confession.

As he took his place in the witness-box he came under eager scrutiny from the onlookers; they saw a dark-haired young man, soberly dressed and sporting an unusually long moustache. The expression on his face was very serious, mournful even, but he appeared to be perfectly composed and gave his evidence in a clear and confident voice.

Examined by Harry Poland, the preacher recalled his first acquaintance with the Bartletts and went on to describe their extraordinary friendship. By way of illustration, the letters he had exchanged with Edwin during the Dover holiday were read to the court. He then stated that after he had moved to his new chapel in Putney he had continued to visit the Bartletts in Pimlico at Edwin's

---

38 This turned out to be chlorodyne prescribed by Dr Leach.

particular request.

Asked to elaborate on these tutorial sessions, he agreed that it was a little unusual for a husband to allow his wife to spend so much time in the company of another man, unchaperoned. He had discussed this with Adelaide:

> I remarked, I remember, how her husband seemed to throw us together and asked how it was. I thought it was remarkable. She told me that his life was not likely to be a long one, and that he knew it, and she repeated what he had told me himself, that his friends were not kind to her – that they did not understand her, being a foreigner; that he had confidence in me and affection for me and that he wished me to be a guardian to her. He knew I should be a friend to her when he was gone.

Dyson went on to repeat what Adelaide had told him during their long hours alone together – about Edwin's mysterious internal complaint and the ominous prognosis of Dr Nichols. The alleged involvement of Annie Walker, in providing chloroform to soothe the fractious patient, came pouring out. The desire for self-preservation had deprived Dyson of any concern for Adelaide's fate. 'I frequently spoke to her about Dr Nichols,' he admitted, 'as I was interested in him.'

George Dyson remained in the witness-box for the rest of the day. It was as if, having seen the folly of his indiscretion and escaped the threat of the gallows, he was cleansing his soul by a public confession: every detail of his gullibility, deceit and criminal involvement must be exposed for examination. Under the gentle prompting of Harry Poland, he described how he had been duped into obtaining the chloroform; how, after Edwin's unexpected death, the realisation had dawned of his implication in the crime he feared Adelaide had committed; and how he had challenged her and reached the decision to confess what he knew. After his early panic he seems to have reached a state of comparative calm, although his confusion of mind during the inquest can be judged from his vague memories of the hearings on 4th and 11th February:

> I was legally represented, and I presume Mrs Bartlett was also represented. The inquest was again adjourned to 11th February. I was called as a witness before the Coroner then, and I presume I was cautioned.

Edward Clarke sat listening carefully throughout the examination. Only occasionally did he interrupt – once to establish how much Edwin had heard of the conversations between Adelaide and Dyson about the advisability of calling in a nurse to avoid gossip. When at last he rose to begin his cross-examination, it was immediately clear that his aim was to probe the more intimate aspects of the friendship between the preacher and the Bartletts, and to destroy the impression of a clandestine affair between Dyson and Adelaide.

'Was there any secret between you, or any secret under-standing between you, apart from her husband?' he asked.

Dyson admitted that he had kissed Adelaide in front of her husband; but on the other hand, he insisted, their intimacy did not exclude Edwin. Although he went on to confess, under pressure, that he had also kissed Adelaide when they were alone, he said that Edwin knew about it and did not object as he trusted him completely with regard to his wife.

'He had implicit confidence in me,' he insisted, 'to the very last hour of his life.'

Clarke then raised the matter, already put to old Mr Bartlett, of Edwin's reputedly strange views about marriage. Dyson was sure that they had discussed the Bible's teaching on the subject quite early in their acquaintance. Edwin had said that a man should have two wives – one for companionship and one for service – and that both should be wives in the 'full and complete sense'. Was this discussed in Adelaide's presence? Clarke wanted to know.

'I think not,' replied the preacher.

Clarke was on to this in a flash.

'One moment. Do you mean to say that there was nothing between you and Mr Bartlett which was kept secret from his wife?'

For the first time Dyson became evasive:

'I am sorry, I cannot undertake to say yea or nay to that.'

Clarke, however, demanded a more positive reply.

'But to the best of your belief, was there any matter of secrecy or confidence between you and Mr Bartlett from which his wife was excluded?'

'Your question does not touch the case,' muttered the witness.

'Will you answer the question, and not judge it?'

Dyson said he knew of no secret. He did, however, admit that Edwin had 'made statements which left no doubt in my mind but that he contemplated Mrs Bartlett and myself being ultimately married. I can remember this; he had been finding some fault with Mrs Bartlett, not angrily, but correcting something, and I said to him, "If ever she comes under my care, I shall have to teach her differently." He smiled and said something to the effect that he had no doubt I should take good care of her.'

Edward Clarke then asked Dyson about Edwin's visit to his lodgings in Putney the previous September, during which he had told him about the new will he had just made. Dyson, however, seemed reluctant to divulge the rest of their conversation.

'This is a very delicate matter for me,' he pleaded.

'No, no,' Mr Justice Wills interrupted, adding sarcastically, 'we have long overstepped the bounds of delicacy.'

This remark left the preacher little choice but to confess that it was during this visit that he had told Edwin about his growing intimacy with Adelaide, to which the Edwin had reacted warmly, with words of encouragement.

Edward Clarke appeared slightly incredulous.

'Just let me remind you,' he said, 'You were telling the husband that you had become attached to his wife, and you say that the husband expected you to continue the intimacy?'

'Precisely,' responded Dyson.

'There is one question I ought to ask you,' continued Clarke. 'I need scarcely ask you, as a gentleman, you had at that time said nothing to Mrs Bartlett about your feelings independent of Mr Bartlett?'

One can imagine Dyson's chagrin as he mumbled, 'I regret to say that I had.'

In the Interests of Science: Adelaide Bartlett and The Pimlico Poisoning

Throughout his lengthy cross-examination Edward Clarke expertly teased out of the preacher a succession of incongruous or inconsistent statements which combined to reduce his credibility in the eyes of the jury. He was obliged to admit that while he had been anxious to recover the poem *'My Birdie'* from Adelaide, 'because it was sentimental', he had not asked her to return his letters. (He had already told Harry Poland, unbelievably, that Edwin had read the poem when he had presented it to Adelaide some weeks before.) He claimed that although Adelaide had told him that the nurse, Annie Walker, had attended Edwin during his illness, she had never mentioned that she had also attended her in her confinement. And although he and Adelaide had often discussed Dr Nichols, they had never done so in Edwin's presence because he was 'sensitive' about his alleged affliction; nor had Dyson, despite his 'true and honest friendship' with Edwin, mentioned this supposed illness and Dr Nichols's prognosis to Dr Leach when the latter was first called – it would have been an impertinence on his part, he said.

Clarke asked him to describe Edwin's emotional state during his last illness. Dyson said that he seemed 'very weary, very much depressed, and suffering from sleeplessness.' He had even seen him crying on one occasion, shortly before Christmas.

Strangely, Dyson seemed unable to remember anything that Edwin had actually said at this time, although on Boxing Day he had told the preacher that he was 'afraid his wife was breaking down in nursing him.' On the Sunday before he died he had asked Dyson if 'anyone could be lower than he was without passing away altogether' – he had thought that the medicine prescribed for getting rid of the worms was the reason for his malaise. Yet Dyson appeared certain that Edwin had been more cheerful that day – 'He did not seem cast down in spirits. He seemed to be bearing up well.'

As for mesmerism, he insisted that, although he and Edwin might have mentioned it casually in conversation, he did not regard him as a 'believer' in mesmerism and had never heard him talk seriously about such things.

Although he had often seen Adelaide studying Squire's *Companion to the British Pharmacopoeia*, it had never occurred to him that she would use the chloroform 'for any dangerous or improper use.' He had, in all innocence, assumed that it was perfectly safe to sprinkle chloroform onto a handkerchief to procure sleep and soothe pain. It was not until the mention of chloroform at the post-mortem that he had felt the slightest anxiety about his purchase of the drug. He had thrown the bottles away in a panic because 'the sight of them was hateful' to him.

'The thought was in my mind at the time,' he said, 'possibly it was the chloroform I had bought had been the cause of Mr Bartlett's death. It would be difficult to say when the thought first came. I think on the Saturday night it grew on me. I thought I should be a ruined man if the matter came out.'

When Edward Clarke at last sat down at the end of the day, the jury was left with much to consider. For all his feeble ways, George Dyson had made no attempt to conceal his misguided attachment to Adelaide Bartlett and had readily admitted buying the chloroform that might have been used to kill her husband. He had confessed, too, that in sheer panic he had thrown away the empty bottles, and that he had deliberately misled the three chemists from whom he had bought the chloroform, excusing this lapse into deceit by saying that he 'did not wish to enter into a long explanation' about his real reason for wanting such a large quantity of a potentially lethal drug.

It was clear that George Dyson was crucially involved in the death of his friend, Edwin Bartlett. His behaviour had been foolish and indiscreet and, in view of his ministerial calling, both scandalous and indefensible.

He was, in his own words, a ruined man, yet one who seemed, at least on the strength of his confession that day, innocent of murderous intent.

CHAPTER 16

Leach in the Limelight

The third day of the trial opened with the examination of the three chemists – Messrs Humble, Penrose and Mellin – by Mr Moloney, for the Crown. One by one they testified that they knew Mr Dyson through his work in the ministry, and all agreed that it was on the strength of this that they had waived any doubts about selling what they considered to be a 'rather large quantity of the drug without a prescription.'

Mrs Alice Matthews then mounted the steps of the witness box and, in answer to questions put to her by Mr Wright, testified that during the five years or so that she had known Mrs Bartlett, the latter had lived with her husband 'on very affectionate terms, and apparently as man and wife.'

At the end of her examination the foreman of the jury requested permission to make a point about Edwin Bartlett's will, which seemed to bear no relevance to Alice Matthews's evidence. He reminded the court that Mr Bartlett, senior, had said earlier that his son had promised to alter his will in his favour, intending to make the alteration on 1st January, the day he died. The juror wanted to know if there was any proof of this intention, beyond the old man's sworn statement.

'I do not think,' interjected Edward Clarke, 'he said he intended to alter his will, but to make him an allowance.'

'To alter his will, I think it was,' persisted the juror, with commendable conviction.

Edward Clarke, however, was equally adamant that Edwin had

intended to start making his father an allowance from 1st January, by way of compensation for the home for life which he had originally promised him.

Mr Justice Wills, having consulted his notes, intervened to say that although Edwin Bartlett had not made his father an allowance as such, over the years he had always been very generous and had been, in the old man's words, 'the tenderest of sons.' But, he added, in support of Edward Clarke, there was nothing said about altering his will.

The juror, on the other hand, was still prepared to dispute the fact:

> We are still under the impression that he stated so, and that it was an allowance. Was there any proof that he promised that besides his own statement?

If a satisfactory answer was given to this important question, it was not recorded.

After this interruption, George Matthews was called to answer questions put to him by Mr Moloney. He said that Edwin Bartlett's general health had been very good and, as far as he could judge, the Bartletts had lived as man and wife; he had not noticed 'anything peculiar about his ideas'. He described the various arguments he had witnessed between George Dyson and Adelaide and then said:

> I saw her with my wife at my house on 20th January. She told us that Dr Leach had said that it would be impossible for her to have given her husband chloroform by inhalation without it showing in the brain, and she could not have given it to him as a drink, because he would have burnt his throat all down, and he would have aroused the house with his cries.

In his cross-examination, Edward Clarke raised the matter of Dr Nichols's book, *Esoteric Anthropology*, which Adelaide had lent Matthews. Clarke asked him what he had thought of it.

'It was a queer sort of book,' he ventured, 'scarcely in my line of business. I did not read it.' Re-examined by Harry Poland he expanded further: 'Mrs Bartlett was a believer in the hydropathic system; and I do not know, but I rather think that the book was about that, and she gave it to me so that I should read something on the subject. I am not certain, because I never read the book but I know so well that it was a book on hydropathy.'

Harry Poland then proceeded to read out the full title and subtitle, to which Matthews responded flippantly:

'If I had read as far as that I should not have read any further!'

'I think you said that you had never seen Mr Bartlett with that book?' asked Poland.

'No, never,' came the firm reply.

The next witness was Annie Walker, who told Harry Poland how she had attended Adelaide during her difficult confinement and how the baby had been born dead. She had seen Dr Nichols, although he had never seen her, and she had certainly not consulted him about Edwin Bartlett. She knew he had written *Esoteric Anthropology*, and she had seen the book lying about at the Bartletts', but had never seen anyone reading it.

Her next statement raised the question of the reliability of Dyson's evidence. Either Adelaide had lied to him or he had fabricated the story of what she had told him.

> I have never had any conversation with Mrs Bartlett about chloroform, nor have I ever got any chloroform for her on any occasion. She has never asked me to purchase any chloroform or any medicine for her. I have never been out of England, and I have never spoken of going to America. I never knew anything of Mr Dyson. I never attended Mr Bartlett at all.

With that, Harry Poland sat down, leaving Edward Clarke to salvage what he could – which he did very neatly, passing quickly from the subject of chloroform to Mrs Nichols and then the book, *Esoteric Anthropology*. Annie Walker said that she had merely looked at it but had not studied it in any depth.

'There is nothing immoral or indecent in this book, is there?' asked Clarke.

'Not anything,' replied the nurse.

Clarke then went on to question her about her relationship with Adelaide, establishing that she had become very fond of her patient and had noticed how attentive and affectionate she was towards her husband.

Re-examined by Mr Poland, Nurse Walker confirmed that, as far as she knew, the Bartletts had shared a bed and, in her presence at least, behaved in a perfectly normal way. Clarke objected to the way the prosecution kept harping on this subject, and Mr Justice Wills instructed the jury to remember that 'among ordinary people you know what passes in the ordinary relations of life, but you know nothing of what passes in the bedroom.' The fact that Mr and Mrs Bartlett had slept in the same bed proved nothing, for it was impossible to guess at the intimate relations between a man and his wife.

'I had a very cursory glance at that book,' he added, pointing to the copy of *Esoteric Anthropology* exhibited in court, 'but there are parts of it which do tell married people how to live together without having children, are there not?'

Edward Clarke rose again in protest:

'Your lordship will find that the book contains nothing objectionable.'

'I will take the opportunity, Mr Clarke, of looking at the book this evening myself. I will just point out to you at once the passage which caught my eye. It was opened there,' he added with a hint of sarcasm, 'that is how I came to see it.'

The judge then passed the book to Edward Clarke, who read the extract to the court:

> Abstinence. – There is one way that is natural, simple and effectual. It is to refrain from the sexual act. It is easily done by most women, and by many men. In every civilised community thousands live in celibacy, many from necessity, many from choice. In England and the other American States there is a large surplus female population. In Catholic countries the whole of the priesthood and a great number of religious of both sexes take vows of perpetual chastity. This practice has existed for at least sixteen centuries. I have shown that in the

> ordinary cases conception can only take place when connection is had a day or two before, or ten days, or, for safety's sake, say, sixteen days after, menstruation. There is then a fortnight each month when the female is not liable to impregnation.

Clarke paused.

'I am much obliged to you,' remarked the judge, with mock gravity.

'"And it is also to be observed,"' continued Clarke, '"that the natural period for sexual union is when it is demanded for the purposes of procreation; and that the use of marriage or the sexual act for mere pleasure, and using any means to avoid impregnation, are unnatural. It is questionable, therefore, whether we can morally justify the use of any means to prevent conception. If it can ever be justified, it is when a woman is unwillingly compelled to submit to the embrace of her husband while her health or other conditions forbid her to have children."'

There was a hush as Edward Clarke resumed his seat.

'I am much obliged to you for correcting my impression; it was formed on hastily opening the book,' murmured Mr Justice Wills, magnanimously.

Thomas Low Nichols himself, author of the controversial book in question, now made his appearance, and was examined by Mr Moloney.

'I was a graduate at New York in 1850,' he said, 'but I have no degree entitling me to practise here. I have been for about twenty-five years in England. I first saw Mrs Bartlett at the Westminster Police Court. I cannot remember having any communication with her or her husband by letter or otherwise. Nor do I know any nurse or midwife of the name of Annie Walker.'

'Did you ever make any statement to anybody that anybody of the name of Bartlett would die within twelve months?'

'Certainly not,' retorted Dr Nichols, 'I could not make any such statement unless I had examined the patient.'

Esoteric Anthropology, he affirmed, had first been published in 1853 and the English edition had come out in 1873, the year that he and his wife left their hydropathic practice in Malvern and moved to London. Though progressive and shocking to many people, it had been welcomed by liberal thinkers all over the world.

Edward Clarke raised the subject of the various other titles penned by the pioneering doctor and his wife, and the court was told that in 1853 they were both lecturing at the American Hydropathic Institute in New York, their subjects including anatomy, physiology and hydrotherapeutics.

One of his wife's books, entitled *Experience in Water Cure,* had, Nichols declared, enjoyed a wide circulation, successfully serving the hydropathic cause and the pursuit of enlightenment. Although he himself was accustomed to a certain amount of scepticism over his work, he insisted that he had honestly tried to make his books 'thoroughly good and useful – true in science, pure in morals, and containing the principles of the highest welfare of man and of humanity.' Although people who had read them occasionally came to see him, his aim was 'not to get consultations, but to prevent their necessity; not to attract patients, but to keep them away and to enable them to get health without my further cure.'

His wife's qualifications had allowed her to work in England and she enjoyed a thriving practice in Earls Court, dealing mainly with women and their specific problems. Unfortunately, she had died two years previously, leaving no record of her patients.

Nichols was adamant that he knew nothing whatsoever about either Adelaide or Edwin Bartlett; it was possible, however, that the prisoner had consulted his wife, and through her, acquired the services of Nurse Annie Walker.

The next witness was Thomas Roberts, Edwin Bartlett's dentist, who, like Dr Leach, lived in Charlwood Street, Pimlico. He outlined the treatment he had given Edwin Bartlett between 16th and 31st December, confirming that on the last occasion his patient's condition was much better. Edward Clarke questioned him about Edwin's reaction to nitrous oxide gas, and there was some discussion about necrosis of the jaw-bone, in which the Attorney General joined. Mr Roberts remarked on the foulness of his patient's breath which, however, had improved by 31st December.

After Mr Roberts had left the witness box, Dr Thomas Green's deposition was read to the court as the doctor was too ill to read it himself. In his statement he gave a detailed account of the post-mortem findings, stating that only the lower part of the gullet was damaged and that the 'contents of the stomach smelt very much like chloroform.' The brain had been carefully examined throughout, cut up and sliced in every possible direction, and there was nothing abnormal about it. The larynx, trachea and kidneys were found to be perfectly normal, but the blood was unusually fluid, in view of the time that had elapsed between death and the post-mortem examination. This, he believed, was a recognised effect of chloroform poisoning, but he himself had no knowledge of it. 'He was a strong, well-nourished, healthy-looking man, powerful, well developed – I should say, as far as I could observe, a man capable of considerable physical exertion.'

Much of Dr Green's deposition proved highly technical, but with regard to the chloroform he made himself very clear:

> Poisoning by liquid chloroform is, I believe, of very rare occurrence. I have never, in the course of my practice, had a case of poisoning by liquid chloroform ... I have not personal knowledge whatever of poisoning by liquid chloroform, nor of the symptoms it produces... I first got a notion of chloroform as soon as we opened the stomach. Before smelling the stomach, no person had suggested to me there was chloroform... What I smelt was almost as strong as a freshly opened bottle.

Had it not been for the smell, he would not have associated the ulcer found in the stomach, and the surrounding inflammation, with chloroform, but they were obviously due to 'recent action by an irritant poison' and chloroform was known to act as a local irritant.

This evidence weighed heavily against Adelaide and the jury was left in no doubt as to the importance of Dr Green's observations. Having already digested a great deal of medical detail that morning, the jurors then prepared themselves for the Attorney General's examination of a key witness – Dr Alfred Leach.

With obvious trepidation the doctor entered the witness box to face Sir Charles Russell. He was a slightly built man, clean shaven except for a thin, waxed moustache, and although he was still young, he was balding prematurely and had the finely chiselled features of a much older man. His face was pale and pinched as he began his evidence in a hesitant, nervous manner.

He had first been summoned to attend Edwin Bartlett on 10th December, having 'never heard of either him or the accused.' He had found his patient 'sitting up on the sofa in the drawing-room. I found that he was suffering from diarrhoea, some pain in the left side, foetid breath, and he was suffering from the signs of indigestion and sub-acute gastritis – one might call it mercurialism.'

Mr Justice Wills interrupted to ask, 'Does that mean that he had taken too large a dose of a blue pill or something containing mercury?'[39]

Dr Leach agreed that the effects could have been from taking one large dose, or equally, it could mean that he had taken small amounts regularly. He then detailed some of his visits to Claverton Street between 10th December and 31st December. After a lengthy description of the medication he had prescribed, he said:

> The last time I saw Mr Bartlett alive was about six o'clock on 31st December, in front of Mr Robert's door, 49 Charlwood Street. He had just had a tooth out, but previous to that I think I may say that he seemed better than I had ever seen him before. He actually said he felt he was better, a thing he was very loath to do.

The doctor obviously thought that his patient had been emotionally disturbed rather than physically ill:

> On the 30th I said I would not continue to visit him, for he had made up his mind to have continual medical attendance, and I was not inclined to continue.

---

39 Mercury, usually, in the form of blue pills, was commonly prescribed in the treatment for syphilis. Edwin, as we know, had actually admitted to swallowing a blue pill found in a drawer in his desk.

So sceptical was he of Edwin's condition that even when Alice Fulcher ran to fetch him at four o'clock on the morning of 1st January, saying that he was dead, he asked her whether 'it was merely one of his notions or whether he was really ill'; and when the maid repeated that Mr Bartlett was dead, he 'scarcely accepted that as true.' Alarmed by Alice's urgency, however, he took a hansom cab to Claverton Street, arriving at about four-thirty.

> I found the deceased lying in his usual place – a camp bedstead near the window. He had on a nightdress, and I think an undervest, and he was lying on his back with his arms across the abdomen. The legs were up a little; the fingers naturally closed, and the surface very pallid and very cold; the eyelids nearly closed, and the pupils, for him, very much dilated: natural for death. The mouth was open, and the tongue was very white. I calculated that he had been dead for two or three hours. A little later, after thinking it over for a day or two, I thought it possible that he might have been dead longer, but I think now, on giving the matter careful consideration, three hours is as nearly accurate as I can give. There was no appearance of a convulsive fit or paroxysm and no froth on the lips.

Dr Leach then described how he had searched the room and found nothing unusual, just that 'natural close odour of a sleeping room, the odour of supper and of condiments and of brandy and of gas.' There was a small bottle of chlorodyne on the mantelpiece, and on the table a brandy bottle and a glass bottle containing carbonate of soda.

'I smelt all the glasses in the room,' recalled Leach. 'I looked around the room with care. The bedroom opened from the drawing-room by folding doors, but I do not think I entered it. I asked Mrs Bartlett to give me an explanation – any assistance, any elucidation of the mystery, but she said she was unable.

'We then discussed several things and I spoke to her in a low voice so that Mr Doggett might take the hint to leave the room. When he was gone I thought perhaps some matters of delicacy which she did not like to mention before him might come out, but she was unable to give me any explanation.'

Asked by Russell if, at any time, he knew that Mrs Bartlett had a quantity of chloroform in her possession, he declared:

'I knew nothing of that till twenty-six days afterwards. It then came upon me as a surprise.'

Mr Justice Wills referred back to the white appearance of the deceased's tongue and Dr Leach admitted that this had puzzled him at the time. Then, to a startled court, he described how he had since experimented on himself using chloroform:

> I took 3½ drachms into my mouth, and, to the best of my belief, swallowed 20 or 30 drops of it; I then ejected the remainder, and was surprised when I looked in the looking glass to find my tongue was very white. The interpretation of what I had then seen in the dead body came to me. I may add that this condition of my own tongue passed off in a few hours.

Young Leach was certainly conscientious, swallowing quantities of liquid chloroform in the interests of science. Unfortunately, even as he grew more experienced in medicine he remained over-zealous, and his recklessness was eventually to culminate in disaster.

Having described his potentially lethal experiments, the doctor went on to the meeting he had had with Adelaide on 26th January, when she had given him a harrowing account of her marriage. This marked the end of the prosecution's examination of the doctor and Edward Clarke rose to question him about Mrs Bartlett's nursing skills. Dr Leach confirmed that he had seen a great deal of the Bartletts during his visits to Claverton Street and, as far as he could see, Mrs Bartlett tended her husband with 'anxious affection.' Asked if he could have wished for a more devoted nurse for his patient, he said:

> No; what I should have wished for was one with a little better memory, that is all.

As the prisoner's memory was so poor, he explained, she had kept a written record of all the treatments she had given her husband 'pinned on the mantelpiece.' She had tended her husband night and day, frequently forgoing her own rest for his sake.

'She never went to bed. I asked her on several occasions to go to bed,' continued Leach, 'but each time she had some excuse. She said she slept comfortably on the chair.'

Eventually, he had thought it best to deal with her a little more firmly and said to her:

'Now, Mrs Bartlett, there is no excuse for you not going to bed.' To this she had replied:

'What is the use of my going to bed, doctor? He will walk about the room like a ghost. He will not sleep unless I sit and hold his toe.' The drollness of the expression had fixed itself upon his mind.

It was becoming clear that Dr Leach was convinced that Edwin Bartlett had been a victim of male hysteria. He believed that his patient had been subject to syphiliphobia and had been treating himself in secret, and he had shown other neurotic symptoms – he had refused, for instance, to leave the house.

'He said it would kill him. He really was so obstinate about going out of doors that he almost at one time made me believe that I had overlooked something serious in him. He was so reasonable on some points that I could scarcely have put it down to sheer folly.' He had, said Leach, 'passively resisted' all attempts to get him outside, saying that he preferred to just 'lie still and feel happy.'

Edward Clarke pressed for further information on the dead man's depressed mental state. He had been improving, said Leach, until the alleged appearance of the lumbricoid worm on 23rd December 'threw everything back again.' The thought of it seemed to increase his hysteria and he appeared 'shocked and upset'. It seemed to confirm his secret fear that there was, indeed, something seriously wrong with him. In the days following the discovery of the worm Edwin's depression had increased dramatically and his mental condition had deteriorated still further. He began to talk about drawing the 'vital force' from his wife as she slept, but both Dr Leach and Mrs Bartlett were of the opinion that this was yet another manifestation of his tortured imagination.

This part of Dr Leach's evidence concluded the proceedings on the third day of the trial. The jury was left with an image of the deceased as a distracted, highly nervous man, certainly suffering from dental ill-health, but little else. Yet by all accounts he was subject to horrendous delusions, feeling worms crawling about inside him and having strange magnetic experiences in the middle of the night. But were these distressing symptoms in their way self-induced, despite the fact that those persons who knew Edwin best had testified that he was a conservative, somewhat prosaic man and certainly not normally given to flights of fancy?

Or had the wretched man been *encouraged* to pursue these fantasies and, tormented by lack of sleep and nervous debility, allowed himself to succumb to a temporary lapse into agoraphobia, obsession with death and terrifying delusions of disintegration and decay?

If this was so, who could have manipulated him so cruelly, and for what purpose?

There seemed to be none – except, of course, to provide a convincing and well-documented prelude to a state of derangement and despair and a possible *suicide*.

CHAPTER 17

Doctors Take the Stand

The fourth day saw Leach recalled for further cross-examination by Edward Clarke, this time on the extraordinary saga of the ineffective purgatives administered on the night of 26th December. Normally, said Leach, if santonine was retained in the body for any length of time, it gave rise to 'green vision, buzzing in the ears and all sorts of troubles.'

The doctor had been very much surprised when his purgatives had no effect whatever, and his patient had suffered no green vision or buzzing ears – in fact, Edwin had said that after the treatment his stomach felt 'warm and pleasant.'

Aware by now of the doctor's intrepid enthusiasm, the court was not wholly surprised to hear that he, too, had swallowed some of the worm powder to determine its effects. But unlike his patient, he had found the result so horrendous that he had vowed to 'avoid letting any patient experience what I experienced on that occasion.' Young Leach's dedication to his patients surely amounts to heroism, so rash was he with his own safety and well-being.

Returning to the subject of Edwin's emotional state during his illness, Clarke's purpose was clearly to underline the impression of a man with abnormal physical reactions and an unbalanced frame of mind. Under his questioning, Leach said that Adelaide had told him her husband often succumbed to crying fits; on one occasion she remarked:

> Edwin sits in his armchair and cries an hour at a time; and when I ask him about it, he says it is because he is so happy.

However, the long ordeal was beginning to tell on the young doctor. When asked to recall the prisoner's reaction to her husband's death and to the subsequent discovery of chloroform in his stomach, he became confused and was obliged to refer again and again to his notes. Clarke prompted him with the statement he had made in the Coroner's court, but he no longer seemed sure of the accuracy of the notes he had written at the time. At this the judge remarked dryly:

> Probably that is all for the best; if you did not think so much of the literary effect, and would tell us what happened, it would be better for everybody.

'My lord,' protested Leach, 'pardon me if I say that it is not the literary effect, but the accuracy, I strive to attain.'

'We do not strive to get any phenomenal accuracy. Just tell us what happened,' came the exasperated reply.

With an effort Leach managed to recover himself and described quite coherently how, after the post-mortem had been completed, Adelaide had selected her hat from the drawer he had brought from the back room. He emphasised that although she had insisted that the bottle of chloroform was still in the chest of drawers at the time, he had been unaware of it. He became defensive, however, over the sealing of the rooms in Claverton Street – apparently some newspaper reporters had suggested a certain negligence on his part – and Mr Justice Wills was provoked to intervene again:

> If you would think less about your own share in the matter, and more about the solemn character of the matter we are engaged in, it would assist us. This perpetual self-consciousness detracts from the value of what you have to say.

Suitably chastened, the unfortunate Leach was given a chance to compose himself while Clarke read aloud a long passage from his statement to the Coroner regarding Adelaide's account of her 'platonic' marriage. How far, asked Clarke, had Leach known of what she told him from personal cognisance, and how far from observation?

Still flustered, and aware of the judge's mounting impatience,

Leach stammered that he had not been entirely surprised by what she had told him, for he knew Mr Bartlett to be 'a man of strange ideas.'

'What ideas?' he was asked.

'Nothing about matrimony,' he replied, 'but very vague ideas about mesmerism and vital force, and things too insignificant to make a note of, which conveyed to my mind that my patient was one of the most extraordinary men I ever had to deal with – though a very pleasant and nice man.'

So strange were these ideas that at one time Leach had begun to doubt his patient's sanity and had tried to find the key to his disturbance. However, he had never heard the deceased talk of having two wives, one for companionship and one for work. 'I never heard him allude to it,' he said.

'That came from her?' asked Clarke, with some scepticism.

'Naturally; not for the first time,' came the unexpected reply. Fumbling and stammering with nervousness, the doctor went on to say that, as far as he had seen, the Bartletts had appeared to live affectionately together.

> With two exceptions, they had no differences and they only quarrelled once; but the terms of their cohabitation remained ultra-platonic. He encouraged her to pursue studies of various kinds and this she did to please him. He desired her to be very learned on all subjects. I remember distinctly on one occasion – I think it was the first time I saw Dyson there. I can see the deceased sitting with a look of being lost in admiration at his wife, while she was discussing some subject or other with Dyson. He sat, never uttering a word, but watching them talking. It was some rather remote subject they were talking about.

Clarke asked if Edwin seemed to welcome Dyson's attentions to his wife, and Dr Leach said that 'he was as welcome to one as to the other, and the deceased had spoken to me of Mr Dyson in terms of the highest admiration and affection, so far as he would be likely to talk on the subject of affection. Oh, yes, they were very proud of Mr Dyson.'

Having whittled Leach's long statement down to the bare bones of what he had actually noticed, Clarke turned to the question of whether or not it would have been possible for anyone in the camp bed to reach up to the mantelpiece without getting up. The doctor stated that, in his opinion, it would have presented no difficulty at all.

The cross-examination now focused on the subject of death from chloroform poisoning. Clarke's long hours of study bore fruit as he pressed Leach, first on the effects of inhalation and then of swallowing. Harry Poland joined in as Leach dithered and hesitated, but the doctor was at last forced to admit that the effects noted at the post-mortem agreed with chloroform poisoning 'as with many other poisonings', and that swallowing chloroform usually caused vomiting, especially after a large meal. He thought it would require great skill to administer chloroform by inhalation if the patient was asleep.

The doctor was then asked to recall the confidential talk he had had with Mrs Bartlett at his surgery on 14th January. He replied that she had only briefly alluded to the relationship between herself and the deceased. Their discussion 'was not about her husband in particular. It was on the general subject of sexual intercourse and her internal conditions; it was in connections with that she consulted me, and then it was that I learned the fact of her having been pregnant once.'

He could not remember whether Adelaide had mentioned the nature of her sexual relations with her husband on that occasion, although she certainly had on 26th January, and he himself could not say whether the Bartletts' relationship had been a sexual one. They seemed very affectionate, but he had seen nothing to prove that the attachment was sexual. He seemed ready to believe Adelaide's story of a platonic marriage, although he found it impossible to offer any observations on which to base that assumption.

The whole subject of Edwin's delusions about mesmerism was thrashed out, and Leach described at length what had been said, and his own research into the subject. Then Harry Poland suddenly asked him if it was true that when he first met the Bartletts, on 10th

December, he had thought they were newly-weds.

'I did,' agreed Leach, 'all this petting, etc., led me to that conclusion.'

This observation revealed a crucial flaw in the doctor's judgement, one that was not missed by Mr Justice Wills.

'You could hardly have supposed then there was anything like brother and sister in their relationship, could you?' he remarked.

'I have distinctly said I did not at that time suppose it, but even going back now to my recollection of that day on which I saw them, and thought they were recently married, I still do not hesitate to say that, after all, it is quite possible that it was an asexual relation,' babbled Leach.

Leach had been the only witness to Adelaide's assertion of a platonic relationship. With the matter thus left open to doubt, Poland returned to the subject of George Dyson and the frequency of his visits. The doctor said that he had seen the preacher at Claverton Street on several occasions and it struck him that 'he was on very intimate terms when there, and that they [the Bartletts] spoke of him a good deal when he was absent.

According to Dr Leach, they usually referred to him as *'Georgius Rex'* when they talked about him but always used the term Mr Dyson when addressing him directly.

When asked about the fire in the front room on the morning of 1st January, Leach said that it was quite a small fire, not sufficient to change the temperature of the room to any great degree, nor affect the condition of the body. On this point, therefore, he was unable to agree with the observations of both Frederick and Caroline Doggett, or the maid, Alice, for they had all said that the fire was banked up and burning well, making the atmosphere in the room extremely hot and stuffy.

This marked the end of Dr Leach's testimony and it must have been with profound relief that the poor man left the witness box at last.

As he stepped down his place was taken by Dr John Dudley, the physician who had been asked to give a second opinion during Edwin Bartlett's illness. In answer to questions put to him by Harry Poland, he described his visit to the house of Claverton Street on

19th December, and his observations that although the patient had seemed very depressed and complained of lack of sleep, he had found nothing wrong with him that could not be cured by exercise and fresh air. Edward Clarke declined to question him, and he was succeeded by Dr Montague Murray, who had attended the post-mortem on 2nd January.

'I did the operative work,' he said, 'while Dr Green watched the operations and dictated the notes which were taken down by Dr Leach.'

He described a small ulceration at the base of the stomach lining which led him to conclude that the deceased had been lying down when the chloroform reached the stomach.

'Supposing,' he went on, 'that the appearances which I saw in the stomach were the result of swallowing chloroform, I am not able to form any opinion as to what period of time must have elapsed between the swallowing and the death and to give time for these appearances to be caused. An hour would certainly be sufficient, I think, between the swallowing and the death.' He had re-examined the stomach the previous night, together with the gullet, and the condition of the gullet showed that the irritant had been taken down the throat. I would say it would show that after it was taken, for the greater portion of the time that life lasted the body was in a recumbent position.'

'How might the liquid chloroform have reached the stomach of the deceased? he was asked.

'Different methods might be employed,' he replied. 'There might be a tube employed – a portion might be poured down gradually.'

A question was then put by the Foreman of the jury:

'If poured down gradually, it would very likely leave some marks on the tongue and throat?'

'No, not necessarily,' came the unexpected reply, and the court was told that liquid chloroform in contact with body tissue did not necessarily have a devastating effect – sometimes, for instance, it would merely cause a slight reddening which would eventually disappear completely.

The doctor admitted that he had never heard of a case of liquid chloroform being poured down the throat of an unconscious person – one who had first been made unconscious by the administration of chloroform fumes. Nevertheless, he said, he thought it *could* be done, without presenting too many difficulties.

He added, however, a vital point regarding such an operation: if a person was totally unconscious, a tube would have to be used as the swallowing reflex would automatically disappear with the loss of consciousness. Any chloroform poured into the mouth would remain there and trickle down the gullet, causing burning.

'By what test would a medical man be able to ascertain that the particular stage had been reached where the reflex action of the muscles continued, but yet there was insensibility which would prevent the burning, and so on?' enquired Clarke.

'Oh, by the presence of reflex in other parts. He would test it by touching the eye, and there would be a closure of the eyelid. That would show that reflexes were present.'

Anxious to emphasise the difficulty of the procedure, Clarke pressed the witness further on this point but Dr Murray could not positively ascertain the precise moment at which a physician would know that the patient was sufficiently insensible to feel no pain, yet sensible enough to be able to swallow. The jury was left in no doubt, therefore, that the dividing line between consciousness and immunity to pain was a very fine one, and that it would require great skill, not only to induce such a state, but, more importantly, to ascertain exactly when that state had been reached.

The next witness was a policeman, Mr Tom Ralph, who had acted as Coroner's officer. He was examined by Harry Poland.

'I went to 85 Claverton Street about half-past nine at night,' he said, when asked about his visit on 4th January. 'I went into the front room, and there I found four glass vessels, jars or bottles, which were covered over with brown paper, and had string tied round them.[40]

At the same time I took possession of thirty-six medicine bottles. I placed the jars and the medicine bottles in two separate hampers and took them to the mortuary at 20 Millbank Street, and placed them in a large safe, under cover, in the back yard. There was no lock to the place, but I put a piece of tape across it and sealed it up.

'On 9th January I went there and found the tape in the same condition. I had been to Claverton Street on the 9th. Mr Doggett, junior, gave me a tumbler which appeared to contain Condy's fluid. There was a small glass bottle inverted in the tumbler, which was open, without any cork in it. As I was moving it into the glass jar that I had taken with me it broke, so that the whole of the broken tumbler and its contents went into the glass jar. I fastened it up, sealed it with Mr Doggett's seal, and took it to the mortuary, and put it with the other things.

'On the 11th I took all the things to Dr Stevenson at Guy's Hospital. I went to Claverton Street again, and met Inspector Marshall. Mr Wood, the solicitor, was there, but not Mrs Bartlett.

'I examined seven boxes on the floor in the front room, and in one of them I found two glass bottles. One of these was like a scent bottle, with a silver top on it, and there seemed to be some white powder in it. I also found in another box a small wooden box containing white powder. I sealed those three things up and handed them to Dr Stevenson on the 16th.[41]

'I found a tin box in the front room containing a man's suit of light clothing, which I examined. In the right hand trousers pocket I found four or five of what are popularly called French letters. I did not take possession of them. I left the clothes with the things in the pocket in the box, I saw on a table in the front room the book Squire's *Companion to the British Pharmacopoeia*.'

The discovery of the 'French letters' in the Bartletts' flat surely caused a ripple of disapproval to pass through the still air of the Central Criminal Court that afternoon. Such things were still relatively new and their use was considered by many to be immoral.

40 These contained the contents of Edwin Bartlett's stomach.
41 The three substances were later identified by Dr Stevenson as toilet powder, pepper and santonine.

Furthermore, the jurors must have felt that the presence of the contraceptives was rather surprising, especially with the story of Adelaide's *platonic* marriage still fresh in their minds. Assuming, that is, that the 'suit of light clothing' in the tin box had, in fact, belonged to Edwin and not to George Dyson, along with the serge coat and slippers kept in the Pimlico flat for his comfort. Alternatively, of course, the condoms may, indeed, have belonged to Edwin, and been kept in his trousers pocket ready for extramarital use.

As the policeman stepped down the examination of the medical witnesses was resumed. According to Edward Clarke:[42]

> The crucial point of the case was reached when Dr Stevenson and Dr Meymott Tidy came into the witness box. They were both men of high character reputation and were probably the best authorities then living upon the qualities of chloroform, and the method and effects of its administration, and their evidence was given with admirable fairness and caution.

First came the evidence of Dr Thomas Stevenson, who was questioned by the Attorney General.

He described himself as one of the analysts usually employed by the Home Office.[43]

He launched into a highly technical account of the post-mortem findings, elaborating on the evidence he had given at the inquest and in the magistrates' court. Relating directly to Mr Doggett's observations, he noted that as well as chloroform 'there was a very small trace of alcohol.'

'When chloroform is swallowed,' he said, 'at first it sometimes produces a state of intoxication, but not always. It then produces insensibility, stertorous breathing, or hard snoring, with muscular relaxation, paralysis, and death. It suspends the operation of the heart – paralyses the heart... It produces a liquid condition of the blood after death, which remains fluid for a long time.'

The doctor went on to describe to the court the sensation of chloroform in the mouth. It would not, he said, be possible to swallow

---

42 'Leaves from a Lawyer's Casebook'. *The Cornhill Magazine*, December 1920.
43 He had also edited *The Principles and Practice of Medical Jurisprudence* by Dr Alfred Swaine Taylor.

it without realising that it was harmful. 'It would produce pain and a hot fiery taste. I have swallowed it myself and I have found that it is very hot and very sweet and burning.'

Dr Stevenson was subjected to probing questioning by both the prosecution and the defence, in which he endorsed the comments made by Dr Murray. Edward Clarke later described the critical moments.[44]

> My cross-examination of Dr Stevenson was long and full of detail and started by eliciting the fact that, although there had been many murders by poisons well known to medical science, there was no recorded case of murder by the administration of liquid chloroform. Then I carefully and gradually made my way until I felt I could ask him the crucial questions.
>
> Now, suppose you had to deal with a sleeping man, and it was your object to get down his throat, without his knowing it, a liquid the administration of which to the lips or throat would cause great pain, do you not agree that it would be a very difficult and delicate operation?
>
> Dr Stevenson's reply was measured:
>
> 'I think it would be an operation which would often fail, and might often succeed.'

Edward Clarke persisted, determined to underline the difficulty an ordinary person would experience in executing such an operation.

'Would you not look on it as a delicate operation?'

'I should look upon it as a delicate operation, because I should be afraid of pouring it down the windpipe.'

'That is one of the dangers you contemplate?'

'Yes.'

'If it got into the windpipe, there would be spasmodic action of the muscles, would there not?'

'At the stage when you had come to the conclusion that you could do it, when there is insensibility, or partial insensibility, the rejection of the liquid by the windpipe would probably be less active than when the patient was awake.'

---

44 'Leaves from a Lawyer's Casebook', *The Cornhill Magazine*, December 1920.

'If the patient got into such a state of insensibility as not to reject it, it would go down his windpipe and burn that?'

'Probably some of it might go down his windpipe.'

'If it did so, it would leave its traces?'

'I should expect to find traces after death, unless the patient lived for some hours.'

In this particular type of poisoning, the doctor went on, there would be very noticeable changes in the post-mortem appearances, not only because of the volatile nature of chloroform, but also in other changes incidental to a post- mortem condition.

Edward Clarke leaned forward.

> And if the post-mortem examination had been performed, as Mrs Bartlett wished it to be, on the very day on which death took place, there would have been still better opportunity of determining the cause of death?

'Yes,' replied the witness – as his questioner had felt sure he would.

At last, it seemed Clarke had managed to expose at least one point in Adelaide Bartlett's favour.

CHAPTER 18

A Powerful Plea

Crowds were again out in force as the trial entered its fifth day. Following Clarke's master-stroke the previous afternoon, Dr Stevenson was recalled for re-examination by the Attorney General. The evidence he gave was both vital and unexpected, for he stated that in his opinion Edwin Bartlett must have been *conscious* when the chloroform entered his stomach, for there was evidence to show that he had *swallowed* the liquid. Had he been unconscious, his swallowing reflex would have failed to function and the chloroform would have remained for some little time at the back of this throat. This would have caused such severe inflammation that it would have shown quite clearly at the subsequent post-mortem examination; as it was, the inflammation had occurred at the base of the gullet and inside the stomach itself, suggesting that the chloroform had been swallowed, not poured.

The next important witness was another much respected expert on chloroform, Dr Charles Meymott Tidy. Harry Poland rose to question him.

Tidy stated that in his opinion chloroform would only cause lasting inflammation if it was in contact with the tissues for some time. He had tried an experiment on himself to test this.

> I put a teaspoonful of pure chloroform in my mouth, and I held it in my mouth for something like five or six seconds; I then spat it out and simply washed my mouth out with a little water. There was a slight redness produced, but it certainly did not last longer than a few minutes at the most, although a certain numbness continued for

something like nearly an hour. I am clear, therefore, that the effect of chloroform on animal tissues will be greatly dependent on the duration of the contact.

Like the other doctors in the case, he would expect to find the blood unusually fluid, for 'one of the peculiar effects of chloroform is its action on the blood including various changes of the blood.'

He went on to suggest that it was extremely difficult to chloroform a sleeping person as in the majority of cases the recipient would wake up suddenly. There were exceptions, however: various attempts to chloroform sleeping children had been more successful than those with adults. Edward Clarke took up this point in his cross-examination and Tidy agreed that most deaths by chloroform were suicides, although there had been cases of chloroform being inhaled accidentally.

The doctor emphasised again that the administration of chloroform was a highly specialised practice, needing great care and precise judgement. The effects of the drug were dangerously variable, even causing death quite unexpectedly in perfectly healthy patients. For this reason alone, many medical men preferred to use ether whenever possible, since its effects were more predictable.

Mr Justice Wills suggested that the effects of swallowing chloroform might be as uncertain as those of inhalation. Indeed so, agreed Dr Tidy, for much less was known about the subject. He did, however, accept a point suggested by a juror, that chloroform was likely to leave a mark on the delicate parts of the mouth.

'There is one other question I want to ask you,' said the judge. 'Dr Leach says that, experimenting upon himself, he produced a mark of whiteness on the tongue when he took chloroform in his mouth. Do you know anything about that?'

'No,' replied Dr Tidy, 'it is contrary to my own experiments, and my own experience. It was a thing I looked for very carefully, but it was a delicate blush of redness.'

Leach, it will be remembered, had actually swallowed some of the chloroform, whereas Tidy had spat it out and rinsed his mouth with water before examining his tongue. His view, however, was likely to carry more weight than that of the nervous young doctor, especially when taken with the lack of evidence of whiteness in the medical literature.

Mrs Mary Ann Furlong, who had been the Bartletts' maid-servant at The Cottage, Merton Abbey, was the next witness. In answer to questions put to her by Mr Moloney, she said that there had been few visitors at The Cottage – as far as she knew, George and Alice Matthews and George Dyson were the only persons who ever went there (the visits of Annie Walker had apparently gone unnoticed). She had made the beds in the house, and swore that the Bartletts had shared the same bed.

> So far as I saw, Mr and Mrs Bartlett lived on very affectionate terms with one another, and, as far as I could judge, they lived as husband and wife.

She was followed by Henry Marshall, the Police Inspector in charge of the case, who told Harry Poland how he had arrested and cautioned Adelaide on 11th February.

'Previous to that date,' continued the Inspector, 'I searched the whole of the railway like from Peckham Rye to Victoria to see if I could find any bottle. I found some bottles, but not the one I expected.

> On 15th February I went to Wandsworth Common with Mr Dyson, and I searched the common for bottles at the place indicated by him. I found the coloured bottle with "*Poison, not to be taken*" on it. I should say that I have searched the Common twice since, but I have not been able to find the other bottles.
>
> On 18th February I received a warrant from the Coroner, upon which I took Mr Dyson into custody and took him before the magistrate. The warrant was for both prisoners, and it charged them with murder.
>
> On 24th February I also searched a number of boxes at Claverton Street. No medicine chest was found; I never could find it either at Claverton Street or at Mrs Matthews', where Mrs Bartlett had been staying. I searched Mrs Bartlett's luggage at the office of her solicitor, and I took possession of a certain number of things – the deceased's

> nightgown and other things – which were handed to Dr Stevenson. The nightgown was cut down the centre. I showed it, the pillow and the other things, to Dr Stevenson. There were stains on the nightgown just above the neck. These were seen by Dr Stevenson.

Dr Stevenson was then recalled for questioning about the nightgown. He reported having seen 'spots and stains' on it. 'But I could not detect any substance beyond a little sugary substance. The stains might have been due to any ordinary article of liquid food, such as beef tea, or it might be the result of perspiration. There was no sign on the pillow case.'

Sir Charles Russell next recalled Caroline Doggett, who told him about the relationship between Adelaide and the deceased.

> The first week that the Bartletts were living with me they had only one bedroom and one bed, which they used together,' she said. 'Afterwards a smaller bed was put into the bedroom, which they continued to occupy up to the time of the illness. The small bed was then moved into the drawing-room. I sometimes went to help the servant to make the large bed, and I found the small one remade, but whether Mrs Bartlett had made it or not, I cannot say. I did not see anything unusual in the relationship between Mr and Mrs Bartlett. I think they were on affectionate terms as husband and wife.

The servant, Alice Fulcher, then faced further questions from Russell. She confirmed the evidence that her employer had just given, adding that during Mr Bartlett's last illness 'Mrs Bartlett used to have a sofa made up in front of the fire, and she slept there.'

Asked about the relationship between Adelaide and Dyson, she said that she had seen some books in the room during the minister's visits, but she 'could not say whether they were open.'

This cheeky comment ended the maid's evidence. It also marked the end of the case for the prosecution.

The witness box stood empty.

Not one person was called in Adelaide Bartlett's defence.

It was unfortunate that, as his judicial adversary on the case happened to be the Attorney General, Edward Clarke would have to deliver his speech for the defence first, leaving Sir Charles Russell the advantage of speaking last.[45] However, it was with an air of complete confidence that he rose to speak, for he knew that his course was now clear.

'In this case,' he began, 'you have heard, in its fullest detail, the evidence which the Crown has to lay before you in support of this charge, and having heard that evidence, and believing that I have been able, to some extent, to trace the effect of it upon your minds, I now, in Adelaide Bartlett's name, claim from you a verdict of "*Not Guilty*".

'Whatever the history of our medical jurisprudence may be, this case will be long remembered. There have been incidents in it, there have been topics dwelt upon, which will not easily be forgotten by any of those who interest themselves in the administration of the criminal law, or in subjects of medical science and of medical jurisprudence.

'We have had certainly strange incidents. I do not speak now of those remarkable relations which appear to have existed between Mr Bartlett and his wife – relations which would be almost inconceivable if they had not been, as here they are, proved to be true.

'It is a marvellous thing that you are asked by the prosecution to accept. You are asked to believe that a woman who, for years, has lived in friendship and affection with her husband; who, during the whole time of his illness, had striven to tend him, to nurse him, and to help him; who had tended him by day, who had sacrificed her own rest to watch over him at night, had spent night after night without going to her restful bed, simply giving herself sleep at the bottom of his couch that she might be ready by him to comfort him by her presence; who had called doctors, who had taken all the pains that the most tender and affectionate nurse possibly could – that woman who had watched over him, had tried to cheer him – you are

45 The Solicitor General was afforded the same privilege.

asked to imagine that that woman on New Year's Eve was suddenly transformed into a murderess, committing that crime, not only without excuse but absolutely without any object – you are asked to believe that by a sort of inspiration she succeeds in committing that crime by the execution of a delicate and difficult operation, an operation which would have been delicate and difficult to the highest trained doctor that this country has in it.

'This is the first case that the world has ever heard of in which it has been suggested that a person has been murdered by the administration of liquid chloroform. There have been cases of death from the swallowing of liquid chloroform. In the great majority of these cases death may have been death by suicide; in all the others, they have been death by accidental taking or administration of that drug.

'During those forty years [since the discovery of chloroform in 1840] there has been no case of the kind, and you are called upon now – it is suggested to you that you should say that Adelaide Bartlett has committed an offence absolutely unknown to the history of medical jurisprudence, and the possibility of which has never been suggested in any book on this subject, so far as we know – never.

'I think you understand the reasons why chloroform never has been used, and probably never will be used, for the purpose of murder, because the administration of liquid chloroform is singularly variable in its effects. Instances are given where large doses of liquid chloroform have been taken and the patient has lived afterwards. There seems no rule at all: one case will give you the instance of a man who swallows liquid and walks for a considerable distance after he has done so; another where a man takes a very much smaller dose of chloroform, and in three minutes he was in a heavy sleep; so that, as to its fatal effects, there are all sorts of variety. No one can define what a fatal does is. A fatal dose has sometimes been very small, and a large quantity has sometimes not produced death; but, for the moment, it seems to me that Dr Stevenson's evidence is conclusive that there was sufficient chloroform in the stomach to indicate that a dose which might have been fatal had been taken, and there are no appearances which point to death from any other cause.'

This said, Edward Clarke launched into a detailed analysis of the findings and the ramifications of the use of chloroform as given in the evidence of Drs Stevenson and Tidy. After this, he refuted the fact that there was anything suspicious about Alice Fulcher being asked to leave the basin outside the Bartlett's room. Edwin Bartlett was by then in bed – what more natural than that his wife should not want him disturbed? Likewise the matter of Adelaide's change of dress: it was her custom to wash and change into something more comfortable before returning to sit through the night with her husband; why should she not have done so on the night of 31st December? Nor did he see anything significant about the fact that the fire in the front room had been banked up and was burning brightly. He did, however, concede one point that he thought might be held against his client.

> It is the matter alleged against Mrs Bartlett of her having made untrue statements to Mr Dyson with respect to Dr Nichols and Annie Walker, and the relation which had existed between herself and them. This matter mainly depends upon the evidence, and upon the recollection, of Mr Dyson, because it is from him that you have got the evidence that Mrs Bartlett told him that her husband had been to Dr Nichols; that her husband was suffering from an internal complaint; that she had administered chloroform for the purpose of soothing him in these paroxysms, and that Annie Walker was the person who had obtained the chloroform for her, and could no longer obtain it because she had gone to America.

Clarke then proceeded to remind the court that George Dyson had also lied about the purpose for which the chloroform was needed; it surely followed, therefore, that had he been tried for murder alongside Adelaide Bartlett, his lies too would have been considered to be indicative of his guilt.

He went on to suggest that Adelaide had told George Dyson that she wanted the chloroform to soothe her husband because she was too embarrassed to mention the fact that Edwin had been keen to reassert his conjugal rights.

'Could any woman with any delicacy at all have explained it so to Mr Dyson?' he asked the jury, confident of its support.

He did not draw the jurors' attention, however, to the fact that the same fastidious lady was quite prepared to have a copy of *Esoteric Anthropology* lying around the drawing room for anyone to see.

After an adjournment, Edward Clarke made a gallant attempt to convey to the jury that his client was the type of woman to gain the affection and respect of her acquaintances. Nothing, however, could conceal the fact that Adelaide had only two women friends, Alice Matthews and Annie Walker – and both of these had given evidence *against* her during the trial!

Without dwelling too long on these unfortunate circumstances, he set out to interpret Adelaide's account of her strange marriage.

> In the first sentence of that statement she said that her husband was a man of strange ideas – that a man might have two wives, one for service and the other for companionship.
>
> If that statement had been made at the inquest for the purpose of diverting suspicion from herself, and of justifying her acts, it might have been the subject of suspicion. But Mrs Bartlett had confided to her doctor that most strange and delicate explanation of the relations with regard to herself and her husband. She stands by that statement now. There was no reason for her to have gone into the witness-box. It would have been to expose herself to a trial as severe and terrible as a woman could ever have undergone, and would have added nothing to the statement she had already made, and which, through Dr Leach's lips, had been made on the public record, of her share of the transaction.

Clarke then began to describe Edwin Bartlett's last illness, emphasising Adelaide's role as a tireless and dedicated nurse. Playing throughout on the jury's sympathies, he came to the fatal night of 31st December.

'Suppose you now sketch in your imagination what took place,' he said. 'Suppose she left the room as usual to wash, and he had placed on the mantelpiece this bottle of chloroform. There was a wine glass there, that wine glass was found afterwards, and while she was away it was perfectly easy for him without leaving his bed, lifting himself only upon his elbow, to put into this wine glass the less than half a wine glass of chloroform which may have constituted that fatal dose, having poured that into the wine glass, having replaced the bottle, then to have taken it off.

'If he swallowed it in that way, and swallowed it up quickly, there would not be, as there were not, appearances of long exposure of the softer substances of the mouth and throat to the chloroform. Having drunk it, he reassumes his recumbent position, the chloroform passes down his throat and reaches the stomach. Within two or three minutes after that he might be passing into a state of coma, that might have been when she came back, or when she awoke.

'Then she herself goes to sleep, and her husband's coma deepens into insensibility and insensibility passes into death. And then the hours go by... she awakens to find that husband apparently cold and dead.

'If you accept that statement, the whole history is clear. There was no scientific miracle worked by the grocer's wife, under circumstances where it could not have been worked by the most experienced doctor. There was unhappily the putting within the reach of a man who was broken by illness, and upon whom there had come this disappointment, and absolute and final severance of the effectual marriage tie between himself and his wife – there was the putting within his reach of the poison which he might have used, and which he probably did use, but there was nothing more, and from that moment there was not a word of hers, there was not an action, not a look, which was not the look, or the word, or the action of the loving wife who had nursed him through his illness to this point, and who now found him suddenly gone forever.

'And from beginning to end her every action and word and thought appears to be the act and word and thought of a woman who is chafing under the cruel uncertainty: what can it be that has suddenly robbed her of her husband?'

The more level-headed members of the jury must have appreciated that Edward Clarke, in this touching piece of melodrama, chose not to dwell on the fact that Mrs Bartlett, whilst 'chafing under cruel uncertainty', had secretly disposed of the chloroform bottle instead of handing it over to the police so that the cause of her husband's death might be determined. Nor did he remind the court that while his tragic client was laying out her husband's body she was already talking about his money...

But Clarke had now reached his peroration, and as he raised his head he was preparing to wring the last drop of sympathy from the all-male jury.

> This woman has not had the happiest of lives. She has been described to you as one who had no friends. She found a friend in Mrs Matthews; she found another friend in continuing the acquaintance of the nurse who was called before you, but beyond that, we know of no friends, and the habits of her husband's life left her much alone. There is no hint of misconduct or wrong upon her part at any time, except the trivial and malignant invention of that witness who came first.
>
> But she had one friend – her husband. He did stand by her, strange as his ideas may have been, disordered as his intellect in some respects must have been. In his strange way he stood by her and he protected her. He was affectionate in manner, and when her reputation was assailed, he defended it as only the husband could defend it. And to her at this moment it may seem most strange that he to whom she had given this persistent affection should be the one of whose foul murder she now stands accused. And if he himself could know what passed among us here – how strange, how sorrowful, it might seem to him – how strange that such an accusation should have been formulated and tried in court in spite of the efforts which he endeavoured to make to prevent it; the precautions which perhaps, by his own rash and despairing act, he too completely defeated.
>
> Gentleman, that husband too has gone, but she is not left without a friend; she will find that friend here today in the spirit which guides your judgement and clears your eyes upon this case. It is a great responsibility for men to be called suddenly from their business and their pleasures, and to be shut off as you have been from the ordinary habits of your life, to decide upon issues of life and death.
>
> The spirit of justice is in this court today to comfort and protect her

A Powerful Plea

in the hour of her utmost need. It has strengthened, I hope, my voice; it will, I trust, clear your eyes and guide your judgement. It will speak in calm and measured tones when my lord deals with the evidence which aroused suspicion and also with the evidence which I hope and believe has demolished and destroyed that suspicion, and that spirit will speak in firm and unfaltering voice when your verdict tells to the whole world that in your judgement Adelaide Bartlett is not guilty!

This highly emotive plea had lasted for six hours, and when the court adjourned for the day, many of its members were visibly moved by what they had heard. Edward Clarke himself must have been utterly exhausted after all his efforts to convince the jury that his client was innocent. As for Adelaide, she could not bring herself to watch Clarke's face as he laboured in her defence, for at one point in the proceedings she sent him a note which read,

Monsieur, I am very grateful to you, although I do not look at you.

CHAPTER 19

The Voice of Scepticism

The following day it was the turn of the Attorney General to make his final speech for the prosecution. Once more the crowds gathered, the women far outnumbering the men. Their presence was commented upon in several newspaper reports, and their demeanour so irritated Mr Justice Wills that he had been arriving at the Old Bailey each morning half an hour earlier than usual, hoping to avoid seeing them jostling around the gates. But by nine o'clock the ladies were already flocking to the court, determined to be there for Sir Charles Russell's reply to Edward Clarke and for the judge's summing up. With any luck, they might also hear the jury pronounce its verdict that day.

The *Daily Telegraph* was moved to comment in forcible terms:

> It is a matter of grave regret to the officials and other gentleman whose public duty compelled them to be present, that so many women besought them for tickets – and, having obtained them, listened to all the painful and revolting details as if they were present at some highly amusing and delightful entertainment.
>
> Nothing more distressing has been witnessed in a court of justice for many years. No more brutalising exhibition has been seen since the days when public executions attracted the roughs of London. The box reserved for the City Land Committee was full of them; and the public gallery was two thirds tenanted by them.
>
> The judge at the outset of his summing up had some strong remarks to make regarding their presence, but not one lady thought it seemly to retire, and the greatest compromise noticeable was the fact that those who had been for the four or five days preceding particularly

diligent with their knitting, laid aside their needles and half-completed work and endeavoured to look unconscious that evidence of a character totally unfit for publication, but considered of the greatest importance, was being tendered and discussed.[46]

The *Evening Standard*, too, remarked on the number of women present, noting that 'the gallery was filled with well-dressed women and girls armed with luncheon packets, sherry, sandwiches and eye-glasses – and, in spite of the plainest hints from the learned judge, they maintained their places, and in the intervals of adjournment, tittered and laughed over the judge's prudery!'[47]

The first task of the Attorney General was to dispel the mood of sympathy created so eloquently by Edward Clarke. His voice, he told the jury, would not be that of passion and prejudice, but of fairness and common sense based on the known facts of the case, and guided by the interests of society and justice. He started by drawing the jury's attention to the fact that, although there had never been a case of murder by liquid chloroform, this did not necessarily mean that such a murder was impossible.

The same, he argued, could have been said of the case of William Palmer who, in 1856, had been tried and convicted at the Old Bailey for murdering one of his victims with strychnine; and of that of Dr George Lamson, convicted in the same court in 1882 of the despicable murder of his crippled brother-in-law. He had poisoned the boy with aconitine, which was a method unfamiliar to medical jurisprudence at the time.[48] Both men had paid the final penalty for their crimes.

He then went on to attack Edward Clarke for his ill-concealed animosity towards Mr Bartlett, senior, pointing out that the old man had quite rightly suspected that his son had died from unnatural causes. He also reminded the jury that old Mr Bartlett had only referred to Adelaide's earlier misconduct with Frederick Bartlett

---

46 *Daily Telegraph*, 19th April, 1886.
47 *Evening Standard*, 19th April, 1886.
48 Aconitine is the poison extracted from the planet Aconitum napellus, otherwise known as wolf's-bane or monk's-hood. Dr Tidy and Dr Stevenson had also given evidence at Lamson's trial.

when he was specifically cross-examined on that point.

These points dealt with, he turned his attention to the question of how Edwin Bartlett had died.

> I noticed that my learned friend did not suggest the question of accident; nor could he. He confined his case to suggesting the difficulties in the way of administering this irritant poison by anyone else, and marshalled his facts and arguments in support of one suggestion, and one suggestion only – suicide, deliberate suicide on the part of the deceased.
>
> Now, let me remind you that this is one of those cases in which you can never have proof to demonstration of the crime committed. Murders by poison are not committed, like crimes of sudden passion, often in the light of day. They are necessarily mysterious and hidden in their operation.

The Attorney General then set out to demolish, by a process of *reductio ad absurdum*, the premises on which Clarke had built his case for the defence. Looking first at Adelaide's marriage to Edwin Bartlett, he described her uncorroborated account of their life together as 'unutterably unnatural', and asked the jurors to use their common sense in deciding whether to reject her extraordinary tale.

'One act of coition in order to gratify her desire to have a child!' he exclaimed, incredulously. 'How did she know that one act of coition would place her in the position to count with certainty or probability on the fruition of her hopes? Yet that is the statement – married in 1875; that in ten years of married life there was one act of sexual intercourse between man and wife, and one act of sexual intercourse only. The birth of that stillborn child – that dead child – seems to have been a source of great physical anguish and trial to her, and she seems to have then expressed the resolution that she would not have any more children. But the language she used to Annie Walker was consistent only with the desire to avoid childbearing. It does not necessarily point to a cessation of marital intercourse; and there is one fact proved in this case – I mean the fact of what was found in the clothes of the dead man at No. 85, Claverton Street, which at least suggested the probability that, while there may have been sexual intercourse, means were resorted to to be prevent any conception from the act of coition. But take the whole of the story. Is there one scintilla of evidence to support the suggestion that Mr and Mrs Bartlett were living upon any other than the ordinary terms of husband and wife?'

Having thus dismissed the story of the platonic marriage, he moved on to the involvement with George Dyson.

> It is quite clear that George Dyson was received upon terms of close intimacy, and I will say dangerous intimacy, by Mrs Bartlett and by Mrs Bartlett's husband. There is no doubt that she was interested in him, and that she probably thought he was equally interested in her [Russell was conveniently ignoring Dyson's own confession to Edwin]; but it is fair to the prisoner to say, it is fair to Dyson to say, that whatever may have been their terms, and their expectations of what was possible in the future, there does not seem to be any just grounds for asserting that she was unfaithful to her dead husband, and that Dyson had, in that particular at least, abused the friendship and confidence which the dead man had shown him.
>
> My learned friend's argument was in effect this: that the dead man saw a growing affection between George Dyson and his wife, which, in the possible event of his death, was to culminate in a closer and nearer relation – that is to say, of man and wife; and that he had so far contemplated the possibility of his own prior death as to have, in that extraordinary language which Mrs Bartlett used to Dr Leach, made over in reversion his living wife to a man whose friendship he was then cultivating. The sequence of that argument is that this compliant husband, when he was told by his wife, 'You have made me over to Dyson; it is unfair to him that you should exercise your rights as a husband' - her husband turns on his pillow, and does an act which removes the only obstacle which stands in the way of the union which he, the dead man, while living had contemplated. I think you will feel the sad necessity of this case, and of her defence, that she should be obliged to cast this grievous stigma, this damaging slur, on the memory of her dead husband.

'What stigma?' demanded Edward Clarke, leaping to his feet.

'My learned friend asks me what stigma?' exclaimed Russell in mock disbelief. 'The stigma that the living husband, with obligations and rights, entered into a compact by which, in the event of his death, his wife was handed over to the embraces of another man, and that he stood by complacently agreeing.'

Treading more warily now, he went on to comment on Adelaide's apparent affection for her husband. She had undoubtedly bestowed every care on him during his last illness (which, he pointed out, was nothing more than an attack of indigestion); on the other hand, if she had decided to kill him, it would have been to her advantage to appear as affectionate as possible, so that nothing would detract from her image as a loving and loyal wife. Perhaps she had rather overdone her affectionate role for Dr Leach's benefit, especially on the last day of Edwin's life, when they were on their way to the dentist. This was hardly the most romantic moment to choose to express her wish that they could marry all over again, as they had been 'so completely happy" nor was it likely that Edwin had 'honestly joined in the expression of the same sentiment.'

With unconcealed cynicism he proceeded to analyse some of the other statements Adelaide had made. Why had she obtained the chloroform? What did she want it for?

'The statement is that she had had no act of intercourse with her husband during the whole of her married life but one; that when he was beginning to get better, about 16th December, he began to show signs of returning passion and desire to have intercourse with her again. Is that likely? Is it likely that passion, which, according to her statement, had lain dormant for all those years, should be again aroused within him? He then lying upon his sick bed, being treated as an invalid – why was it that at this time this passion manifested itself? How came it that it occurred to her that she should sprinkle chloroform upon a handkerchief, and, when he was seeking to approach her, wave it over his head?' The jury was welcome, he said, to ignore the dictates of common sense and accept that story at face value.

Russell then went on to propose a new theory as to how the chloroform reached Edwin Bartlett's stomach on the night he died:

'If the draught had been handed to him in a glass, and given to him as if for an ordinary purpose, with drops of chloroform in it, and water or some other thing, to drink then it was conceivable that the dying man would have gulped it down, believing in its innocence, and not suspecting that the prisoner had administered something which was wrong and injurious.'

This theory was far too plausible for Edward Clarke to entertain – in fact, it constituted the only real threat to his defence. He rose quickly to raise his objection.

'My lord, I protest against any such suggestion being put forward, for the first time, at this stage of the case, when it was not even hinted at by the learned counsel for the prosecution in his opening, or in the examination of any of the witnesses.'

'I am not making any suggestion,' countered Sir Charles, 'but when my learned friend is erecting one theory – namely, the theory of suicide – I am entitled to submit any theory which would point in a more probable direction.'

Turning back to the jury, he asked them to consider why suicide should be rejected as a logical answer to the problem before them. Edwin had been prosperous in business and, until 10th December, in good health. By Christmas Day he had been almost recovered and very cheerful, and on 31st December, he had been also 'in good spirits, on good terms with himself, and on good terms with his wife.' Did common sense allow them to accept that, even supposing Adelaide had spurned his advances, he had reached for the bottle of chloroform when she had left the room, drunk it down, and then replaced the stopper before returning the bottle to the mantelpiece – all so that, after his death, his wife might find happiness with her new-found admirer?

'She then is supposed to have come back,' he continued. 'And recollect, this theory falls to pieces and crumbles up on examination, unless you are also prepared to believe that when she comes back – the man having taken the fatal dose; she has meanwhile heard no sign, no utterance of pain or distress – she finds him apparently tranquilly sleeping in his bed in such a condition that she, the anxious, the affectionate wife, is able to compose herself at the foot of the bed, and go to sleep.'

He reminded the jury that the chloroform bottle had been removed before the household was aroused – and by whom but the defendant, since both Leach and Doggett had sworn that there was no bottle of chloroform in the room at four-thirty that morning? Moreover, had she not kept quiet about her possession of poison until 26th January, when she knew for certain that chloroform had been named as her husband's killer?

And what of her motive? Here Russell was as realistic as ever:

> One cannot but see, looking at his physical condition, the state of his gums, the state of his teeth, the offensively foetid breath, that her husband may have become personally distasteful to her; that she had begun to see in Dyson a man of superior education, although, apparently, of no physical attractions;[49] a man with whom her husband unfavourably compared; may she not have felt this feeling growing upon her? And when she knew that the will had been made in the September previously by which she was benefited, that the will was free from the restriction in the earlier will, namely, that she did not receive the benefit merely during her widowhood, but was absolutely the beneficiary – in this condition of things, the evil comes into her mind to avail herself of this illness, that she might take advantage of the opportunity of ridding herself of a husband who had become distasteful to her, and for whom she had ceased to care, that she might clear the way to a union with a man for whom she had of late conceived admiration and apparently affection.

Having presented the jury with a coldly logical view of the facts before them, the Attorney General closed his speech with a statement that was a model of fairness.

> My learned friend has said that the spirit of justice in the jury-box will be the friend and protector of the prisoner at the bar. Let me say the spirit of justice, and whose friend it is to be proved to be, depend upon the antecedent question which is not yet determined – is there guilt here, or is there innocence here?
>
> The spirit of justice, if there is guilt, cannot be invoked to conjure up doubts or to protect a criminal. Even as justice is blind, so ought

---

49 Sir Edward Clarke, however, later described George Dyson as 'goodlooking'.

justice to be deaf to appeals, to prejudice or to passion. Justice is open to the impression of the truth.

The truth is the point upon which your attention is to be fixed. The law requires that you should give the benefit of any fair and reasonable doubt which remains in your minds. I ask you to give the benefit of that doubt, if that doubt does remain, but it must be a doubt which presents itself to your minds as reasoning men, anxious to discharge your duty between the prisoner and the public – the Crown, whom we represent – a doubt which you cannot overcome.

Apply your minds, I pray you, gentlemen, in that spirit; consider and weigh the facts of the case in that spirit; and if you come to the conclusion that still a doubt remains, in God's name give this woman the benefit of that doubt. But if, after you have heard my lord, and you have retired from that box, and find yourselves face to face with the responsibility of the duty that devolves upon you, and the conviction is borne in upon your minds that you cannot receive this theory of suicide; if the conviction remains in your mind, although you may not be able to state with accuracy the exact methods or means by which it is accomplished, that guilt lies at this woman's door, then I ask you, by the duty you owe to your oaths, and to the country which you represent, not to shrink from the responsibility which in that event will be cast upon you.

Sir Charles Russell then sat down and prepared to listen to Mr Justice Wills's address to the jury. However, before the judge could begin his summing up, Edward Clarke interrupted to announce that he had received a communication from Nurse Annie Walker.

I don't know whether your lordship, before beginning to sum up, would ask Annie Walker one question with regard to anything she knew as to the single act – your lordship will know what I mean. I say no more.

Robert Wright rose to say that the prosecution would be happy with whatever his lordship thought right and fair, although the recalling of a witness at this stage in trial proceedings was most unusual. Mr Justice Wills did not object.

'It is very late but I think we should never shut out anything that is material,' he said. 'Let Annie Walker step up.'

In the Interests of Science: Adelaide Bartlett and The Pimlico Poisoning

Clearly convinced that the nurse would provide positive evidence for the defence, Edward Clarke asked:

> At the time you nursed Mrs Bartlett in her confinement, did you become aware from anything she said to you with regard to its having been the result of a single act?

'Yes, sir,' replied Annie Walker.

This seemed to corroborate the prisoner's extraordinary story about her platonic relationship with her husband. Edward Clarke sat down again, satisfied that he had scored a vital point for the defence. Unfortunately for him, but fortunately for the sake of the truth, Mr Justice Wills decided to ask Annie Walker what exactly had been said with regard to that delicate matter.

'That it happened only once – on a Sunday afternoon,' she replied.
'She said so?'
'Both of them; that there was always some preventative used.'
'You say you had that from both of them?' persisted the judge.
'Both of them.'

The bluntness of this statement came as a devastating blow to the defence. Clearly, the Bartletts' marriage had not been platonic at all, and Adelaide's story had been a fanciful fabrication devised to arouse the sympathy of the chivalrous young Dr Leach – and, of course, to provide a plausible reason for her possession of a bottle of deadly poison.

Surely no jury could now acquit her in the face of this damning evidence?

CHAPTER 20

Extraordinary Scenes

Annie Walker's unexpected statement, following on from the impassioned plea of Edward Clarke and the coolly rational argument of Sir Charles Russell, must have left the jury in a whirl of confused impressions. Much now depended on the judge's ability to make a balanced assessment and offer the guidelines for reaching their decision.

It was eleven o'clock in the morning when Mr Justice Wills began his summing up, and the *Pall Mall Gazette* was afterwards loud in its praise:

> No one who was in the court of the Old Bailey on Saturday is likely ever to forget the lucid, the impressive, and the eloquent summing up of Judge Wills. He will remember the grave but kind voice which rose to vehemence and sank to a whisper in his analysis of the evidence. The prisoner meanwhile sat statue-like. Mr Clarke, with tightened lips, leaned forward, with his hand to his forehead, listening intently, as though his own life had been at stake, sometimes shifting his hand to his cheek and digging his fingers into the flesh.[50]

'At times,' commented the reporter from the *Evening Standard*, 'he allowed the assembly to feel optimistic about the outcome of the trial; and yet, as his speech continued he showed equal emphasis on the facts in the case he thought might be construed against her. This was done with such eloquence that his audience swung between feelings of optimism and extreme pessimism; yet he himself seemed

---

50 *Pall Mall Gazette*, 19th April, 1886.

impartial as a great judge must.'[51]

In his opening comments he addressed the equivocal position of George Dyson, expressing his view that it had been to Adelaide's advantage that Dyson had appeared in the witness-box and been subjected to cross-examination. As to the reliability of the resulting evidence he was clearly less sanguine, and he was totally dismissive of the spiteful testimony of old Mr Bartlett, whose name inevitably cropped up in his brief outline of the Bartletts' life together. Ill-feeling had obviously existed on both sides, he noted, but 'there is something that calls to one's lips unbidden the name of Judas in the kiss with which he parted from his daughter-in-law on 1st January. Fortunately, as it seems to me, very little indeed depends upon the evidence of the senior Bartlett, and I shall have no occasion further to refer to him.'

When he came to Dr Nichols's 'very unpleasant' book, *Esoteric Anthropology*, the judge made no attempt to disguise his disapproval.

> One can scarcely think that in any decent household, and with any decent husband, such books should be put before the wife. Apparently, there are people who can read these books and see no shame in them. Annie Walker seems a respectable woman, and she says there is not a word immoral or improper in the book.
>
> Gentlemen, it has been my unpleasant duty to look at this book. I entertain myself an entirely different opinion, and there is one passage, notably, which instructs the ladies and gentleman of our land in the last invented means of procuring abortion; and yet we are invited to look upon this book as an effusion of purity, and an honest attempt to help people in the conduct of their lives. I cannot have such garbage passed under my eyes and then allow it to go forth that an English judge concurs in the view that it is a specimen of pure and healthy literature. It is one of those books, in my judgement, which, under the garb of ostentatious purity, obtains entrance into many a household from which it would be otherwise banished. It scatters its poison and does its mischief.

Modern women, he declared, aiming a swipe at the pre-dominantly female audience in the public gallery, had been depraved by being

---

51 *Evening Standard*, 19th April 1886.

given access to shocking literature, 'and it is such reading as this that helps to unsex them, and to bring them day after day to listen willingly to details which even to men of mature life, are distasteful and disgusting.'

Despite this bitter reproach, he did concede that the passage read out by Edward Clarke was more praiseworthy, although 'one has learnt today what is the natural and to be expected consequences of indulgence in literature of that kind.'

In 1885, he resumed, the Bartletts had had 'the great misfortune to make the acquaintance of the Rev. George Dyson.' His thundering tirade directed against the morals and character of the young preacher left the jury in no doubt about the judge's opinion of his influence on a previously happy marriage. There was nothing sinister, however, in the making of a new and wiser will, and nothing against Adelaide in her complaint against the old one: it was only to be lamented that the man in whom Edwin Bartlett had placed such confidence as to make him his executor, should have been so unworthy of trust.

As for the conversation supposed to have taken place at Putney, 'I confess to my mind,' declared the judge, 'it presents some features of almost revolting improbability. The Rev. George Dyson would have you believe that Mr Bartlett invited him to continue his intimacy with both of them. If there is anything in the atmosphere of this case which ought to make one part with the ordinary faculties which God has given us, and by which alone we can hope to test the truth of stories which are placed before us, by all means accept that statement.'

The letters exchanged between Edwin and Dyson shortly afterwards were, he felt, open to misrepresentation. When taken in their own social and moral context, there was nothing extraordinary about them. They were sentimental and lacking in taste, but there was nothing to be read into them of a salacious nature.

'We now come to Claverton Street,' the judge continued, as he embarked on a discussion of the possible truth in Dyson's statement that Adelaide had talked of Edwin's imminent death. 'Again, I say, receive what he says with caution, not to say mistrust.' He conceded, however, that as Alice Matthews had corroborated Dyson's version (although in his confusion over some of the points in Mrs Matthews's testimony the judge had to be corrected by Edward Clarke) it did appear that Dyson had been telling the truth here.

What was certain was that those who had known Edwin for many years agreed that he had generally enjoyed good health, despite the punishing regime he had imposed on himself in relation to his business affairs. His illness in December had been unpleasant and debilitating but not unduly serious and, moreover, had been well past its peak by the last night of the year. After his visit to the dentist he had been cheerful and optimistic, with a robust appetite; there was nothing to suggest that he had fallen into a suicidal melancholy.

The judge was generous in his praise of Adelaide for her care of her husband throughout a particularly trying illness. 'She seems to have been entirely true to her trust and her duty. She performed the most disagreeable duties, doing everything with patience and devotion. That must never be lost sight of. She was perfectly devoted, perfectly affectionate, perfectly natural in her conduct.'

Nor was there anything suspicious in the events and reported conversations of the night of 31st December. The question to be answered was how the chloroform which killed Edwin had found its way into his stomach. There was strong evidence that the glass later found on the mantelpiece had once contained chloroform, but the jury should not entertain the theory so lately advanced by the Attorney General.

'I do not suppose that you will consent to approach this subject as against the prisoner from any other hypothesis than that originally put forward, on which alone the examination and cross-examination of the medical witnesses has been conducted.'

In giving this advice the judge was acting correctly and with scrupulous fairness; one can only deplore the fact that the last-minute theory had not occurred earlier to the Attorney General and formed the main thrust of his case – as no doubt he would have agreed. It was perhaps an indication of the extent to which affairs of

State had diverted his energies from Adelaide's trial.

Returning, therefore, to the first hypothesis – that Edwin would have had to be rendered partially insensible but still able to swallow – Mr Justice Wills expressed grave doubts whether a woman without medical experience could have successfully poured liquid chloroform down the throat of a sleeping man.

'The attempt would be surrounded by so many difficulties, and open to so many chances of failure, that no skilled man would venture upon it unless he were a madman. The ignorant and presumptuous will sometimes attempt that which no human being who understood the conditions of the problems would think of trying, and will sometimes blunder into success. But, if she did succeed in that fashion, it was a most extraordinary piece of cruel fortune.'

If the jurors could not accept that the chloroform had been criminally administered, they might like to examine a theory of his own - that it had been taken by Edwin Bartlett of his own volition, as a sleeping draught. This gave his lordship the opportunity to expand on the misery of insomnia, which could easily drive one to despair as he himself had cause to know. Some years before he, too, had suffered from prolonged bouts of sleeplessness and knew only too well how desperate a person might become to obtain the oblivion of sleep. One might speculate, he suggested, that Edwin Bartlett had resorted to drinking chloroform to procure sleep.

'I know the uncommon strength of mind, will, and resolution which it takes to resist that impulse,' he said. 'Fortunately for myself, I soon became aware that one had better undergo any misery than resort to the fatal practice of taking narcotics, but it takes a very strong-minded man to come to that decision, because the sufferings of that state of mind are greater than any person who has not gone through such an experience can imagine.

'All this,' he went on, 'leaves behind the question – to my mind, by far the most important part of this inquiry – and that is, what is the history of that chloroform bottle?' Disregarding Dyson's statement about how and where it was handed over, and assuming that it was not criminally administered, it must at some time have been on the mantelpiece, as Adelaide had said, and some of its contents must also have been in the wine glass.

'A very strong fact in her favour,' stressed the judge, 'is that there had been no attempt to clean out that glass. It is a fact which strikes my own mind as one of considerable weight, and one that ought not to be lost sight of; and it does seem to me strangely unlike the conduct of any criminal in any case of which I have had experience to betray no anxiety to get rid of every trace of the actual method of which administration had taken place.'

On the other hand, how could one account for the disappearance of the bottle? 'There were drawers in the room behind, and there was her pocket. We can never know for certain in which of these two places it was. We shall never know for certain whether the way in which that bottle got out of the house was that it was in her pocket on 1st January, or that she had put it into the drawer on that night, and left it there until the seals were taken off the room.'

It was Dr Leach who had sworn that the bottle was not on the mantelpiece when he searched the room at five o'clock in the morning; Dr Leach who had reported Adelaide's assertion that she had left it there. Mr Justice Wills heaved a sigh.

'One must make great allowance,' he warned the jury, 'for a man who is evidently possessed of a self-consciousness that not even the solemnity of this inquiry could still for a moment, and which undoubtedly detracts from the value of his evidence, because one never knew when one was getting the unvarnished efforts of memory or the impressions of a not very strong-headed man painfully haunted by the idea that he is the central personage in a drama of surpassing interest.'

There were many anomalies in this part of the case, and the judge highlighted them expertly. If Adelaide was innocent, why did she make no mention of the chloroform when she saw Dr Leach searching the room and even discussed with him the possibility that Edwin had swallowed chlorodyne? That only made sense if the story she told to Leach on 26th January was true – which would also explain the false statements she was said to have made to Dyson when she asked him to procure the chloroform for her. In both cases modesty and delicacy might have prevented her from revealing the truth.

If she was guilty, however, why did she urge so anxiously for an immediate post-mortem examination? 'There is no doubt about this,' said the judge, adding wryly, 'it does not depend on Dr Leach's anxiety to construct a drama which will look as if it came out of a sensational novel.' It was a point, he emphasised, 'of extreme importance in her favour.'

By now it was a quarter to two in the afternoon, and the judge announced that there would be a short adjournment for lunch. As few people were willing to forfeit their coveted seats in court most remained where they were, eating what food they had brought with them. There was a loud buzz of conversation as the morning's proceedings were eagerly discussed between mouthfuls.

After half an hour the court reassembled. Curious eyes watched as Adelaide was brought back into the dock. The terrible reality of her situation and the anguish she was suffering had begun to show on her face. She was led in looking very pale, supported on either side by a wardress, whilst a prison officer stood behind her chair. All faces were turned towards her, some reflecting compassion, others suspicion and scorn.

Mr Justice Wills returned briskly to the matter before them, picking up the threads with the post-mortem examination on the 2nd January. He was still occupied with the missing bottle of chloroform, which Adelaide had stated was then in the chest of drawers in the back room.

'There were two drawers,' he pointed out. 'You remember Dr Leach said so. In the second of them he did not look.'

He described how George Dyson had escorted Adelaide to East Dulwich, skating over their alleged conversation since it had come from a 'tainted source'. Their meeting the following Monday was more worthy of attention, as part of the conversation had been overheard by Mrs Matthews. The judge felt that there was more to be learned to explain Dyson's cry of 'Oh, my God!' in response to Adelaide's denial that she had told him Edwin was likely to die soon – 'perhaps it does not suit Mr Dyson's purpose to give it to us.'

That same day the Coroner's officer, Tom Ralph, had removed 36 medicine bottles from the flat in Claverton Street but had failed to make a thorough search, 'so depriving us of the advantage of knowing what the contents of the room were at the time.' Two days later, on 6th January, Adelaide had returned to the flat and claimed to have removed the chloroform bottle which she later tossed into the pond at Peckham Rye.

Sticking closely to corroborated events and utterances, the judge moved on to Adelaide's barely credible story given to Dr Leach on 26th January. If the jury believed that, they might also believe Adelaide's explanation for the purchase of chloroform, but his lordship left them in no doubt about his own opinion.

> I do not know what you think of the evidence you heard this morning [referring to Annie Walker's last-minute statement about contraception]. It is difficult after that to elevate these people into the hero and heroine of an extraordinary and sensation romance. It looks more as if we had two persons to deal with abundantly vulgar and commonplace in their habits and ways of life.

With blistering scorn he tore up the saga of 'a man with such exalted views of matrimony that he thought the wife whom he had elected for his companion too sacred to be touched'. If the French letters found in Edwin's pocket 'were destined for external use, as they very likely may have been, they were also used at home.' And so he wound up to the most damning indictment he had yet made against Adelaide.

> If the one little grain of truth which is generally to be found in any romance, in any story of falsehood, be found in these articles and in the use habitually made of them between husband and wife, what becomes of the whole story of the use for which the chloroform was wanted? Does it not go by the board? And if that story be exploded,

what, after all, are you left to face? Chloroform procured for an unexplained and an inexplicable purpose; death by chloroform; the bottle disappearing, and, by the statement of this woman herself, emptied and thrown away by her; and when at last the state of things has been set up which renders it no longer possible to keep silence, an explanation given, which is a tissue of romance such as, if the evidence of Annie Walker can be accepted, could deceive no one but the ecstatic person to whom it was originally detailed.

The judge paused, and a hush fell on the court-room as the implications of his words sank in. The reporter from the *Pall Mall Gazette* was quite caught up in the drama:

> As the afternoon grew older and the shadows deeper the tone of the judge seemed to increase in solemnity, until the faintest sound, the shutting of a door, the fall of a book, the scratching of a pen, became an irritant, so tense had the occasion become.
>
> The judge was no believer in colourless summing-up, and the hope for the prisoner's life now rose, now fell, as he weighed the evidence in the scale.[52]

Mr Justice Wills looked round the court, then turned his gaze to the jury again.

'Gentlemen,' he began, 'this is the stress of the case against Mrs Bartlett. I am anxious not to make too much of this disappearance of the bottle. The conduct of people who suppose that state of circumstances has arisen, or is going to arise, which may place them under suspicion, is apt to be the same whether they are guilty or innocent.

> But after all you are faced with these facts, which there is no getting out of – chloroform handed to her; chloroform in her possession; chloroform killing the man; the bottle of chloroform disappearing, and no account of it save the one we have been discussing. That account, no doubt, is extremely material if you can believe it, because it would dispose of every circumstances of suspicion as to the purchase of the chloroform and as to the subsequent silence about it; but it is for you to say whether you can possibly, consistently with your oaths and consistently with your consciences, accept it,

---

52 *Pall Mall Gazette*, op. cit.

or whether you must not look at it as the expression, in adorned and imaginative language, of the simple and vulgar fact that they had come to the determination to have no more children, and that their intercourse from that time forward was upon that footing, and whether in that event, the statement made to Dr Leach is anything more than an amplified and etherealised version of that vulgar fact.

Gentlemen, if you think you ought not to believe it – if, in the face of Almighty God, before whom we are performing this solemn duty, you feel that you cannot do so, you must not flinch from the consequences. Give to the prisoner the full benefit of those circumstances of exceptional weight to which I have drawn your attention. Give her the full benefit of all such considerations. But remember, after all, we are dealing with the case of a married woman who had fallen into a perilous friendship with a man who was not her husband, whose husband could have been, in the latter portion of his life, no attractive object, either mentally or physically, and as to the most important circumstances connected with whose disappearance from this world the only explanation you have been enabled to get is one which, as it seems to me, cannot stand in the presence of these vulgar facts.

If you think it can stand, by all means take a different view. Upon some points I am sure we are all agreed – such, for instance, as her own conduct and the difficulty of the operation involved in the theory of murder. Strong they are, undoubtedly. If you think I have not made sufficient allowance for phases of life which I have not understood, if you think that anywhere or in any way I have erred on the side of severity, the last thing that would occur to my mind would be to feel any tinge of regret.

But you must do your duty; and if you think that, after all is said and done, the facts are too cogent, and that, when you come to balance the probabilities and the improbabilities, your minds are really in no suspense – then it would be your bounden duty to act upon your convictions, however painful the consequences.

If your state of mind should fall short of that; if either you can concur in the emphatic appeal by the learned counsel for the defence to acquit his client because you believe her innocent, or if you are still unable, after facing the question like men and, after looking at these difficulties from all sides, to make up your minds, and you remain in a state of honest and conscientious doubt, why, then, in that case also, the prisoner would be entitled to her acquittal.

Again the judge paused, his eyes resting on each member of the jury in turn. They sat motionless, unwavering in their concentration.

'Gentlemen,' he said, gravely, 'my task is done. I now dismiss you to yours. Be pleased to retire to perform your task in this difficult and anxious business.'

It was seven minutes to three.

The following extract from the *Daily Telegraph* describes the scene in court as the assembly waited for the jury to return:

> With the want of management which seems to characterise those responsible for the arrangements of the Old Bailey, the windows of both sides were thrown up, producing draughts which presently induced Mr Clarke to petition the judge, who explained that he had given no order for such unnecessary ventilation.
>
> In the draughty court the scene was an extraordinary one. Everybody had risen from their seats, put on their overcoats and hats, and gentlemen with collars up excitedly debating the points of the case. The dock had, for the moment, no attraction for the curious, the prisoner having been allowed to escape from the keen observation to which she had been exposed.
>
> A disgraceful incident had led to her withdrawal. Immediately the jury retired, ladies, and others near to it, crowded and stood up on the little hustings seemingly erected for this especial object, and from this elevated post rudely peered through the glass panes of the dock. One lady held up a gold pair of eye-glasses and watched Mrs Bartlett's every movement. There between two attendants sat that lady, with drooping head, apparently unaware of the staring crowd. A warder spoke to her, and with a half smile upon her face, she composedly retreated below. At five minutes past four there was a sudden hush and a whisper spread that the jury had some questions to ask. The three knocks announcing the judge's approach were given at the door and Mr Justice Wills, reappearing, took his seat...[53]

Here the *Pall Mall Gazette* takes up the story:

> Suddenly the chatter of tongues ceases and every eye is directed towards the passage on the right of the jury-box. 'Here they come!' cry some, and the procession of jurymen files up into their box and

---

53 *Daily Telegraph*, op. cit.

take their seats. The blanched face and fragile figure in black staggers up the steps, almost carried by the two women warders, followed by an officer, and almost falls on her seat. Every head cranes towards the dock, then turns to the jury, until the intense silence is broken by the judge. The prisoner looks down, ghastly pale; her body seems to move to and fro, her lips twitch convulsively – but these agonies were not yet relieved: the jury had not come to give her life or death, but merely to ask a question. [They wanted to know what time the occupants of the house went to bed on the night Mr Bartlett died.]

It was answered. They march solemnly with heads down, and again disappeared. The jury retired and again the Court was a Babel... The prisoner was carried down the steps to undergo afresh the tortures of expectancy.

Slowly, the fingers of the clock went on – the quarter; the half-hour; the three-quarters; five o'clock and the Court was in deep shadow.... Outside the sky is black with clouds and the rain is dripping down. One heard the peculiar roar of the crowd in Newgate Street. Within, the insatiable crowd is growing more impatient.

As the fingers of the clock pointed to five minutes past five some subtle movement at the door told that the jury had done their work.

'Here they come!' was again the cry, which almost grew to a shout. 'Here they come!' It is such a cry as one hears at the finish of the Derby or the Boat Race...

All eyes were once more fixed on the twelve men who ascended to the pew-like seats with eyes down and solemn faces as though they were following a body to the grave. Some tried to read their verdict in their eyes.

The judge took his seat, his flowing red robes about him, the gold chains and the violet costumes of the sheriffs helping to relieve the gloom. Once more the terrible silence was broken by the clicking of the dock handle as it turned to give passage to the prisoner, whose face was now livid, her eyes closed, her lips glued together – and scarcely alive.

Carried to the front of the dock, she stood supported on either side by the faithful women warders. Two spruce doctors and the grave chaplain stood on her left, and behind her again the sturdy policeman.

> The tenseness of the terrible scene was prolonged by the delay in calling over the names of the jury; even the most hardened in criminal cases felt his pulse beat quicker, while many were half-choked with the emotion of the critical moment. The prisoner gasped...[54]

At last the Clerk of the Court asked the question, the answer to which had become of paramount importance to every person in the room – and half of London besides.

> Do you find the prisoner, Adelaide Bartlett, guilty or not guilty?
>
> We have well considered the evidence, and, although we think grave suspicion is attached to the prisoner, we do not think there is sufficient evidence to show how or by whom the chloroform was administered.
>
> Then you say that the prisoner is not guilty, gentlemen?
>
> *Not guilty.*

As the Foreman of the jury uttered these words, Edward Clarke, experienced counsel though he was, leaned forward in a gesture of relief, his arms stretched out across the table and tears streaming down his face.

Even before the words *'not guilty'* were spoken, someone had slipped out of the court and spread the news to the crowds outside. The *Daily Telegraph* described what followed:

> It was amid a scene of the wildest excitement such as the Central Criminal Court has rarely presented, that the verdict of 'not guilty' was returned in the trial of Adelaide Bartlett.
>
> The demonstration of approval took its key-note from the premature burst of cheering in Newgate Street, and it evoked from Mr Justice Wills an emphatic protest, in most indignant tones. There had been premonitory symptoms that popular feeling, which from day to day throughout the week had gradually intensified, would vent itself at the earliest opportunity. During the speech of Mr Edward Clarke for the defence, passages had been applauded, denoting the conclusions at which the spectators had already arrived and the prejudices they had conceived, and this disposition was again manifested when the

---

54 *Pall Mall Gazette*, op. cit.

learned judge addressed the jury.[55]

The majority of those in the court-room were definitely in favour of the verdict:

> The feeling which had been so long pent-up burst out, shocking the judge. Loud cheers, distant hurrahs, waving of pocket handkerchiefs, of hats, of newspapers, the noise of people jumping up and down, made up a hubbub which the shouts of the usher's 'Silence!' were vain to quell.[56]

The judge took a dim view of the uproar.

'This conduct is an outrage,' he declared. 'A Court of Justice is not to be turned into a theatre by such indecent exhibitions.'

Again, in the *Daily Telegraph*:

> But few heeded him and it was difficult to catch the few sentences he afterwards uttered, thanking the jury for their attention and again protesting against the 'insult' he had received. Mrs Bartlett received the verdict calmly. She had stood – the only woman in court with an uncovered head – at the front of the dock, a hectic flush on her usually sallow and colourless cheeks, but during the painful scene she held her head down and merely moved it a little aside when the verdict was delivered. The attendants supported her down the steps, making some believe that she had fainted – but their assistance was not absolutely necessary.[57]

After Mr Justice Wills had formally thanked the jury, he left the court in a bad humour on account of the riotous scenes that had occurred. Many of those present throughout the trial may have felt that, though anxious to appear unbiased, he was in fact of the opinion that Adelaide Bartlett was guilty.

According to Sir John Hall in his introduction to *Trial of Adelaide Bartlett*,[58] when dismissing the jurors, 'whether by accident or design, he omitted to say that he concurred with their verdict.'

---

55 *Daily Telegraph*, op. cit.
56 Ibid.
57 Ibid.
58 *Trial of Adelaide Bartlett*, edited by Sir John Hall. William Hodge & Company, Ltd., 1927.

Extraordinary Scenes

The scene outside the court that evening, however, was jubilant. The reporter from the *Daily Telegraph* was there:

> Meanwhile, the crowd in the street cheered and cheered and enthusiasm had scarcely a limit when Mr Clarke drove out of the grim, grey yard of Newgate. A few minutes later, Mr Justice Wills went off in a cab, unrecognised. The crowd still thronged the street, and spectators loitered in the yard, despite the cold drizzle which was falling, whilst at the windows of the neighbouring warehouses, men and women gathered in the expectation of seeing Mrs Bartlett leave the jail. A hansom cab had been driven up to a small, arched door through which she was supposed to be coming, and the city constables roughly cleared the precincts. Thus diverted, the attention of the onlookers was not directed to the front exit from the sessions house, where Mrs Bartlett emerged twenty minutes after her discharge from the dock, and, entering a cab, drove away unrecognised, notwithstanding the fact that hawkers were selling her photograph to bystanders.[59]

Undoubtedly, Adelaide Bartlett must have realised just how incredibly lucky she had been to escape justice thanks to the efforts of Edward Clarke who had successfully secured her release and ultimately saved her from the gallows.

---

59 *Daily Telegraph*, op. cit.

CHAPTER 21

Verdict of the Press

Adelaide's strongest line of defence during her trial had been Edward Clarke's apparent conviction that she was innocent of murder, combined with the points in her favour emphasised by Mr Justice Wills. For all that, not one witness had come forward to speak for her. Even her friend, Annie Walker, whom Clarke must have considered to be the only sure witness for the defence, had turned out to be, at the last minute, a trump card for the prosecution.

The verdict, therefore, though obliquely worded, came as a personal triumph for Edward Clarke. Some thirty years later, in *The Story of My Life*, he vividly described the stress and anxiety he had endured.

> I do not think anyone who has not been through it himself can realise the mental strain of the last day of a trial for murder upon the counsel for the defence. As he listens to the reply for the Crown and to the judge's summing up, he finds little comfort in the thought that he has done his best, and that the responsibility for the result lies not so much with him as with the judge and the jury. He hears the arguments he has pressed most strongly answered in the reply, perhaps ignored or made light of in the summing up, and he cannot help feeling that there may have been some failure on his part, of clearness or of force, and that an adverse verdict and the inevitable sentence may possibly be the consequence of that failure.

> The week was to me one of very great strain. I made a point of being at my place in court every morning before the judge came in, so that when the fragile, pale little woman came up the prison stairs to take her place in the dock she should see in the crowded court at least one friendly face.

As the days went on, the public excitement grew; and on Saturday morning there were restless crowds in the Old Bailey, and the quiet tones of the judge were sometimes disturbed by the tumult outside.

On the Saturday I sat for five hours listening to Sir Charles Russell and Mr Justice Wills, recognising the strength of the one and the scrupulous fairness of the other, yet quite unable to free my mind from the apprehension that the life of Adelaide Bartlett might be in the greater peril through some defect of mine. Then, when the summing up was over there were two hours of tense anxiety.[60]

When the words *'not guilty'* rang through the court he was quite overwhelmed:

For the first and only time in my fifty years of advocacy the suspense, and emotion as I saw my client go from the dock to freedom broke me down. I found myself sobbing; I dropped my head on the desk before me, and some minutes passed before I regained my self-control. Then came the hour of triumph. When I had unrobed and came down to the courtyard, I found the jury waiting at the foot of the steps to shake hands with me and to congratulate. When the gates were opened to let my brougham out, a cheering crowd came round me and ran beside it, shouting, up the Old Bailey and along Holborn, while the passers-by on foot, or on the omnibuses, took up the cry.

I went to the Lyceum that night to see Henry Irving and Ellen Terry in *Faust*, and I was cheered when I entered the theatre.

The Adelaide Bartlett case was an extremely important mile-stone in Edward Clarke's life and he was the first to admit that it played a vital part in his subsequent career:

The results of a conspicuous success such as this do not show themselves in professional advancement only: my name had become more widely known than ever before, and I felt the assistance of this during all the political activities of this eventful year.

The press, however, was less enthusiastic over the verdict, expressing its scepticism in no uncertain terms. *The Times* was particularly censorious:

---

60 *The Story of My Life*, Sir Edward Clarke, John Murray, 1918.

> We do not much admire the modern practice on the part of juries to append to their verdicts riders which often betray a lack of courage and go far to stultify their conclusions. But such qualifications may be excusable and we can understand the statement on Saturday by the Foreman of the Jury... This is, or ought to be, a verdict of 'not guilty'. How Mr Bartlett met his death the Jury do not know; the Pimlico Mystery, at the end of six days' trial, remains a mystery still. Whether on the theory of guilt or innocence the whole story is marvellous. Three or four very commonplace persons are actors in it, and they weave a plot which in all probability will never be unravelled.[61]

The verdict came as a surprise to many in court; even the jurors had reservations as illustrated in the following letter published in *The Times* on 20 April, 1886:

> Sir, - The expression of the jury preceding the verdict upon which you comment in your leader to-day was in this, as in many cases, the result of compromise. Eleven of our number were in favour of the verdict of "Not guilty," with a rider that "we were of the opinion that, considering the state of health Mr. Bartlett was in, or imagined he was in, and the state of mind the evidence showed him to be in, he administered the chloroform to himself with the view of obtaining sleep or committing suicide," but the twelfth juryman would only consent to the verdict in the form in which it was given, and the majority, rather than subject Mrs. Bartlett to all the agony and expense of a second trial, gave way upon the point.
>
> >Your obedient servant,
> >F. E. Elton, Foreman of the Jury.
>
> The Chesnuts, Garrett Great Green, Lower Tooting, April 19.

A week later, this article appeared in *The Lancet*:

> By the verdict of the Jury at the Central Criminal Court on Saturday last another celebrated case has been, legally speaking, removed from the catalogue of crimes, though left by that verdict in an atmosphere of suspicion. However strong was that suspicion, there was certainly not sufficient evidence to prove beyond all reasonable doubt that a murder had been committed...
>
> If the evidence bearing upon Mr Dyson's position in the home of the

---

61 *The Times*, 19th April, 1886.

Bartletts be accepted as true, there was room for grave suspicion against the two persons originally charged in the indictment, considering the facts which transpired on and after the 28th December...

In the Scotch Courts, the verdict on Saturday would have been 'Not Proven' – certainly a more logical way of recording the finding in the present case... The purchase of chloroform by Mr Dyson at the request of Mrs Bartlett, the certain death of Mr Bartlett by swallowing the drug, and the disappearance of the bottle which contained it, formed a chain of events which required all the forensic talents of Mr Clarke to loosen and unlink to the satisfaction of the Jury.

That the chloroform gained admission to the stomach of Mr Bartlett during his lifetime there can be no shadow of doubt, for there were unequivocal signs of its irritant action upon the mucous membrane...

Mr Clarke, in his able address, asked the Jury to believe how utterly unlikely it was that Mrs Bartlett should select for the carrying out of her alleged purpose a drug which hitherto had not been employed to encompass homicide. The pleading on this point was not devoid of all show of reason, but to adopt it as unanswerable, if followed to its logical conclusion amounts to this: that a jury ought not to convict a prisoner of the crime of murder because there was not precedent as regards the means recorded in the history of forensic medicine.[62]

So the debate continued.

Following suggestions from some doctors that the case should prompt the drawing up of restrictions on the sale of chloroform, *The Globe* commented on 21st April:

> The Medical Press seems disposed to get an anti-chloroform panic, based on the Bartlett case. It actually suggests there may be a 'run' of this particular 'lethal weapon', by means of which, as is clearly suggested, you can kill a person without being found out.

On 24th April, *The Penny Illustrated Paper* stated that Mrs Bartlett had received seventeen offers of marriage at the Old Bailey the previous week, among the suitors being 'an ex-MP, a foreign marquis, a clergyman of the Established Church, and three members of the medical profession.' And *The Globe* added vindictively:

---

62 *The Lancet*, 24th April, 1886.

> How can any young lady of possibly more than average attractions, who desires to have an exceptionally large number of matrimonial proposals made to her, fulfil her ambition? The answer is obvious. By being accused of having poisoned a man, by being acquitted, and by being advertised in the newspapers. It is quite possible that neither Mrs Bartlett nor Madeleine Smith, a quarter of a century ago, had such an ambition, but both discovered the solution to the problem.

But the general feeling and attitude of the public at the time may be summed up in the following passage from *The Life and Famous Cases of Sir Edward Clarke*:[63]

> Despite the popularity of the verdict, contemporary feeling was that Mrs Bartlett was somewhat lucky. This is summed-up in the postscript of a letter to Clarke from Lord Chief Justice Coleridge, in which he congratulated him on the result of the case: 'I hear a good thing attributed to Sir James Paget[64] that Mrs Bartlett was no doubt quite properly acquitted, but that now it is to be hoped *in the interests of science* she will tell us how she did it!'

---

63 *The Life and Famous Cases of Sir Edward Clarke*, Derek Walker-Smith and Edward Clarke. Eyre & Spottiswoode, 1939.
64 *Sir James Paget*: Sergeant-Surgeon to Queen Victoria and Consulting Surgeon at St Bartholomew's Hospital.

Part Four

'... the presence of the chloroform in my drawer troubled my mind. And I was also troubled by some scruples as to whether putting my plan into practice would have been right.'
Adelaide Bartlett's statement to Dr Leach

CHAPTER 22

The Poisoner's Craft

As *The Times* had predicted, Edwin Bartlett's death has remained a mystery, for Adelaide never did, so far as we know, tell anyone how she did it – if indeed she did. It is therefore left to those of us who believe her guilty to fathom how she managed to pour liquid chloroform down her husband's throat that night without causing him to protest loudly enough to alert the rest of the household. One thing is certain: however she did it, she was the first person to be accused of using chloroform as an instrument of murder.

Of equal importance to the criminologist is her pattern of behaviour prior to Edwin's death. In retrospect, her actions are open to quite conflicting interpretations – from one viewpoint the classic poisoner at work, but from another the loving if over-solicitous wife. For instance, she took sole charge of nursing her husband twenty-four hours a day, refusing to employ anyone to assist her, and she restricted all visits to the sick-room, especially from close relatives. She never left Edwin alone with visitors and even answered questions on his behalf, appearing over-protective and showing excessive anxiety over his illness. Were these actions engendered by caution, or by concern?

Dr Leach turned out to be both inexperienced and gullible. Was he carefully chosen, or picked at random? That the chloroform was acquired by lies and subterfuge is undeniable. Was it delicacy and modesty that guided her tongue, or did her deceitful words hide a darker intent?

More incriminating, perhaps, was her invention of a terminal illness – for what reason but to prepare the ground for Edwin's sudden death? On the other hand, how much reliance can be placed on the evidence of George Dyson in this respect? When we come to Edwin's mental instability and depression we have the support of more than one witness; but was it Adelaide who made known and even encouraged his phobias as a foundation for possible suicide? Did she cultivate the trust of both doctor and patient to facilitate a sinister purpose?

What cannot be disputed is that she was intimately involved with a young man who would soon be free to marry, and that in the event of her husband's death she stood to gain not only her freedom, but his entire fortune.

Despite all his efforts, Edward Clarke was unable to convince the jury that they were dealing with a case of suicide. Had he succeeded, Adelaide would not only have escaped the hangman's noose, but would have managed to have her victim posthumously blamed for his own death.

The question remains: if Adelaide murdered her husband, how was this extraordinary crime committed in the early hours of 1st January, 1886?

During the trial, Sir Charles Russell,[65] though unable to obtain a verdict of guilty, appears to have solved the mystery of Edwin Bartlett's death, for in his closing speech he put forward the most plausible theory as to how the murder was committed; naturally, since he raised it so late in the proceedings, there was an immediate objection from the defence. His theory, as we have seen, was this:

If the draught had been handed to him in a glass, and given to him as if for an ordinary purpose, with drops of chloroform in it, and water or some other thing, to drink then it was conceivable that the dying man would have gulped it down, believing in its innocence, and not suspecting that the prisoner had administered something which was wrong and injurious.

---

65 Russell also failed in his *defence* of Florence Maybrick in 1889, though convinced of her innocence. She was charged with poisoning her husband with arsenic and served a fifteen year prison sentence.

Sir John Hall, writing on the case in 1927 in the *Notable British Trials* series, seemed to agree with this hypothesis for in his introduction he wrote:

> It is interesting to wonder whether the trial might have had another termination had the Crown proceeded on the supposition that Mr Bartlett allowed himself to be 'chloroformed'. The general circumstances are by no means inconsistent with that possibility.

Indeed, the circumstances within the strange relationship that existed between Adelaide Bartlett and her husband were entirely consistent with that possibility.

But why on earth would Edwin willingly swallow a glass of brandy laced with liquid chloroform?

To find the answer we must first consider his state of mind at the time, which was well-documented despite Adelaide's attempts to restrict visits. His symptoms seem to point to a nervous collapse, a recurrence, perhaps, of his previous breakdown in 1881, when his doctor had recommended a fortnight's convalescence. He had returned, apparently, 'wholly restored', yet four years later he was cracking up again, suffering from, amongst other things, lassitude, weakness, hysteria and a desperate need for sleep. Had these symptoms been solely the result of his hypochondria, as Adelaide herself suggested, they would surely have been chronic, not sudden. Yet his friends confirmed that he was generally in excellent health and had a strong constitution. So what had triggered the weakness, insomnia and dreadful state of his teeth and gums? And what had caused his disturbing psychological symptoms to emerge – a sudden, irrational fear of leaving the house, for instance?

In her book *Poison and Adelaide Bartlett*, Yseult Bridges would have us believe that Edwin was confined to his room by an hypnotic force exerted on him by George Dyson, using Adelaide as his medium. She even interprets Edwin's eagerness to get back upstairs after his enforced outing with Dr Leach on 28th December as further evidence of this strange magnetic pull.

This seems a rather fanciful explanation but one that would have sufficed perfectly well in 1886; mesmerism and animal magnetism were much favoured by certain quasi-medical men of the day and were believed to be the cause of a plethora of bizarre phenomena. Subjects such as these, along with spiritualism, homeopathy, hydropathy and phrenology, were very much in vogue as topics of stimulating conversation over the tea cups in middle class Victorian drawing-rooms, and no doubt Adelaide, Edwin and George Dyson discussed them frequently and at length. Although mesmerism sounds infinitely more exciting and mysterious, it seems far more likely that Edwin was suffering from – amongst other things – nervous exhaustion, and had succumbed to a temporary lapse into agoraphobic behaviour, due to the debilitating effects of his illness; he was displaying all the distressing and inexplicable fears that seem so bizarre to non-sufferers, fears that were aggravated by the deluded and fragile state of his mind, not by mesmeric forces outside himself. He *was* afraid of leaving the house and, as he tried to explain, he felt that he would die if he went outside without Adelaide to support him; not, however, because he was being hypnotised but because of fears within himself and his own feelings of inadequacy, cruelly fostered by Adelaide masquerading as his devoted and dedicated nurse.

Mr Justice Wills seems to have suspected that Edwin's death may have been caused by an accidental overdose of chloroform used as a sleeping draught. He told the court in his summing up that he himself had suffered a twelve-month period of insomnia and knew only too well the 'uncommon strength of mind, will, and resolution' it took to resist resorting to narcotics to secure sleep.

At the time of his death Edwin was not only weakened by his illness and riddled with deep-seated fears, manifest in his feeling that he was crawling with worms, but his insomnia was, literally, driving him mad. Thus it may have been that on the last day of the year Adelaide promised him a safe, euphoric passage into the blessed oblivion of sleep, and to his jaded mind this must have seemed an exquisite prospect after so many sleepless nights.

He had already lost his fear of anaesthetics: earlier that evening, after his visit to the dentist, he had talked enthusiastically about the gas he had been given, and for her part, Adelaide had urged Mrs Doggett to confirm that chloroform was nothing to be afraid of – 'Is it not pleasant?' she asked in front of Edwin, perhaps anxious to reassure him. This, however, was quite unnecessary, for Edwin's trust in her was unshakeable; he had every confidence that she would give him just enough chloroform to allow him to drift safely into sleep. During his illness Edwin had said as much to George Dyson, during a conversation in the flat at Claverton Street. 'Oh, yes, you may trust her,' he had said, 'if you had twelve years' experience of her as I have, you would know you could trust her.'

Whilst not taking Adelaide's fanciful tale of their platonic marriage as sacrosanct, the lack of sexual harmony in the marriage may well have been a source of frustration to Edwin and could have been partly responsible for his nervous condition. Yet, shortly before his death, Adelaide had hinted that things might be different in future. That same day, for instance, on their way to the dentist, she had encouraged him in this belief, flirting with him and building up his hopes.

She may even have suggested that the use of chloroform might not only cure his insomnia but also dramatically enhance their sex life. In 1984, a research chemist, David Harvey, was convicted of the manslaughter of his mistress, Mrs Betty Amor, by chloroform. The couple had been used to inhaling the drug, sprinkled on a piece of cloth, to improve their sexual performance. According to Harvey, on the night of the tragedy they had fallen asleep after a session of lovemaking, and when he awoke Mrs Amor was dead, with the cloth lying across her face.

It is possible that Adelaide, bearing in mind her cloistered, religious upbringing, may have had an aversion to sex and in the earlier days of her marriage done her best to avoid it – at least where Edwin was concerned. Moreover, whenever she was unable to repel his advances she had insisted on 'some preventive being used', so great was her fear of another pregnancy.

And was it perhaps *Adelaide*, not Edwin, who held unorthodox views on marriage, suggesting that a man should have two wives, one for use and one for companionship? Dr Leach testified that this idea '*came from her*' and both Mr Bartlett senior, and Edward Baxter insisted that Edwin never had 'ideas about anything different to other people.'

If this is the truth of the matter, Adelaide's coldness may well have caused friction in the marriage. If Edwin did his best to establish a normal relationship after the birth of the stillborn child, he failed dismally. It could be that at times Adelaide made him feel so repulsive that he began to wonder if he really *was* diseased, especially when the mysterious worm appeared and he fancied he felt them crawling like snakes inside him.

Dr Leach said in evidence that Edwin's hypochondria may have led him to believe that he was suffering from syphilis – a condition he called syphiliphobia – and that in consequence he had been dosing himself with mercury for some time. Necrosis of the bone, which was present in Edwin's jaw, may be caused by syphilis or mercury, but as Edwin did *not* have the disease this might indicate that his use of mercury was confined to that one sample blue pill which he found in his drawer at work and swallowed as a tonic.

Yet nothing he did seemed to please her. Overcoming his morbid fear of dentists, he had all his rotten teeth out to solve the problem of his foetid breath. Still that was not enough. Yet on the surface, all seemed well. Everyone who knew them testified that they appeared to live together normally as man and wife, although Mr Justice Wills, in his wisdom, pointed out during the trial that 'the real relations between a man and his wife can only be guessed at.'

Although they had always shared a bed prior to their move to the flat in Claverton Street, from the onset of Edwin's illness they had slept separately – as many couples do in these circumstances. Did Adelaide, one cannot help wondering, initiate the first bout of sickness early in October, as a temporary respite from Edwin's restlessness and bad breath – or was it a trial run for murder?

Did she, in fact, start feeding him small doses of lead acetate, which Victorian ladies used to mix with opium, warm water and vinegar to make astringent and sedative lotions? Was this the reason for the mysterious blue line around Edwin's gums? Dr Stevenson, in evidence at the trial, clearly confirmed that Edwin had been, initially, a victim of lead, not mercurial poisoning, as diagnosed by Dr Leach.

Furthermore, Dr Green, in his evidence, was of the opinion that some of the damage to the tissues of the lining of Edwin's stomach, as revealed at the post-mortem, was 'characteristic of *an irritant poison antecedent* in causation to that caused by the chloroform, and not to disease.'

Despite the use of relatively unsophisticated methods of analysis, discernible traces of lead were found in Edwin's body, indicating that there was an unusual amount of lead present. Did Adelaide, therefore, having made up her mind to kill him, and knowing that traces of lead would be found if a post-mortem was subsequently made, suggest to her husband, his doctor, family and friends, that his mysterious illness might have been caused by handling lead-lined tea-chests at work?

But what made her progress from administering small, debilitating doses of lead to killing Edwin outright with a lethal dose of chloroform? Perhaps, during his illness, she had so enjoyed freedom from his advances that the very thought of his recovery was repellent – or was her involvement with George Dyson the reason? Was she, at that time, passionately in love with the preacher or just enjoying the excitement of an affair? Did she really consider marrying *Georgius Rex,* and if so, did the idea of marriage to him provide sufficient incentive to kill her husband? Whatever her feelings for him at the time of the murder, these changed dramatically in the face of Dyson's infuriating moral qualms after Edwin's death. From that time there was nothing in her behaviour to suggest that she ever wished to see George Dyson again.

Alternatively, did young Frederick Bartlett feature in Adelaide's plans? We know that he returned to England on 5th January, 1886, but whether for Adelaide or for the manager's job Edwin had offered him, we cannot know.

And yet we have Dr Leach's testimony that, after Edwin's death,

Adelaide went to see him on 14th January; during their conversation they discussed sexual matters at some length, without reference to her marriage to Edwin, which leads one to believe that re-entry into a convent did not feature in her future plans.

What were her reasons for killing Edwin? Was it illicit love, a violent aversion to sex with him or, simply that his dull lifestyle and pernickety ways had driven her to desperate measures? Whatever her reason, she must have callously planned and executed his murder whilst posing as his loyal and devoted wife. Clearly, she was not in love with Edwin and never had been, but the fact that she chose a method of killing him that was, if any instrument of death may be so named, humane, would lead us to believe that she did not harbour any great hatred for him either.

She chose, after all, not the knife thrust, the hammer blow or the bullet, but liquid chloroform, knowing that once swallowed, it would produce intoxication and a relatively easy drift into unconsciousness, paralysis and death.

But why did Adelaide decide to kill her husband on that particular night? On a purely mercenary level, she must have known that Edwin was going to start giving his father an allowance the following day, 1st January, and Adelaide would have relished the chance to get the better of the old man. Furthermore, as Dr Leach was determined to send Edwin away to convalesce on his own within the next few days, she had little time left in which to carry out her plan. Edwin's health was steadily improving, and if his death was to appear as suicide it had to happen soon, while his health, especially his state of mind, was uncertain, not when he was fully recovered.

These factors, and the conveniently noisy party going on downstairs that evening, may well have determined that it was time for Edwin Bartlett to die.

Let us now imagine the scene in the first floor flat at Claverton Street that night. The old year was on its way out and the New Year, 1886, was about to begin. Having drawn the heavy winter curtains against the cold night air, the Bartletts were warm and cosy, completely cocooned from the outside world. From the street below came the echo of horses' hooves clattering against the cobbles and the low rumble of cab wheels as they ferried late revellers to their midnight celebrations. The gas jets hissed gently as Adelaide and Edwin sat by the fire, the heat from the flames making them pleasantly drowsy. The remains of supper were still on the table; they had eaten well, treating themselves to a few little luxuries – slices of rich fruit cake, a bowl of choice nuts and a bottle of best brandy. Excited bursts of laughter rose from the room below, somehow emphasising their isolation. But the Bartletts were quite content to sit alone, for Edwin, at least, was at last feeling much happier. His health was improving daily – he was even talking about going back to work after his trip to Torquay. One way and another, he was beginning to feel more optimistic about the future, and the only thing that prevented him from making a complete recovery was his chronic insomnia: if only he could get some sleep and renew his former strength and vitality. Dr Leach had prescribed bromide, morphia and other sleeping draughts but without success – sleep still eluded him and he had become desperate. There were two opium pills, also prescribed by the doctor, locked away in the small cupboard by the fireplace, but Adelaide had decided not to use them. She had read all about chloroform in her medical book - one to five minims to be taken as a sedative in a teaspoonful of brandy – and had suggested they try that instead.

    Edwin needed little persuasion to change into his nightshirt and climb into bed to await his wife's ministrations. He lay back contentedly and watched as Adelaide sprinkled a few drops of liquid from a fluted glass bottle onto her handkerchief. A slight movement of her wrist and the lace square brushed against Edwin's cheek. Within seconds he became drowsy; the warmth of the room, the effects of the brandy, the lingering smell of supper, Adelaide's gentle mood, all these things combined to make him feel relaxed and happy – positively euphoric, in fact.

    And was it then, as the clock on the mantelshelf began to strike twelve, that Adelaide suggested they drink a toast to the New Year? Did she then hand him the glass of chloroformed brandy to toast their future happiness? And was there a loving smile on her pretty face as she watched him swallow it gladly, settle back on his pillow and drift into sleep – and death?

Had Edwin cried out as the chloroform reached the back of his throat and into his stomach, the sounds of celebration from the party below would have drowned his cries, although both Dr Stevenson and Dr Tidy testified that the pain of swallowing chloroform was *not* excruciating, as one might expect, describing it, in fact, as having a 'hot, fiery taste.'

Did Adelaide then sit and watch her husband die, or did she, knowing that death would soon follow once the stertorous breathing had begun, go into the back room and there wash the sickly smell of chloroform from her hands, change her dress and tidy her hair? Then, returning to the front room, did she check that her husband was dead, close his eyes, and proceed to pour brandy into his mouth and over his chest to mask the pungent smell of chloroform and vomit – at the same time making a mental note to get the bedclothes washed first thing in the morning?[66]

And finally, did she go into the back room once more, open the window and pour the remaining chloroform into the yard below? It would have evaporated almost immediately, leaving no trace. This done, she could have rinsed out the empty bottle and hidden it amongst the clothes in one of her drawers.

It seems likely that Adelaide spent the early hours of the New Year sitting by the fire near her husband's body, waiting for a suitable time to waken the household. This gave her the chance to decide upon the story she would tell once the alarm had been raised and the body found. Sitting there for four hours with her mind, no doubt, on many things, she kept the fire going to warm her, and at four o'clock it was still banked up and burning brightly.

66 Vomiting is a symptom of chloroform poisoning. Annie Best, the charlady's maid, who washed Edwin's bed linen the morning after he died, said in evidence in the magistrate's court that there was a 'gummy froth' on the pillowcase. This was probably vomit.

It was done. Edwin was dead. She was free. For the first time in her thirty years she would be able to control her own life – no nuns, no paternal agents, no husband, no meddling father-in-law, and, if all went according to plan, Edwin's money at her disposal as well.

CHAPTER 23

The Marriage Trap

To fully understand what led Adelaide Bartlett to commit murder it is essential to look more closely at the development of her character during the ten years she was married to Edwin. Not long after the marriage she became acquainted with the ideas of Dr Nichols and his wife, and her attitude to life underwent a fundamental change. Gone were the characteristics of a convent-educated girl – obedient, passive, content to play an unquestioning and subordinate role. The more she aligned herself with feminist philosophy the more dissatisfied she became with the life Edwin had to offer. She may also have found that she objected to the sexual obligations of marriage, especially with Edwin, for it must be remembered that she had not *chosen* to marry him.

Involved as she was with the Nichols' doctrine, it was only natural that Adelaide, caught in what she no doubt saw as a marriage trap, should confide in Mary Nichols, for had not she, too, suffered the misery of a loveless marriage? It was most probably after consulting her that Adelaide decided motherhood might provide the solution to her problem, for there is a passage in *Esoteric Anthropology* which states:

> It is only for the continuation of the species that indulgence in sexual passion is permissible; the moment the indulgence is supposed to have resulted in a natural and legitimate consequence, from that moment the wife is sacred from the husband until the time of the nursing of the child has expired.

Knowing that Edwin had great respect for learning, she may have gambled on the fact that he would accept medical opinion, no matter how unorthodox, and leave her unmolested throughout the period of pregnancy and nursing. It seems likely that she followed Mary Nichols's advice and became pregnant, only to see her plan misfire, for the child was stillborn. She suffered badly in childbirth and was left with nothing, not even a sexual reprieve to compensate for all the pain and sadness caused by her bereavement. Thus thwarted, she would have been obliged to steel herself against her aversion to sex with Edwin during the years that followed. We cannot know Edwin's feelings in the matter, but it would have been only natural for him to want a normal marriage and the prospect of sons to inherit the family business he had worked so hard to build.

Adelaide, however, became even more wedded to the feminist philosophy; her ideas would have been lost on Edwin, for he was a much simpler character than his wife, although at the same time he wanted a wife who was accomplished and well-read. He was proud of Adelaide in this respect and other people's admiration of her erudition gave him pleasure, even though her studies had encompassed a way of thinking that left him hopelessly confused.

Perhaps, as Adelaide probably told him many times, he could have done with two wives – one for companionship, the role she chose to play, and one for use, the role to which she strongly objected. No doubt Edwin did his best to divert her need for feminist literature, perhaps discussing the problems with his friend George Matthews. It is possible that Adelaide lent him her copy of *Esoteric Anthropology* in order to convince him that, despite Edwin's misgivings, the book was quite harmless.

George Matthews said in evidence that 'she was always talking about Dr Nichols and his theories' although they did not appeal to him personally. Nor did he have a chance to become converted to the cause, for Alice Matthews returned the book unread, regarding its presence in her house as insulting. The fact that Adelaide had shown the book to a gentleman friend was indelicate and, to some, a sure indication that she lacked the modesty of her middle class contemporaries.

Alice Matthews's reaction to finding *Esoteric Anthropology* in her house was immediate, direct and typified the attitude of most men and women in 1885, an attitude that was shared by Mr Justice Wills and others who were present at the trial.

Adelaide's adherence to the Nichols' cult had changed her entire thinking and it might well be that, had she been introduced to the feminist doctrine earlier in her life, she would not have married at all. Keen to broaden her horizons and embrace new ideas, she found herself rejecting the usual subservient role given to women at that time. Yet hers was a complex psyche for she also loved to use her charm and feminine guile to full advantage – as she did so successfully with both George Dyson and Dr Leach: she seemed to enjoy exploiting both sides of her nature, fully aware of her charm yet eager to indulge in profound conversations with men whom she considered to be her intellectual equals.

Today she would have been able to capitalise on both aspects of her personality, as many women do with great success; but in 1875, when she married Edwin Bartlett, no such choice was open to here. She had no alternative but to be kept by her husband, and as little more than a chattel she was expected to be content with a dependent and subordinate role.

It could be that, determined to wean her from what he considered to be the ungodly influence of the new wave of liberal thinkers, Edwin cultivated the acquaintance of the Reverend George Dyson expressly for that purpose, encouraging him to visit Adelaide as often as he could, inviting him into his home as a 'friend and spiritual adviser.'[67]

George Dyson was, to Edwin's mind at least, well-educated, and as a man of religion likely to hold traditional views regarding a wife's duty to her husband – a duty which included the bearing of a clutch of healthy children. Early in their acquaintance, Edwin had asked Dyson whether the Bible 'permitted polygamy', only to be told that the Church would never condone such an arrangement.

---

67 From the *Llanelli and County Guardian*, 25th February, 1886.

Much relieved, Edwin must have hoped that under the minister's guidance Adelaide would reject such outrageous ideas and return to the innocent compliance she had displayed when they were first married – studious, grateful and devout, allowing him to guide her in everything. In desperation, he looked to George Dyson to reverse the contamination of Adelaide's mind, writing him letters that expressed his trust and hope that he could bring her to her senses.

For that reason, while they were in Dover, he left them alone as much as possible, and when he went to see Dyson at his lodgings he begged him to continue with his mission, saying that 'his sermons had affected his wife in a way no other preacher's had done and that she was a better and nobler woman since he had been there.'[68] He showed him one of Adelaide's earlier 'highly devotional' letters, written from the convent in Belgium, saying that he hoped Dyson could *'bring her back into the same line of thought and devotion.*[69]

During his questioning at the Old Bailey the preacher said that the letter he had sent to Adelaide while she was in Dover, which had caused her to 'overflow with joy' when she read it, was a letter of 'that character' – in other words, a pastoral epistle, heavy not with verbal passion but with noble thoughts! No wonder Edwin was so delighted with Adelaide's reaction to these evangelical overtures. There is nothing unnatural about his expressions of gratitude and brotherly love when one realises that his plans for his wife and the preacher were not carnal at all, but spiritual.

George Dyson, too, was most probably a little shocked by Adelaide's progressive views, although his disapproval was soon diluted and eventually drowned by the charm she turned on him. And from that moment, Edwin's enlistment of the young minister began to go sadly wrong, for he had overlooked one fundamental fact – that the austere Wesleyan frock concealed a man, albeit a morally weak one. Consequently, instead of coaxing Adelaide back into the safe fold of submissive thought, the poor man was drawn into a scandalous affair, became involved in the murder of one of his closest friends

---

68 From the *Llanelli and County Guardian*, op. cit.
69 Ibid.

and was left with his clerical career in ruins.

Adelaide, it seems, was a difficult woman for a young man to handle. She was a tease, a coquette, preferring the dropped handkerchief to the athletics of the bedroom, and apparently content to sit at George Dyson's feet, either gazing at him with her large brown eyes or coyly resting her head on his knee. This coquettish side of her nature, coupled with her strident intelligence, created a dichotomy in her character which she used to great effect when she set out to charm *Georgius Rex*. But it may be that by December of that year she and Dyson had become lovers, so that the thought of Edwin's recovery and renewed sexual advances became even more repugnant to her. Perhaps, like many women, she was unable to cope with more than one emotional involvement at a time and that one, she may have decided, would be with George Dyson, not Edwin. Having made her decision, any sexual activity with her husband would have seemed, quite simply, adulterous, and it was *she*, not Edwin, who considered herself to be 'promised to Dyson.'

Adelaide appears to have made a habit of twisting the truth to suit her own desires; she chose, therefore, to ignore the real reason why Edwin encouraged Dyson to frequent the house and give her instruction. She preferred to believe that Edwin wanted them to come together in a romantic sense because that was what she herself wanted, and by believing this she was able to justify her adulterous affair and physical rejection of her husband.

There are other aspects of Adelaide's character that might assist a better understanding of her strange story. Her insistence that she was a Roman Catholic seems, at first, to have little bearing on the case, but in fact it is extremely important. She declared herself a Catholic despite the fact that she had, at her own request, spent a year at a Protestant convent after her marriage, attended a Wesleyan Chapel and been tutored by a Wesleyan preacher. It was only by doing so that she could justifiably deny any use of the contraceptives found in the flat at Claverton Street. If she was suspected of having recourse to such devices her story about a platonic marriage would be instantly invalidated and her avowed reason for needing the chloroform – to suppress her husband's sexual demands – would become very suspect indeed.

Perhaps Adelaide fervently wished that her ten-year marriage to Edwin had been platonic – maybe she had even convinced herself that it was – but Annie Walker shattered the illusion once and for all with her final damning statement.

Is there anything that emerges from the shadowy uncertainty of truth and fiction to enable us to suggest a rather different interpretation? It may be that Edwin was unconventional in contemporary terms, that he disliked children and, with no wish to have a family, always insisted on using condoms. Perhaps, on that Sunday afternoon, fresh from his holiday in Scotland, he was so relaxed and so pleased to be with Adelaide again that she was able to persuade him to make love to her without taking any precautions, *just that once.* The result of this union being disappointment and pain, the couple might both have agreed not to risk having more children. Was it at this point that Adelaide lost interest in the sexual side of marriage? Edwin certainly seems to have been more interested in his business and in his dogs than he was in family life.

In a letter to the *Daily News,* published in the *Westminster Times* on 24th April, 1886, the ever voluble Dr Leach felt moved to express his feelings about the case and about Edwin:

> I may state that there are undisclosed facts in this case too strange for belief by any but eye-witnesses, and though all within my knowledge are distinctly evidence in favour of Mrs Bartlett, her legal advisers evidently considered them too strong a food for the digestion of a British judge and his jury. In one respect experience has justified their opinion. This much I feel it a duty to state in vindication of my patient's widow. In conclusion, one word concerning the dead man. Much has been written in the papers and much said from the Bench tending to present the late Edwin Bartlett in a very odious light. I knew him only during the last 21 days of his life; I must state that he was not so black as he has been painted. He was a man of the most extraordinary ways and ideas, and since his death we have all learnt that his ideas were stranger than even I knew them to be. He was shy and reticent, especially before strangers, but once he believed in anybody his belief became an implicit faith, and, to use a metaphor,

> his whole heart seemed to go out to them, and his gratitude for trifles was unbounded. There was, too, something peculiarly 'taking' in him, and, although a self—made man, he was retiring, diffident, and in no sense unmannerly. I confess that, with all his oddity, I took more than an ordinary interest in the welfare of my late patient.

One cannot help but feel that, had the Pimlico murder happened a hundred years later, Dr Leach would have been unable to resist selling his story to the popular press.

For all his 'more than ordinary interest', even the good doctor was in no position to speak with authority about the couple's sexual relations, and it is always possible that Edwin, faced with his wife's coldness, may have been far less of a gentleman than he appeared in the eyes of his colleagues, friends, and, indeed, his doctor. He was described by Dr Green as powerful and well-developed, and in the privacy of the bedroom who can know what he was really like prior to the illness that he had reduced him to a jelly of a man before he died? His family, after all, were far from mild-natured – his father was decidedly aggressive and Frederick, by all accounts, had the makings of an arrogant scoundrel. It is possible, therefore, that the last view we have of Edwin Bartlett – weak, dependent, ineffectual – may not have been the true picture of the man.

Yet knowing a little of Adelaide's nature, one is tempted to believe that, had he behaved in a brutal manner towards her, she would have wasted no time in exposing him after his death. The image of herself as a misused maiden would have been guaranteed, after all, to send both Dr Leach and George Dyson into a frenzy of chivalrous indignation and would undoubtedly have ensured the profound sympathy of the all-male jury at her trial.

But she was far too clever for that, too cunning to provide her detractors with a possible motive for killing her husband. She knew only too well that if she denounced him as a brute the whole mystery of his sudden death would dissolve, exposing it as a very ordinary case of murder, even though the method used was both original and ingenious. It can be safely assumed, therefore, that if Edwin misused his wife during their ten years together, her silence was quite deliberate and carefully calculated.

Instead, Adelaide cleverly compounded the mystery by spinning a tangled web of bizarre half-truths –a platonic marriage, a terminal illness from which Edwin would die within a year, the premature engagement to George Dyson – around a case that was in fact very simple. Though prepared to tolerate a loveless marriage, she could no longer accommodate her husband's sexual demands. As she saw it, her only escape was to kill.

It seems incredible now, for modern wives need never resort to such drastic methods of refusal; the divorce courts are kept busy, year in and year out, freeing women from marriages which, a century ago, might well have driven them to murder.

CHAPTER 24

Loose Ends

Edward Clarke, in his speech for the defence at Adelaide's trial, said of the Reverend George Dyson:

> I think Mr Dyson will never in his life read the account of a trial for murder without thinking how heavily his own rash, unjustified conduct would have told against him if he had been put upon his trial.

Certainly, George Dyson had been extremely lucky to escape the consequences of his foolish behaviour, although his involvement in the Pimlico affair did have a drastic effect upon his career in the ministry. Having lost all credibility and respect by his conduct, his future in the Methodist church was ended even before the case came to trial. A statement in *The Globe,* on 19th April 1886, underlines his ruin: 'The Reverend George Dyson has sent his resignation to the Wesleyan body. He intends going abroad for a few months and will, in all probability, study for the law after taking his MA Degree in Dublin.'

However, despite Dyson's histrionics in the Matthews' drawing-room and in the court at the Old Bailey, his humiliation may not have been as devastating as he led people to believe. This letter appeared in *The Globe* on 27th April from a lady in Pontypridd:

> The Rev. George Dyson is now staying at Llanelly where his sisters reside. He has abandoned the ministerial costume but his identity has not been lost. On Sunday he attended two of the churches in the town and attracted considerable attention. He appears to have recovered from the effects of his recent incarceration and does not shun the notice of the people among whom he once lived.

George Dyson's father, Rev. John B Dyson, had been a well-known and much respected member of the Llanelly community before his move to Poole, in Dorset. Not surprisingly, therefore, the local newspaper, the *Llanelli and County Guardian*, had taken up the story of Dyson's arrest on 18th February and this article, published on 25th February, gives a further insight into the young preacher's character:

> Mr Dyson was for several years resident at Llanelly, his father, the Reverend George Dyson [sic] having charge of the Wesleyan Church in Hall Street and occupying a house in New Road. The young man made many friends in this place. Studiously inclined, he was reserved in manner and his private life was exemplary in every respect. He was, for a considerable period, engaged in the South Wales Works, where he was apprenticed as a pattern maker. Sympathy is generally expressed with Mr Dyson, who is now so critically situated, and it is sincerely hoped that he will be able to exonerate himself entirely from participation in what would appear to be a wilful murder. I remember young Dyson well, a most estimable and pleasant gentleman.

The Wesleyan Archives have no record of George Dyson after June 1885, when he obtained his MA Degree at Trinity College, Dublin. However, a booklet on the history of Putney Methodist Church states that after his resignation George Dyson emigrated to Australia.

According to recent researches into Wesleyan history by John A Vickers, however, George Dyson settled in America after the trial at the Old Bailey. He changed his name to John Bernard Walker, married and had a child, George, and in 1898 acquired American citizenship. He became a prolific and respected journalist writing on engineering and technical aspects of the military, specialising in naval history. In 1912 he published *An Unsinkable Titanic*, the first in-depth scientific study of the construction techniques used in the building of the *Titanic*. Today it is one of the rarest and most sought after books on the subject. He wrote a number of other books and became contributing editor of Scientific American, and died in 1928.

As for the intrepid Dr Leach, he died on 14 September 1892, aged thirty-five. In addition to his obituary in the *British Medical Journal* the following announcement appeared in the magazine, *Tit-bits*:

> The Death of Dr Leach
> Fatal Medical Daring
>
> Dr Leach, who figured in the Bartlett case, known as the Pimlico Mystery, has fallen a victim to his own daring in his medical duties. He died through inhaling sewer gas while investigating the causes of a patient's diphtheria. It was considered surprising that he did not kill himself in his Bartlett case experiments, when he actually took chloroform to see if it occasioned the symptoms noticeable in the dead man.

There is nothing one can add about the unfortunate Dr Leach, except to say that he left a wife and two children and had seemed, by his very nature, destined to die young.

Although George Dyson may have enjoyed a successful career in America and the wretched Leach paid dearly for his folly, what of the *femme fatale* of the piece? After the strain of her imprisonment, trial and fortunate acquittal, Adelaide stayed for a while with her solicitor, Mr Wood, and his sister at 66 Gresham Street in the City of London. From there she wrote this letter of thanks to her defence counsel, Edward Clarke.[70] It was dated 24th April, 1886:

> Dear Sir
>
> Forgive me for not earlier expressing my heartfelt gratitude to you, I feel that I owe my life to your earnest efforts, and, though I cannot put into words the feelings that fill my heart, you will understand all that my pen fails to express to you. Your kind looks towards me, cheered me very much, for I felt that you believed me innocent. I have heard many eloquent Jesuits preach but I never listened to anything finer than your speach [sic.] My story was a very painful one, but sadly true, my consent to my marriage was not asked, and I only saw my husband once before my wedding day.... I am much gratified that Dr Stevenson has written to say that he concurs in the verdict, he wrote so kindly of Miss Wood, who has been a true friend. I received

---

70 This abridged version of the letter was published in Sir John Hall's *Trial of Adelaide Bartlett*, Notable British Trials series, William Hodge & Company, Ltd. 1927.

great kindness at Clerkenwell, from the Governor to the lowest, they did their best to comfort me.

Assuring you that I shall ever remember you with feelings of deepest gratitude,

I am,
Sincerely yours,
Adelaide Bartlett

Undoubtedly Adelaide *was* treated inordinately well during her detention, at a time when incarceration in a city gaol was, for most people, a far from pleasant experience. This could point to some intervention from her father who, it must be said, though not prepared to acknowledge her, did his utmost to protect her by providing the money to retain Edward Clarke for her defence.

Nor was it just a question of money. Her father must have been a man of considerable influence, a man for whom Edward Clarke, though renowned for his conscientious endeavours on behalf of his clients, was prepared to postpone some cases and return several lucrative briefs in order to defend his client's illegitimate daughter.

Yet Adelaide herself was of little social importance: she was merely a grocer's wife and, moreover, one whose standard of morality had been publicly questioned. It is a measure of his professionalism and skill, therefore, that Edward Clarke, a staunch Anglican, renowned for his unerring code of Christian behaviour, should have set aside his feelings sufficiently to concern himself, on a personal level, with a lady involved in a bizarre affair with a minister of religion and who indulged a reading preference that many considered scandalous.

Certainly, the fact that her natural father was in the position to enlist the services of Clarke had been crucial and without it the outcome of the trial might well have been a sentence of death.

It may be surmised, therefore, that there are certain aspects of Adelaide Bartlett's life which show clearly the benefit of privileged, though covert, connections. Anyone attempting to speculate on Adelaide's origin must first consider the time of her conception. She must have been conceived in the spring of 1855 which coincided with Napoleon III's State visit to Windsor. Clara and her husband, the Comte d'Escury, parents to young Henry, were living in London at the time but returned to France for the birth of Adelaide in December, 1855.

Thirty years later, at the time of Adelaide's trial, it was rumoured that her father had been a member of Queen Victoria's entourage and many aspects of the mystery point to that conclusion. Devotees of the case will surely continue to speculate on his identity, for it provides a puzzle that has a peculiarly Victorian flavour. After all, what kind of man would have been so bold, or so reckless, as to dally with young Clara under the aristocratic nose of her husband, the Comte de Thouras, formerly a man of arms who bore one of the most illustrious names in France?

What *was* the truth of the matter?

Who did young Clara fall for in the spring of 1855? Was it a romantic seduction or a sordid affair, or something between the two?

Thousands of Londoners who followed Adelaide's dramatic story in 1886, and thousands since, have been intrigued by it yet no one knows the answer, nor has any previous writer attempted to solve the mystery and suggest a possible name.

Being the soul of discretion, Edward Clarke kept his silence and made no reference to Adelaide's family during the trial. It was not until he wrote his memoirs,[71] more than thirty years later, that he referred to any irregularity in her birth. Even then he remained cautious, describing her, as we have noted, as the 'unacknowledged daughter of an Englishman of good social position.'

It is possible, of course, that Clarke did not know who her father was, receiving his brief and remuneration through the man's representatives. After all, Adelaide's marriage to Edwin had been conducted in a secretive manner, the whole transaction being arranged by her father's agents.

One of the unusual features of the marriage settlement was the stipulation that Edwin, after taking full responsibility for her, should never refer to her past. This would suggest that he knew something of his wife's origins but had been sworn to secrecy – having, of

---

71 Sir Edward Clarke, QC, MP, *The Story of My Life*, John Murray, 1918.

course, first satisfied her father that he was a man of honour. The same may be true of the solicitor, Edward Negus Wood, who drew up the marriage contract in 1875 and was ordered to enlist the services of Clarke in 1886.

Adelaide's birth in Orléans, the death of her mother, Clara, when she was eleven years old, her sheltered adolescence, her cloak and dagger marriage at nineteen and the sudden flow of money for her defence when she was charged with murder – would suggest that her biological father came from a family of some prominence, one that would be especially anxious to avoid any living proof of illegitimate progeny in its ranks.

One must therefore search for a family that was considered by contemporaries to be both proud and licentious. The Pagets were such a family, and a likely contender for the dubious honour of Adelaide's paternity might be the dashing Lord Alfred Paget.[72] He was undeniably 'an Englishman of good social position', and, like many of the Pagets, known to enjoy romantic intrigues. By the mid-nineteenth century his family was so firmly entrenched in the Royal Household that on at least one occasion, when Queen Victoria and Prince Albert gave a party, several Pagets were summoned from London to swell the ranks.

Indeed, Queen Victoria surrounded herself with Pagets. One of her oldest and most intimate friends was Lady Constance, daughter of Lord Uxbridge,[73] and both she and her sister, Elenora, became members of the Court of Windsor.

Their behaviour, however, often gave rise to criticism. In his book, *The Prince Consort*,[74] Roger Fulford records that 'On one occasion the Queen was much annoyed when two of the Ladies Paget, during a Drawing Room, remained close to her, chattering and giggling and making a great disturbance.' Yet evidently the Queen was prepared to overlook the roguish reputation of her friends. Emphasising the

---

72 Lord Alfred Henry Paget (1816-1888). In 1847, he married Cecilia Wyndham and they had fourteen children.
73 Lord Uxbridge was afterwards the Marquess of Anglesey and head of the Paget family. He held office as Lord Steward and later Lord Chamberlain.
74 *The Prince Consort*, Roger Fulford. Macmillan, 1966.

extent of their influence at Court, Roger Fulford comments:

> Almost all the best places at Court were occupied by members of a single Whig family – the Pagets. This family was likened, not unjustly, by the Press, to a 'swarm of locusts'... The dominance at Court of the Paget family – haughty, self-seeking and raffish – gave the impression that morality and respectability counted for nought with the Queen. Whiggery was alone the password to admit the bearer to the charmed presence of the Queen of England.

E. S. Turner's description of the Court confirms this state of affairs:[75]

> [Queen Victoria's Court] contained an inordinate representation of Pagets, a high-spirited family which according to Lord Melbourne, made a point of never learning anything... Of the three great offices, the Lord Steward was a Paget and the Lord Chamberlain was married to a Paget; these were, respectively Lord Uxbridge and Lord Conyngham... both these gentlemen installed their mistresses on the Household staff. Not the least noteworthy of the family was Lord Alfred Paget, the Queen's Equerry, a dashing horseman whom the Queen thought 'remarkably handsome in his uniform of the Blues.' Court gossip said that the Queen admired more than Lord Alfred's horsemanship. Certainly she took pains to admire his dog...

In his book, *Queen Victoria: A Personal History* Christopher Hibbert states that some courtiers even thought the Queen might marry Lord Alfred Paget, who had a portrait of her tied around his dog's neck.

The amatory exploits of various Paget gentlemen were, of course, kept from the Queen, though it is difficult to imagine how this was accomplished. Yet E. S. Turner writes:

> Without a doubt the Queen was ignorant of the cynical way in which the Lord Chamberlain and Lord Steward had made their amatory dispositions under her roof.

But according to Roger Fulford:[76]

---

75 *The Court of St James*, E. S. Turner. Michael Joseph.
76 Roger Fulford, op. cit.

These matters were not, of course, known to the general public but they were whispered by busybodies outside, and the scurrilous newspapers used to refer to Windsor Castle as the Paget Club House. The loose habits of these eminent courtiers did not encourage a high tone of morality among the Queen's guests, and on one occasion Lord Palmerston, who was staying at the Castle... burst into the bedroom of Mrs Brand, one of the Queen's Ladies of the Bedchamber... Her protests roused the Castle (though happily not the Queen) and Palmerston, caught red-handed, passed it off with a nonchalant air.

However, despite their reputation for reckless living, the Pagets continued to hold positions of power and prestige throughout Queen Victoria's reign. During Napoleon III's visit to Windsor in April 1855, their attendance at official functions was all too conspicuous. It is possible that this visit coincided with Adelaide Bartlett's conception, for she was born in December of that year, some eight months later. In the spring of 1855, Lord Alfred Paget was forty-one years old and given the honour of personally attending the Emperor during his stay at Windsor. He was exceedingly impressive and suitably experienced in turning the head of any young girl – Clara Chamberlain, for instance, married two years before to a man sixteen years older than herself. Yet how could Lord Alfred Paget and young Clara have met that spring?

There is one possibility. The State visit of the French Emperor and his wife, Eugénie, was a magnificent affair, its programme featuring a number of splendid balls and banquets which must have afforded Lord Alfred every opportunity to show himself to great advantage. One such occasion was a grand banquet held at the Guildhall, where many City dignitaries were invited to honour the Emperor's visit.

Could it be that Clara's father, William Robinson Chamberlain, and her brother, William, both Members of the City Stock Exchange, were among the guests that evening – and did they bring with them young Clara and her husband, the Comte de Thouars D'Escury? Bearing in mind the fervent Anglo-French climate at the time, it is certainly possible that Clara's attendance at the ball that evening had been sought because of her recent marriage into the French aristocracy.

And was it here, in the magnificent setting of the Guildhall, that young Clara met the flamboyant Lord Alfred, whom the Queen thought so remarkably handsome?

It is certainly tempting to imagine that Clara, perhaps already disenchanted with marriage to a teacher of mathematics, was seduced by the handsome courtier during the heady celebrations of that festive spring.

Evidently, though adventurous and sometimes rash in their amatory pursuits, the Pagets had somehow managed to avoid testing the Queen's tolerance too far. We can assume that Lord Alfred, if he were the father, would have made quite sure she knew nothing about young Clara's pregnancy. The scandal, had it been known, would have been extremely damaging to his reputation, for besides being a man in high office, he was also married. More importantly, perhaps, the Queen, anxious to maintain the delicately balanced relationship she had with the French Court, would not have welcomed the embarrassing news that a French aristocrat had been cuckolded by one of her own Household.

It is hardly surprising, therefore, if Lord Alfred Paget was, indeed, Adelaide's father, that he was so anxious to guard his identity when, thirty years later, she embarrassed him still further by turning up at the Old Bailey on a charge of murder.

It is not known for sure but after her release from Clerkenwell Prison Adelaide probably went to America where the Paget family had strong connections. One of Lord Paget's sons, Sir Arthur Henry Fitzroy Paget, had married the American heiress, Minnie Stevens, in 1878. It must have been a great relief for those responsible for Adelaide when she crossed the Atlantic and, it seems, settled into obscurity. She certainly covered her tracks well for the remainder of Adelaide's life remains a mystery. She was, indeed, an extraordinary woman, one who possessed a reckless personality which the restrictions and alienation of her early years could not subdue.

It is somehow easy to forget that Adelaide Bartlett was also a woman of great cunning who seems to have been quite prepared to kill an innocent man to gain her independence. In doing so, she earned herself a unique place in criminal history by getting away with such a memorable murder with both ingenuity and consummate skill.

It seems fitting to allow Adelaide the last word. The letter of thanks she wrote to Edward Clarke after her release, which first appeared in Sir John Hall's *Trial of Adelaide Bartlett,* in 1927, had three important lines missing. It was not until 1939 that the complete document was published in a book entitled *The Life and Famous Cases of Sir Edward Clarke.* This time the missing lines were included and in them Adelaide confesses:

> I have not been a good woman and my temptations have been terriable [sic] ones, but though I have not kept my vows as I should have done, you will judge me mercifully.

We can, at least, do that.

Bibliography

Trial of Adelaide Bartlett, edited by Sir John Hall.
Notable British Trials Series. William Hodge & Co., 1927

The Trial of Adelaide Bartlett for Murder, edited by Edward Beal.
Stevens & Haynes, 1886.

Poison and Adelaide Bartlett, Yseult Bridges.
Hutchinson, 1962.

The Story of My Life, The Rt. Hon. Sir Edward Clarke, KC.
John Murray, 1918.

The Life and Famous Cases of Sir Edward Clarke,
Derek Walker-Smith and Edward Clarke.
Eyre & Spottiswoode, 1939.

The Court of St James, E. S. Turner.
Michael Joseph, 1959.

The Prince Consort, Roger Fulford.
MacMillan, 1966.

The Pilgrim Daughters, Hesketh Pearson.
Heinemann, 1969.

Jennie – The Life of Lady Randolph Churchill, Anita Leslie.
Hutchinson, 1969.

The Greville Diaries, edited by P. W. Wilson.
Heinemann, 1927.

Victorian Murderesses, Mary S. Hartman.
Robson Books, 1977.

Gladys, Duchess of Marlborough, Hugo Vickers.
Weidenfeld & Nicolson, 1980.

Victoria and Albert, Joanne Richardson.
Dent, 1977.

World Famous Acquittals, Charles Franklin.
Odhams, 1970.

Queen Victoria and the Bonapartes, Theo Aronson.
Cassell, 1972.

The Court of St James, Christopher Hibbert.
Weidenfeld & Nicolson, 1979.

Eugenie and Napoleon III, David Duff.
Collins, 1978.

Chloroform: The Quest for Oblivion, Linda Stratmann.
Sutton Publishing, 2003

Queen Victoria-A Portrait, Giles St Aubyn.
Sinclair-Stevenson, 1991

Periodicals

The Cornhill Magazine
The Daily News
The Daily Telegraph
The Globe
The Illustrated Police News
The Lancet
The Llanelli County Guardian
The Nursing Record and Hospital World
The Nursing Times
The Pall Mall Gazette
The Penny Illustrated Paper
The Times
The Westminster Times

National Archives

CRIM 1/23/7

Index

Note: AB stands for Adelaide Bartlett

aconitine poisoning, 171
Amor, Betty, 205
animal magnetism, 146–7, 203–4
Armstrong, Major Herbert Rowse, 28
Attorney General *see* Russell, Sir Charles

BARTLETT, ADELAIDE (*née* de la Tremoille): appearance, 21, 91, 105, 107, 110; family background, 1–2, 223–4; birth and early life, 2; parentage, 2–3; meets and marries Edwin Bartlett, 3–6; marriage contract, 5, 224–5; education, 5–6; enters convent in Belgium, 6; religious beliefs, 6, 216; married life, 6–8, 14, 18–19; affair with Frederick Bartlett, 8–10, 126; relations with father-in-law, 9, 10–11, 17, 19; embraces feminist ideas, 13–14, 212–14; consults Mary Nichols, 16; pregnancy and stillbirth, 16, 99, 138, 172, 213; moves to Merton village, 18–19; husband's will, 19, 24, 73, 75, 109, 124n; affair with Dyson, 20–7, 30–2, 127–8, 129, 130–3, 215–16; and husband's 'mysterious' terminal illness, 23, 31, 55–6, 83; moves to Claverton Street, 28–30; calls in Dr Leach, 34–5; nurses Edwin, 37–8, 40, 44, 46–55; imposes visitor restrictions, 38–9, 41–3, 45, 55, 58; obtains chloroform from Dyson, 55–6, 63–4; knowledge of drugs, 23, 56; orders bottle of brandy, 59–60; rift with Dyson, 64, 81; accompanies Edwin to dentist, 65; and Edwin's death, 67–73, 74; her account of the tragedy, 68–9, 75; seeks to expedite post-mortem, 72, 77; learns of Frederick Bartlett's return, 73–4; relations with father-in-law, 76, 78, 79; shops for widow's weeds, 77; at post-mortem, 78–80; secretly removes chloroform bottle from flat, 80–1; leaves for East Dulwich, 80–2; quarrels with Dyson, 83–6; contacts solicitor, 85, 86, 93; recovers belongings from Claverton Street, 86–7, 89, 94; meetings with Dr Leach, 86, 87–8, 96–7; public fascination with, 90, 105, 107, 117–18; at inquest, 90–1, 102, 105, 106; last meetings with Dyson, 91–2, 93–5; at Edwin's funeral, 92; disposes of chloroform, 94–5, 98; leaves East Dulwich, 96; precarious position, 98–9; her 'extraordinary story', 99–101, 149–50, 151, 166, 172–4, 178, 186–7, 205–6; refuses to give evidence at inquest, 102, 106; arrested and charged, 106–7; privileged treatment during detention, 109–10, 223; at Westminster Police Court, 110; committed for trial at Old Bailey, 111; trial (*see entry for* trial); marriage

Index

offers, 197–8; considered lucky to be acquitted, 198; assessment of case against, 201–8; motive for murder, 208, 218–19; probable actions on night of murder, 208–11; her character and nature, 212–19; sexual relations with Edwin, 6, 99–101, 151, 172–3, 174, 178, 186–7, 205–6, 212–13, 216–17; possibly misused by Edwin, 218–19; letter to George Clarke, 222–3, 229; her natural father, 109, 116, 223–8; in later life, 228; cunning and criminal eminence, 228–9

Bartlett, Caroline *see* James, Caroline

Bartlett, Charles (AB's brother-in-law), 3, 9

Bartlett, Edwin (AB's husband): appearance and character, 3–4, 35; grocery business, 4–6, 34, 118n; marriage to AB, 4–8; and AB's affair with Frederick, 8–9; and father's apology, 10–11, 125; dental troubles, 11, 33; nervous collapse, 11–12; and AB's pregnancy, 16; his will, 19, 24, 73, 75, 109, 124, 136–7; relations with Dyson, 20–2, 23–7, 30, 31–2, 130–1, 132–3, 150, 181, 214–15; moves to Claverton Street, 29–30; illness, 33–40, 41–5, 59, 143, 206–7; dental treatment, 40–1, 45–6, 141–2; mental and nervous state, 33, 35, 39, 44, 46–9, 125–6, 127, 134, 146–7, 148, 203–4, 206; treated for worms, 47–52; delusions, 52–5; outing with Dr Leach, 58; last visit from father, 58–9; returning health, 63, 64–5, 143; visit to dentist, 65–6; last hours, 66–7; death, 67–73, 74–8, 108, 144–5; post-mortem, 74, 76–7, 78–9, 83, 142, 153–4; stomach contents analysed, 87–8, 91, 96, 103; inquest into death, 90–1, 102–4, 105–6, 107–9; funeral, 92; cause of death, 103, 111; theories of how died, 122–3, 166–8, 172, 174–5, 182–3, 202–5; estate, 124n; Dr Leach's opinion on, 217–18; possibly misuses wife, 218–19; and AB's origins, 224–5

Bartlett, Edwin, Snr (AB's father-in-law): tradesman, 4; and son's marriage, 5, 9; relations with AB, 9, 17, 19; issues apology, 10–11; banished from son's flat, 17; visits Edwin in illness, 38–9, 45–6, 58–9; barred from seeing son, 39, 41, 43, 55; demands second medical opinion, 42; and Edwin's death, 76, 78; at post-mortem, 78–9; evidence at inquest, 90–1; contests Edwin's will, 109, 124, 136–7; evidence at trial, 123–7, 180

Bartlett, Frederick (AB's brother-in-law), 3, 218; affair with AB, 8–10; letter and return to England, 73–4, 126, 207

Baxter, Edward: relations with Edwin, 4–6, 11, 25; visits Edwin in illness, 38, 39, 45, 54–5, 64–5; visits restricted by AB, 41, 43; AB orders New Year treats from, 59–60; and Edwin's death, 74, 75; breaks news to Edwin's father, 76; unable to put up AB, 80; and Edwin's business letters, 86; evidence at trial, 127, 206

Beal, Edward, 86, 90, 91, 93, 102, 106

Belgium: AB enters convent in, 6

Bellin, Mr (dentist), 11

Best, Annie, 210n

birth control literature, 13–14, 139–40, 180–1 *see also* contraceptives

Boulter, Ann, 72–3, 74, 130

brandy: as solvent for chloroform, 60, 103

Bravo, Charles, 15, 118n

Bravo, Florence, 15, 28, 115

Bridges, Yseult: *Poison and Adelaide Bartlett*, 3, 203–4

British Equitable Insurance Company, 11, 130

Brixton, 6

Index

capital punishment, 115
Central Criminal Court: celebrated murder trials at, 115, 118–19, 171 *see also* trial
Chamberlain, Clara (*later* de la Tremoille; AB's mother), 1–2, 223–4, 227–8
Chamberlain, William (AB's uncle), 2, 5, 227
Chamberlain, William Robinson (AB's grandfather), 1, 5, 227
Cheyne, Dr (of Mandeville Place), 76, 78
chlorodyne poisoning, 71, 80, 87–8
chloroform: as an aphrodisiac, 205; brandy as solvent for, 60, 103; as cause of death in Bartlett case, 103, 111; dosage effects, 160, 164; effects of swallowing, 142, 153, 156–7, 159–61; how administered in Bartlett case, 108, 122–3, 153–4, 157–9, 160, 183, 201; poisoning symptoms, 156; sale of, 197; as a soporific, 100–1; unprecedented in murder, 99, 103, 142, 157, 164, 196–7; and vomiting, 108, 151, 210n
Clapton, Dr William, 11, 130
Clarke, Sir Edward: retained for AB's defence, 109, 223; researches and prepares case, 116–17; life and earnings, 118–19; and withdrawl of case against Dyson, 122; cross-examinations, 125–7, 128, 130, 132–5, 137, 138–9, 141–2, 145–6, 148–51, 154, 156, 157–8, 160; and jury question, 136–7; and *Esoteric Anthropology*, 139–40; writes on Tidy and Stevenson, 156; closing speech, 163–9, 191, 196–7, 220; his suicide theory, 166–8; protests at Russell's new theory, 175; recalls Annie Walker, 177–8; description, 179; sobs at verdict, 1, 191; leaves court, 193; mobbed, 195; thanked by AB, 169, 222; reflections on trial, 194–5; letter from AB, 222–3, 229; and identity of AB's true father, 224; *The Life and Famous Cases of Sir Edward Clarke* (with Derek Walker-Smith), 198, 229; *The Story of My Life*, 2, 116n, 117, 194–5, 224
Clarke, Chief Inspector George, 119n
Claverton Street, Pimlico: situation, 28; rooms and servant, 28–9; Bartletts rent first floor flat, 29–30; scandalous affair between AB and Dyson, 30–1, 127–8; no dogs at, 34; sick-room and reception area, 37–8, 77; night of murder, 208–11; death scene, 68–9; fire in front room, 69, 128, 152; post-mortem at, 78–9; AB leaves, 79, 80–1; flat locked and sealed, 79, 149; flat searched, 81n, 154–6, 161, 186; AB recovers belongings, 86–7, 89, 94; demolished, 28n
Clerkenwell Prison, 107, 223
Companion to the British Pharmacopoeia (Squire), 60, 104, 134–5, 155
contraceptives: Nichols's advice, 13, 14; found at Claverton Street, 155–6; used by the Bartletts, 172–3, 178, 186–7, 216–17
Coroner *see* Hicks, Braxton
The Cottage, Merton, 18–19, 20–3, 124, 161
Croydon, 5, 42

Daily News, 120, 121, 217–18
Daily Telegraph, 121, 170–1, 189, 191–2, 193
de la Tremoille, Adolphe Collet (AB's legal father), 1–2, 223–4
de la Tremoille, Clara (AB's mother) *see* Chamberlain, Clara
de la Tremoille, Clara (AB's sister), 2
de la Tremoille, Frederick (AB's brother), 2
de la Tremoille, Henry (AB's brother), 2
Deronda Road, Herne Hill, 80
Dilke, Sir Charles, 116
Dodd, Miss (headmistress), 5

Index

Doggett, Caroline: rents flat to Bartletts, 28–30, 34; witnesses intimacy between AB and Dyson, 30; as exemplary landlady, 38, 79–80; food for Edwin, 45, 65, 67; AB speaks to about chloroform and sleeping drops, 66–7; and Edwin's death, 69–70; ordered to have bed linen washed, 74; AB discusses money concerns with, 75; evidence at inquest, 103; evidence at trial, 127–8, 129, 162

Doggett, Frederick, 28; and Edwin's death, 68–70, 71–2, 130, 144; sends telegrams, 74; evidence at inquest, 103, 107–8; evidence at trial, 127

dogs, 7, 18, 34, 48, 51–2, 124

Dover, 23–4, 25, 27

Dudley, Dr John: examines Edwin, 44–5; attends post-mortem, 78–9; evidence at trial, 152–3

Dyson, Rev. George: appearance, 20, 110, 130; academic ambitions, 20; affair with AB, 20–7, 30–2, 127–8, 129, 130–3, 215–16; Edwin appoints executor, 24; correspondence with Edwin, 26–7, 181; visits to Claverton Street, 34, 45, 50, 65, 134, 150, 152; hypnotic influence, 52, 203–4; procures chloroform for AB, 55–8, 63–4, 134–6; deteriorating relations with AB, 64, 81; at post-mortem, 78–9, 80; escorts AB to East Dulwich, 81–2; questions her about chloroform, 81, 92, 94–5; mounting anxieties, 82–3; gets rid of empty chloroform bottles, 82, 98, 135, 161; quarrel and rift with AB, 83–6; his poetry, 84; accompanies AB and Mrs Matthews to London, 86–7; unburdens himself to Mr and Mrs Matthews, 88–9; last meetings with AB, 91–2, 93–5; at Edwin's funeral, 92; discusses predicament with father, 95–6; urges Mrs Matthews to testify against AB, 97; confesses to Wesleyan authorities, 97; and AB's 'given to Dyson' story, 100, 173–4; scorned and ridiculed, 105–6; at inquest, 106; charged and taken into custody, 108–9, 161; at Westminster Police Court, 109–10; committed for trial at Old Bailey, 111; in court, 120, 121; case against dropped, 121–2; evidence at trial, 130–5; judge's opinion of, 181–2, 185–6; Edward Clarke on, 220; after trial and in later life, 220–1; character, 221

Dyson, Rev. John B, 95–6, 97, 221

Elton, F.E. (Foreman of the Jury): letter to *The Times*, 196

Esoteric Anthropology (Dr Nichols), 14, 16, 137–41, 166, 180–1, 212–14

ether, 68, 69, 103, 160

Evening Standard, 171, 179–80

feminism, AB's interest in, 13–14, 212–14

French letters *see* contraceptives

Friern Road, East Dulwich, 16, 82, 83–6, 96, 97

Fulcher, Alice, 38, 50, 65, 78; servant, 28–9; witnesses intimacy between AB and Dyson, 30, 31; works late on New Year's Eve, 67, 165; fetches Dr Leach, 67–8, 70, 144; her suspicions, 68; earnings, 118n; evidence at trial, 129–30, 162

Fulford, Roger: *The Prince Consort*, 225–7

Furlong, Mary Ann, 18, 21–2, 161

Globe, The (newspaper), 197–8, 220

Green, Dr Thomas: called in by Dr Leach, 74–5, 76–7; post-mortem, 78, 80, 83, 153; deposition, 142, 207, 218

Gully, James Manby, 15

Guy's Hospital, 88

Hackett, Mr (visitor to Claverton Street), 63–4

Index

Hall, Sir John (ed.): *Trial of Adelaide Bartlett,* 10n, 192, 203, 222n, 229
Hartman, Mary S.: *Victorian Murderesses,* 3
Harvey, David, 205
Herne Hill, South London, 4, 7, 34, 80
Hibbert, Christopher: *Queen Victoria: A Personal History,* 226
Hicks, Braxton (Deputy Coroner of Westminster), 90–1, 102–4, 106, 108–9
Home Rule Bill (1886), 116
homeopathy, 14–15, 204
Humble, Mr (chemist), 56–7, 136
hydropathy, 14–15, 137–8, 140–1, 204
hypnotism, 203–4

inquest (into death of Edwin Bartlett), 90–1, 102–4, 105–6, 107–9
insomnia, 39, 183, 203, 204–5, 209

James, Caroline (*née* Bartlett; AB's sister-in-law), 5, 42

Lamson, Dr George, 171
Lancet, The (medical journal), 3n, 35, 46–7, 196–7
Leach, Dr Alfred: called in to attend Edwin, 35; misdiagnoses mercury poisoning, 36–7, 111; treats Edwin, 37, 39; conversations with AB, 39–40, 42, 54; examines Edwin with Dr Dudley, 44–5; opinion on Edwin's mental state, 46–7, 206; recommends trip to Torquay, 47, 54; treats Edwin for worms, 47–52; discusses mesmerism with Edwin, 52–3; takes Edwin for drive, 58; suggests house calls no longer necessary, 63; assists dental treatment, 65–6; and Edwin's death, 70–2, 108; his chlorodyne poisoning theory, 71, 80, 87–8; arranges post-mortem, 74–5, 76–7; at post-mortem, 78–9, 80, 153; overlooks chloroform bottle, 80–1, 149; discusses post-mortem findings with Dyson, 83; meetings with AB, 86, 87–8, 96–7; and AB's 'extraordinary story', 99–101, 149–50, 151; evidence at inquest, 103–4, 106; evidence at trial, 143–6, 148–52, 176, 184; samples poisons, 145, 148, 160–1; judge's opinion of, 184–5; reflections on case, 217–18; death, 221–2
lead poisoning, 37, 59, 111, 206–7
leasing (of property), 28
Lewis & Lewis (solicitors), 109
Llanelli and County Guardian, 214n, 215n, 221
Llanelly, South Wales, 220–1
Lockwood, Francis, 118, 121
Lordship Lane, East Dulwich, 6, 17, 124
lumbricoid worm, 47–8, 53–4, 146
see also worms

Malvern, 14–15, 140
Married Women's Property Act (1882), 19
Marshall, Inspector Henry: at inquest, 104; arrests and cautions AB, 106–7; takes Dyson into custody, 109; evidence at trial, 161–2
Mathews, Charles, 118
Matthews, Alice: reaction to *Esoteric Anthropology,* 16, 213–14; relations with the Bartletts, 18, 21; and Edwin's death, 74, 75, 77–8; witnesses quarrel between AB and Dyson, 83–4; accompanies AB to Claverton Street, 86–7; and Peckham Rye Pond, 87, 94–5, 97, 102; Dyson unburdens himself to, 88; doubts and suspicions, 93, 95; asks AB to leave, 96; persuaded by Dyson to testify at inquest, 97; evidence at trial, 136, 182
Matthews, George: AB lends *Esoteric Anthropology* to, 16, 213; relations with the Bartletts, 18, 21, 93; visits Edwin in illness, 40; and Edwin's death, 77–8; takes AB in, 80, 82;

Index

Dyson confides in, 89; AB and Dyson call on, 93–4; evidence at trial, 137–8
Maybrick, Florence, 115, 202n
Mellin, Mr (chemist), 57–8, 136
mercury poisoning (mercurialism), 35–7, 38–9, 40–1, 44, 59, 111, 143, 206, 207
Merton, near Wimbledon: The Cottage, 18–19, 20–3, 124, 161; Wesleyan Chapel, 20, 57
mesmerism, 52–3, 125, 127, 134, 150, 151, 204
Millbank mortuary, 88, 91, 96, 155
Moloney, Mr, 118, 136, 137, 140, 161
morphia, 39, 45, 209
murder, death sentence for, 115–16
Murray, Dr Montague, 76, 78, 157; evidence at trial, 153–4

Napoleon III, Emperor, 223, 227
necrosis (of the jaw), 66, 141, 206
Nichols, Mary Gove, 13–14, 15–16, 141, 212–13
Nichols, Dr Thomas Low, 13–14, 15; AB claims to have consulted, 23, 31, 138; evidence at trial, 140–1
see also Esoteric Anthropology
nitrous oxide gas, 65–6, 141

Old Bailey: celebrated murder trials at, 115, 118–19, 171 *see also* trial
opium, 206–7, 209

Paget family, 225–7
Paget, Lord Alfred, 225, 226–8
Paget, Sir Arthur Henry, 228
Paget, Sir James, 198
Pall Mall Gazette, 179, 187, 189–91
Palmer, William, 171
Palmerston, Lord, 227
paregoric, 69, 103
Partridge, Mr (magistrate at Westminster Police Court), 107, 109–10
Pay, Esther, 119
Peckham Rye Pond, 8, 87, 94–5, 98, 101, 102
Penny Illustrated Paper, The, 81n, 107, 197
Penrose, T. (chemist), 57, 136
Poland, Harry, 118, 123–4, 127, 129, 130–1, 137–8, 139, 151–2, 154, 159–60, 161
post-mortems: carried out in home, 77

Ralph, Tom (Coroner's officer), 81, 154–6, 186
Roberts, Thomas, 40–1, 45, 111; evidence at trial, 141–2
Rochester Row Police Station, 107
Russell, Sir Charles (Attorney General), 118; appearance and manner in court, 116n; lack of case preparation, 116, 182–3; submits no case against Dyson, 121, 122; opening speech, 122–3; examinations, 143–5, 156–7, 159, 162; closing speech, 171–7; offers new theory of Edwin's death, 174–5, 182, 202–3; suggests motive for murder, 176

santonine, 50, 51, 53, 148, 155n
Smith, Madeleine, 115, 198
Station Road, Herne Hill, 4, 7, 11, 123
Staunton, Patrick, 118
Stevenson, Dr Thomas: analysis of Edwin's stomach contents, 88, 91, 96, 103, 155; evidence at inquest, 103, 108; evidence at police court, 111; analysis of powders recovered from Claverton Street, 155n; reputation, 156; evidence at trial, 156–9, 162, 164–5, 207, 210; evidence in Lamson trial, 171n; concurs with jury verdict, 222
Stoke Newington: girls' boarding school, 5
Styles, Theodore, 56
syphilis, 36, 143n, 146, 206

Thompson, Edith, 115
Tidy, Dr Charles Meymott: reputation,

Index

156; evidence at trial, 159–61, 210; evidence in Lamson trial, 171n
Times, The, 1, 84n, 102, 103, 105, 109, 195–6
Tit-bits, 222
Titanic (liner), 221
trial (for murder of Edwin Bartlett): attendance and public interest, 117–18, 129, 170–1, 185, 189; legal teams, 118, 119–20; AB's appearance and demeanour in court, 120–1, 185, 189, 190, 192; juror substituted, 121; application to try prisoners separately, 121; arraignments and pleas, 121; case against Dyson dropped, 121–2; opening speech for the prosecution, 122–3; evidence for the Crown, 123–46, 148–62, 177–8; jury question, 136–7; speech for the defence, 163–9; closing speech for the prosecution, 171–7; judge's summing up, 179–89; deliberations and verdict, 189–91, 196; uproar in court, 191–2; AB's reaction to verdict, 192; crowds outside, 193; AB leaves court, 193; Edward Clarke's reflections on trial, 194–5; reactions to verdict, 195–8; letter from Foreman of the Jury, 196
Turner, E.S.: *The Court of St James*, 226

Uxbridge, Lord, 225, 226

Vickers, John A, 221
Victoria, Queen, court of, 224, 225–7

Walker, Nurse Annie: recommended, 16, 141; attends AB's confinement, 16, 134; AB's relationship with, 16–17, 18, 19, 166, 194; alleged involvement in supplying chloroform to AB, 31, 55–6, 88, 131, 165; evidence at trial, 138–9, 177–8, 217; judge's opinion of, 180; unknown to Dr Nichols, 140
Walker-Smith, Derek and Edward Clarke: *The Life and Famous Cases of Sir Edward Clarke*, 198, 229
Wandsworth Common, 82, 161
water cure treatments, 14–15
Wesleyan Church, 97, 221
Westminster Police Court, 107, 109–11
Westminster Times, The, 5n, 7n, 217–18
Weymouth Street, Portland Place, 96
Wilde, Oscar, 119
Wills, Sir Alfred, Judge, 22, 31, 206, 214; appointed Bartlett case, 118; career, 119; first day of trial, 120; instructs jury on Dyson, 121–2; second day of trial, 133; third day of trial, 137, 139–40, 143, 145; fourth day of trial, 149, 152; fifth day of trial, 160; irritated by crowds and spectators, 170–1; sixth day of trial, 177–8; summing-up, 179–89; his 'accidental overdose' theory, 183, 204; condemns outburst in court, 191–2; fails to concur with jury verdict, 192
women: and divorce, 219; and early feminist literature, 13–14, 180–1; fascinated by AB, 118; and hydropathic treatments, 14–15; married women and property rights, 19; as spectators in court, 170–1, 189; subservient role in marriage, 214
Wood, Edward: Edwin's solicitor, 5, 10; and Edwin's new will, 24; notified of Edwin's death, 74; at post-mortem, 78, 80; AB engages, 85, 86, 93, 155; at inquest, 90; at police court, 107; instructed to retain Edward Clarke, 109; AB stays with after trial, 222; sworn to secrecy, 225
worms, 47–50, 51–2, 53–4, 55, 146–7, 204, 206
Wright, Robert, 118, 136, 177

www.ingramcontent.com/pod-product-compliance
Lightning Source LLC
Chambersburg PA
CBHW062156080426
42734CB00010B/1711